Jewish Feminism in Israel

The Hadassah International Research Institute on Jewish Women, established at Brandeis University in 1997 by Hadassah, the Women's Zionist Organization of America, Inc., supports interdisciplinary basic and applied research as well as cultural projects on Jewish women around the world. Under the auspices of the Institute, the Brandeis Series on Jewish Women publishes a wide range of books by and about Jewish women in diverse contexts and time periods.

Marjorie Agosín, *Uncertain Travelers: Conversations with Jewish Women Immigrants to America*, 1999

Rahel R. Wasserfall, *Women and Water: Menstruation in Jewish Life and Law*, 1999

Susan Starr Sered, *What Makes Women Sick: Militarism, Maternity, and Modesty in Israeli Society*, 2000

Pamela S. Nadell and Jonathan D. Sarna, editors, *Women and American Judaism: Historical Perspectives*, 2001

Ludmila Shtern, *Leaving Leningrad: The True Adventures of a Soviet Émigré*, 2001

Jael Silliman, *Jewish Portraits, Indian Frames: Women's Narrtives from a Diaspora of Hope*, 2001

Judith R. Baskin, *Midrashic Women*, 2002

ChaeRan Y. Freeze, *Jewish Marriage and Divorce in Imperial Russia*, 2002

Mark A. Raider and Miriam B. Raider-Roth, *The Plough Woman: Records of the Pioneer Women of Palestine*, 2002

Kalpana Misra and Melanie S. Rich, *Jewish Feminism in Israel: Some Contemporary Perspectives*, 2003

JEWISH FEMINISM IN ISRAEL
SOME CONTEMPORARY PERSPECTIVES

KALPANA MISRA
MELANIE S. RICH
Editors

BRANDEIS UNIVERSITY PRESS
Published by University Press of New England
Hanover and London

Brandeis University Press
Published by University Press of New England, Hanover, NH 03755
© 2003 by Brandeis University Press

Printed in the United States of America   5 4 3 2 1

Library of Congress Cataloging-in-Publication Data
Jewish feminism in Israel : some contemporary perspectives / Kalpana
Misra, Melanie S. Rich.—1st ed.
    p. cm.—(Brandeis series on Jewish women)
Includes bibliographical references and index.
ISBN 1-58465-324-8 (cloth : alk. paper)—ISBN 1-58465-325-6 (pbk. :
alk. paper)
1. Feminism—Israel. 2. Jewish women—Israel—Social conditions. I.
Misra, Kalpana. II. Rich, Melanie S. III. Series.
HQ1728.5.J49 2003
305.42'095694—dc21
2003007368

The art that appears on pages 146–68 has been reproduced with the permission of the
artists.

This book was published with the support of the Jewish Federation of Tulsa Foundation
and Temple Israel, Tulsa, Oklahoma.

CONTENTS

ACKNOWLEDGMENTS   vii

CONTRIBUTORS   ix

Introduction
Kalpana Misra   xiii

Theorizing Israeli Feminism, 1970–2000
Marcia Freedman   1

Women and Religion in Israel
Naomi Graetz   17

**Women, Law, Religion, and Politics in Israel:
A Human Rights Perspective**
Marsha Freeman   57

**Gender Equality in the Kibbutz—
From Ideology to Reality**
Michal Palgi   76

Mizrahi Feminism: The Unheard Voice
Henriette Dahan-Kalev   96

The Women's Peace Movement in Israel
Gila Svirsky   113

Violence Against Women
Irit Umanit   132

**"Bad Girls"—The Israeli Version:
Contemporary Women Artists in Israel**
Tami Katz-Freiman   141

Epilogue
Melanie S. Rich   172

INDEX   179

ACKNOWLEDGMENTS

We have accumulated many debts in planning and compiling this volume. First and foremost we extend a special thanks to Sara Sanditen, who through Partnership 2000 opened up a whole new world of friendships, contacts, and opportunities for involvement in Israel. The inspiration, encouragement, and introductions provided by Terry Greenblatt were also deeply appreciated. Our contributors brought the highest levels of enthusiasm and dedication to this project, and we are enormously grateful to them and to one another for the multiple pleasures of collaborative work. Shulamit Reinharz, Dena Scher, and an anonymous reviewer generously gave of their time to read the manuscript and it has been immeasurably improved by their valuable comments and insightful suggestions.

This book would not have been possible without the interest and generosity of the Jewish Federation of Tulsa Foundation, the Charles and Lynn Schusterman Family Foundation, the University of Tulsa, the Haddassah International Research Institute on Jewish Women at Brandeis University, and Temple Israel of Tulsa. For their support and facilitation special acknowledgment is also due to Tom Horne, Martin Belsky, Eldon Eisenach, Michael Mosher, and the Women's Studies Governing Board at the University of Tulsa. We are grateful also to Perry Simons for his technical assistance and to Phyllis Deutsch for her expert editorial supervision. Toy Kelley provided timely and efficient secretarial support.

Finally, for their boundless enthusiasm and exuberant encouragement through every stage of this project we owe a special debt of gratitude to our husbands, Perry Simons and Murali Iyengar, and to our children, Josh, Ali, Kabir, and Karnika.

CONTRIBUTORS

Henriette Dahan-Kalev is a lecturer in the Department of Public and Policy Administration at Ben Gurion University of the Negev. With a doctorate in political science from Hebrew University, her areas of teaching and research interest are Israeli politics, ethnic politics, feminist political theories, and globalism and the welfare state. Dr. Dahan-Kalev is also a women's and human rights activist.

Marcia Freedman taught philosophy at Haifa University and women's studies at Oranim Teacher's Seminary throughout the 1970s. In the early 1970s, she was one of the founders and leaders of the Israeli feminist movement in its second wave. Freedman was elected to the Knesset and served from 1973 to 1977, where she provided a rare voice for women's issues, raising concerns that had never been spoken of publicly in Israel before—domestic violence, breast cancer, rape, incest, and teenage prostitution. She introduced legislation that led to reform of Israel's then highly restrictive abortion law. In 1977 she cofounded the Women's Party. She currently divides her time between Berkeley, California, and Jerusalem. In Israel, she serves as a consultant to Kol Ha-Isha, the Jerusalem women's center, and is a founder of the newly established Community School for Women's Studies. She is also an active member of the Israeli Women's Coalition for a Just Peace and the president of Brit Tzedek V'Shalom (Jewish Alliance for Justice and Peace). In Berkeley, she is a frequent lecturer and an advocate for Israeli women's and peace issues in the North American diaspora. She is the author of *Exile in the Promised Land*, a memoir, as well as a number of articles and reviews.

Marsha Freeman is a Senior Fellow at the Humphrey Institute of Public Affairs, University of Minnesota, and director of the International Women's Rights Action Watch (IWRAW), an international gender and human rights resource center that provides information, training, and technical assistance to activists, scholars, UN experts, and government officials concerned with implementing women's human rights. For the last fifteen years Freeman has worked with women all over the world in their efforts to identify and claim their rights. She holds a law degree from the University of Minnesota and a doctoral degree in English and American literature from the University of Pennsylvania.

Naomi Graetz was born in New York City and has been living in Israel since 1967. She serves on the faculty at Ben Gurion University. She is the author of *S/He Created Them: Feminist Retellings of Biblical Stories*, and *Silence is Deadly: Judaism Confronts Wifebeating*. Her many articles on women and metaphor in the Bible and Midrash have appeared in such journals as *Conservative Judaism* and *Shofar*, and in anthologies including *A Feminist Companion to the Bible*, *Gender and Judaism*, and *Jewish Mothers Tell Their Stories*. She was the founder of the Negev branch of the Israel Women's Network and has been a strong proponent of women's rights. She is an active member of the Masorti (Conservative Judaism) movement, and served on the committee that was instrumental in the decision to ordain women as rabbis in Israel.

Tami Katz-Freiman is a Tel Aviv/Miami–based independent curator, art historian, and art critic. For over ten years she held several positions at the Tel Aviv Museum, including curator. After leaving the Tel Aviv Museum in 1989, she curated exhibitions for several of Israel's most prominent museums and institutions, including *Meta-Sex 94: Identity, Body and Sexuality* for the Ein Harod Museum of Art. In addition to essays for the catalogues and books published in conjunction with the exhibitions she has curated, Ms. Katz-Freiman has written numerous articles, essays, and reviews addressing various issues in contemporary art for *Studio Art Magazine*, Israel's foremost art publication, and for *Art Papers*. Following five years of living and working in Miami, she is currently teaching at the Camera Obscura School of Photography and Filmmaking in Tel Aviv.

Kalpana Misra received her doctoral degree from the University of Michigan in 1992 and is an associate professor of political science at the University of Tulsa. She is the author of *From Post-Maoism to Post-Marxism: The Erosion of Official Ideology in Deng's China* (Routledge, 1998). Her articles have appeared in the *Routledge International Encyclopedia of Women*, *Women in Politics*, *Contemporary South Asia*, *Strategic Analysis*, *China Report*, *Economic and Political Weekly*, and other anthologies and periodicals.

Michal Palgi is a sociologist and senior lecturer and chair of the Department of Gender Studies at Yezreel Valley College. Following postdoctoral study at Harvard University supported by the Fulbright Foundation, Dr. Palgi has taught at a number of universities in both Israel and the United States. These include Tufts University, Ruppin College, Haifa University, Oranim College, and Harvard University. She has published prolifically on sociological issues of the kibbutz. She is a coauthor of *Participation and Control* and a coeditor of *Sexual Equality: The Israeli Kibbutz Tests the Theories*. She has published several articles in edited volumes and refereed journals. She has held innumerable administrative and scholarly positions on boards and committees and has also served as guest editor of *The Kibbutz in Transition*, a special edition of the *Israel Social Research Journal*.

Melanie S. Rich is a licensed clinical psychologist who has been in practice in Tulsa, Oklahoma, for the past nineteen years. She did her training at the Berkeley campus of the California School of Professional Psychology, where she received both her masters and doctoral degrees. Her dissertation in 1982 was one of the early research projects on the transmission of trauma in Holocaust survivor families. She has for the past three years chaired a Partnership 2000 Women's Forum under the auspices of the United Jewish Communities and the Jewish Agency for Israel, which included a four-city cooperative effort to begin a partnership project to address women's issues in the Kinneret region of Israel.

Gila Svirsky is a peace and human rights activist in Israel. She is a cofounder of the Coalition of Women for a Just Peace, which has engaged in a number of dramatic acts of resistance to end Israel's occupation of the Palestinian territories. She has also been executive director of Bat Shalom of the Jerusalem Link and of B'Tselem, two leading Israeli organizations that advocate an end to human rights abuses and a just solution to the conflict. For six years, she has also served as director in Israel of the New Israel Fund. Ever since its founding in January 1988, Gila Svirsky has been a member of the Women in Black vigil in Jerusalem. She was born in the United States and has lived in Israel since 1966.

Irit Umanit serves as the chair of the Forum of Shelter Directors in Israel. A long-time activist in the Israeli women's movement, she was hired as the director of the first short-term crisis shelter for women in 1994. In that capacity Ms. Umanit is responsible for the establishment and daily operation of the shelter, including supervising the shelter's staff, coordinating work with other battered women's shelters, and conducting public education in Israel about the subject of domestic violence. She brings to her work at the Women's Crisis Shelter the conviction that violence against women is a direct result of gender inequality, and that through public education, support, and outreach current trends can be overcome. Her educational background is in special education, with many years of experience teaching special education in Israel and the United States. She is the recipient of an award from the Seattle Jewish Federation for a special education Jewish Sunday school curriculum that she developed while living in Seattle.

Introduction

Kalpana Misra

The late nineteenth and early twentieth centuries witnessed growing and activist feminist movements in many different parts of the world. Most of these movements arose in the context of nationalist movements emphasizing self-determination, secularism, democracy, and socialism. The "logical" and organic links between feminism and anticolonialism, feminism and constitutional democracy, feminism and socialism seemed obvious not only to women but also to broad sections of men as well in their opposition and resistance to oppression and discrimination based on class, race, ethnicity, and religion. Women's participation in broader struggles for national liberation or revolutionary socialism brought forth at least a formal recognition, if not commitment, to women's right to legal, political, economic, and social equality in public discourse. The criterion for modernization for societies and states became, in many instances, the extent to which public policies and political platforms alleviated gender-based inequities and promoted the empowerment of women as a group. The association of women's movements with larger struggles had disadvantages as well. "Narrowly feminist" concerns were not always taken into consideration and gender issues could be and were subordinated frequently in the interests of unity. Nonetheless, in general, secular nationalism overall provided a favorable impetus to the placing of women's issues on the public agenda.

Nationalism based on politicized religious identities has had a far more adverse effect on the rights and status of women worldwide. The intensification of intercommunity conflict and close interaction of politics and religion, a marked feature of the second half of the twentieth century, has brought about a preoccupation with community identities, religious traditions, and cultural practices that seeks to negate and suppress divergent interests and rights of individuals and social collectivities. The politics of religious self-assertion and exclusion marginalizes and subordinates women in the very process of identifying them as the cultural signifiers and custodians of community identity. The articulation of a traditional communitarian discourse centers on areas of marriage, divorce, inheritance, reproductive rights, and sexuality, and in doing so legitimizes gender inequities embodied in specific family and social structures. The role of the state acquires a crucial significance under these circumstances. The state can actively serve as a guarantor and protector of women's rights and interests or collude in the subordination and oppression of women either through regressive legislation or by "noninterference," which essentially transfers state authority to customary or personal law enforced by patriarchal religious establishments.

Within the context of these developments the status and experience of women in Israel pose an especially interesting agenda for research on the links between gender, religious community, and the state. Although often erroneously lumped together with other industrialized democracies, the Israeli state and society have a unique identity and existence, which make them a particularly fascinating unit for analysis. The liberal democratic polity of Israel differs fundamentally from Western democracies whose politics functions on the basis of secular or civil legal codes. Israeli citizens are governed by personal law; that is, Israeli Jews are subject to rabbinical law and Muslim or Christian minorities to their own respective laws. Such a policy sanctions not simply the separation of communities but a pattern of divisive politics as well. The implications of this arrangement are, however, most pronounced in the area of gender issues, where the state comes to play an ambivalent role, premising political equality and providing space for the articulation and aggregation of women's interests on the one hand, and, on the other, legitimizing and preserving institutionalized discrimination based on religion or custom.

The politicization of religious identities and the emergence of the national security imperative as the most crucial and overriding concern of the Israeli state further undermines women's rights by positing a conflict between personal and group/collective interest. The strategic need for a unified community translates into a demand for coherence and homogenization and the denial of social diversities and cultural pluralism, along with the subordination of gender and class loyalties. Ultimately, the discourse and conflicts over tradition and identity come to be centered on the female, not only in minority communities of Arab Muslims and Christians, but also within the majority Jewish population.

The State of Israel was founded on the promise of nondiscrimination and the egalitarian socialist orientation of its initial wave of settlers assured an early recognition of gender equality, albeit more at the theoretical level than that of practical policy. As the Jewish state completes the first fifty years of its existence and enters the twenty-first century, it is particularly pertinent to assess its performance specifically in the area of women's rights. The justification for such a focus rests on the assumption that "the woman question" is not simply a single or even isolated issue of the oppression of women as a particular group, but one that links up with all other issues related to the social, political, economic, and cultural makeup of any society.

The eight essays in this volume provide a contextualized and nuanced understanding of the complex interconnections between gender, state, nation, religious community, and culture in contemporary Israel. Collectively, they address four main questions. What are the obstacles to achieving gender equality in Israeli society? Where are Israeli Jewish feminism and the women's movement today? How do Jewish feminists conceptualize women's issues and interests, and what kind of strategies have they devised for promoting fundamental change beyond just gaining visibility and "adding women in"?

The nexus between ultra-Orthodox Judaism and the state is highlighted by Naomi Graetz's and Marsha Freeman's articles. Beginning with David Ben-Gurian's compromise with the National Religious Party and the omission of civil marriage and divorce provisions from the Equal Rights for Women Act of 1951, Israeli politicians through the 1990s have repeatedly emphasized political and national unity at the expense of women's rights. According to Graetz, political support for constructing the myth of a structured and homogenous Jewish community has enabled the ultra-Orthodox religious establishment to enforce a monolithic version of Jewish identity and religious practice. The functioning of Orthodox Judaism as an official state religion provides the cultural and legal basis for discrimination against women as well as against secular, liberal, Reform, and Conservative Jews in general. The essentialism projected by the state and by Orthodox rabbis oversimplifies a complex and highly diverse Israeli reality, while promoting a static and one-sided interpretation of tradition. Such essentialism obstructs domestic legal reform and Israel's conformity with international standards of human rights, as Marsha Freeman demonstrates. In the particular context of the Jewish nation, the State has not simply endorsed but actively supported the development of a hegemonic political culture in which challenges to discrimination are perceived as affronts to the essence of national identity. Women find themselves disadvantaged legally, politically, and economically, with little opportunity for fair negotiation.

The interplay of social, economic, and political forces and their consequences for women is addressed by Michal Palgi's article. The kibbutz experience in Israel has provided an illuminating example of the achievements of a consciously designed program to eliminate general disparities in status, income, and political authority; however, its record on erasing gender-based inequalities has been a mixed one. Palgi's essay focuses on the socioeconomic transformation underway since the beginning of the economic crisis in the 1980s and its specific implications for women. Her analysis also revisits a number of questions that are central to feminist theory and practice. Does the continuing division of labor—with men pursuing careers in agricultural and industrial sectors and women clustered in education- and service-oriented occupations—point to a "natural" tendency for men and women to gravitate toward earner/spender and producer/caregiver roles? Does differentiation of gender roles necessarily lead to inequality?

The kibbutz experience has been particularly noteworthy in addressing such issues as the feminization of poverty, the economic independence of women, and the recognition of household labor as socially useful. Nevertheless, over the several decades of its evolution, women's status, roles, and authority have undergone only modest transformation. Economic development and technological advances have not automatically brought equality for women in the absence of gender-sensitive policies. As the kibbutz responds to its economic crisis and decline with measures of liberalization, and as the occupational boundaries between the kibbutz and the broader Israeli society become more porous, inter- and intragender inequalities are likely to increase.

The expansion of feminist consciousness in response to politics, militarization of nationalist ethos, and ethnic division is a thread that runs through the entire volume. Marcia Freedman, who provides an overview of second-wave feminism since 1973, alludes to the complex ways in which Zionism and Israeli nationalism have become gendered and attributes the reemergence of feminist activism to the experience of the Yom Kippur War and its aftermath. Freedman's survey of the early phase of the movement and Gila Svirsky's account of the development of Women in Black record the evolving strategies and consciousness of Jewish feminism in Israel. The 1970s were characterized by militant and confrontational tactics and by an extensive reliance on imported American models of feminist organization and ideologies. The 1980s witnessed both a reorientation toward indigenous modes of resistance, signified by the pacifism and nonviolence espoused by Women in Black, and also an increasing recognition that women's identities are constituted in complex ways. Israeli feminists could not promote their interest as women qua women and as mothers, sisters, wives, and girlfriends by staying apolitical in light of the most pressing question facing the country— the Intifada in the Occupied Territories and the repression unleashed by Israeli security forces in response to it. Nor could they in all consistency with feminist beliefs condone or overlook the impact of Israeli militarism on Arabs and Palestinians both within Israel and in the Occupied Territories.

Taking a stand in the public arena against aggression and militarism also facilitated the acceptance of domestic violence and sexual abuse as an issue within the realm of public discourse and state policies. Irit Umanit draws connections between the phenomenon of domestic violence and both the Israeli culture and collective psyche of a community under siege in need of constant military preparedness. The valorization of young Israeli male soldiers as well as popular attitudes of not merely accepting but celebrating aggression would appear to be the most serious obstacles to facing and addressing systematically the problem of violence against women.

Tami Katz-Freiman's description and analysis of the avant-garde feminist art exhibit *Meta-Sex* further expounds on the impact on feminist identity of "myths of masculinity, heroism, and masochistic patriotism." Judging by the work of feminist artists who came of age in the 1980s, there was in the following decade a firm rejection of any compartmentalization of gender relations and other social, political, and economic concerns. As in the case of the symbolism of Women in Black, there is in these works a powerful critique of the "public body of Zionism." One can see parallels also in the artists' deconstruction of the "mythical heroic public body" and empty "staged rituals" with the initiatives of the religiously observant women discussed in Naomi Graetz's article. As feminist artists honor the personal, individual, and private over the public and collective, Orthodox and Conservative women reject their prescribed identities to affirm themselves as Jewish women who individually and as a group will resist their exclusion from the process of recording, interpreting, and vitalizing their religious traditions.

Henriette Dahan-Kalev's research on Mizrahi feminism deconstructs and debunks the myth of universal gender interests as the often-idealized self-perception of feminist organizations regarding their democratic structure and functioning. Her contribution to this volume documents the emergence of

Mizrahi activists and theorists within the mainstream Israeli feminist movement, and analyzes the effects of their critical intervention on feminist organizations and strategies. The ethnic and racial blindness that has characterized the Ashkenazi-dominated movement, Dahan-Kalev argues, is not simply a benign neglect of issues that are of less concern to the movement's leadership and the majority of its membership. The questions of discrimination and marginalization that have been raised by Mizrahi feminists address the problem of asymmetrical power relationships and hierarchies even within the women's movement, and bring to the fore the issues of hegemony, subordination, and exclusion based on difference. Mizrahi and Palestinian feminists challenge the legitimacy and authenticity of "Israeli" feminism's claim to represent women from all sectors of Israeli society.

Marcia Freedman also faults liberal feminism for its dilution of feminist critiques of unequal relations within the family and of social constructions of gender, and for doing little to expand the basis of the movement beyond Ashkenazi women. The alienation of broad masses of Mizrahi, Palestinian, Bedouin, Ethiopian, and other groups of women reflects the deep chasm between the "first world assumptions" of Ashkenazi feminism and the harsh realities of the socially oppressed and economically underprivileged non-Ashkenazi women. The narrowness of the mainstream feminist agenda, its ideological framework, and its values have fractured the Israeli feminist movement and led many Mizrahi and Palestinian feminists to the creation of separate organizations and programs that affirm their ethnic identities and focus on issues of racial and cultural oppression that are central to them. Their alternative voices have enriched Israeli feminist discourse by bringing into the open the ethnic divide that characterizes Israeli society and finds reflection in the movement as well. A major criterion for assessing Israeli women's organizations in the future will be the extent to which they can become more inclusive and accommodate demands for justice and fair distribution of resources and power. The breakdown of the peace process and the resurgence of violence in the region have made the task more challenging. However, these crises also make it more imperative than ever to address and overcome the issues of exclusion and the separation of communities.

Collectively, the essays in this volume present a systematic, critical, and dynamic view of Israeli Jewish feminism within its specific social and political context. The book, though regrettably limited in its scope and representation (for reasons related to wider political and social processes and to the return of conflict and instability), fills a crucial gap in existing scholarship on Israeli

Jewish feminist theory on women's issues. Its strength and particular significance lies in the multiple ways it addresses women's experiences in Israeli
society, focusing both on the obstacles to equality and on the creative ways
in which women are coming together to pursue change and transform their
environment.

Jewish Feminism in Israel

Theorizing Israeli Feminism, 1970–2000

Marcia Freedman

The defining national moment of the period during which feminism resurfaced in Israel is the Yom Kippur War and its aftermath. The 1973 war left Israelis shaken, not only because of the long days when it wasn't clear whether the army could defend the country, and not only because this was Israel's longest war, tying up men and resources for months, but also because of the unforgivable failure of the intelligence services to forewarn of the attack.

The war had important consequences for the nascent feminist movement: it exposed the ways in which Zionism and Israeli nationalism are gendered. Male Israeli soldiers, the contemporary embodiments of Zionist machismo, were so caught by surprise that they literally had to run barefoot from the oncoming enemy army as Israel's frontline positions were overrun. The army high command, Moshe Dayan among them, had been asleep at the wheel. For at least a week, Israelis did not know whether the army was going to be able to defend the borders. The high number of dead and wounded was unprecedented, as was the incidence of post–traumatic stress disorder (then still called shell shock) following the war. Israeli men had been shamed and frightened by the Yom Kippur War.

At the time of the war, Israeli women for the most part were either still unaware of feminist issues or were in denial about the relevance of such issues to their own lives (even though the facts of their lives, if looked at, revealed glaring inequality). But the war was very close to home, and there was no way for women to take part in the defense of their homes. They felt

1

frustrated and helpless. The absence of men between eighteen and fifty-five on the home front caused most businesses and institutions to remain closed for months. Women could not help noticing that with the men gone, the country all but shut down. It became immediately noticeable that there was not a single female bus driver in all of Israel. It didn't take long for the amazing fact to emerge that Egged, the country's only bus service (a cooperative remnant of Zionism's early flirtation with socialism) had a charter that explicitly and blatantly barred women from becoming bus drivers. In this situation of female idleness and frustration, the government's call to women to contribute to the war effort by knitting woolen caps and baking cakes for the soldiers was a profound insult.

At the time of the war, only 27 percent of Israeli women worked outside the home, and virtually all Israeli women did all of the housework and childcare for their families. The average female wage was less than the amount needed for a single adult to support herself. Marriage rates were very high and divorce rates very low, women married early, they had an average of three to four children, and, if they worked outside the home at all, it was often only part time, a fact of life dictated by Israel's short school day. Women's work outside the home was limited to a small number of the 350 official job categories of the Ministry of Labor—the usual women's job market of teaching, nursing, childcare, clerking, light factory work, office work, domestic work, and retail sales. Nothing was yet known about the extent of violence against women, but soon would be. No one, except the radical feminists, questioned the distribution of labor within the family or the social construction of gender, and when the feminists did so, it was shocking. As Natalie Rein, an Anglo-Saxon participant in and observer of the earliest years of the feminist movement, notes, the "new [feminist] ideas . . . were looked on as nothing short of blasphemous. The Zionist ethos has always thought of itself as advanced, one of the myths being that its men and women were equal. Now it was suddenly being faced with contradictions."[1]

Feminism had been on the scene for only a few years before the Yom Kippur War. The earliest feminists in Haifa, Tel Aviv, and Jerusalem had been meeting in small groups since 1970 and were very loosely organized and informally connected. It was a radical movement that based itself on models of feminism imported largely from the United States via both the growing body of feminist literature as well as a growing network of contacts between Israeli and American Jewish feminists.

The literature came in ones and twos—books and articles sent by friends abroad, books purchased when traveling abroad, books left behind by visiting feminists. These books and magazines were passed from hand to hand, one friend to another. Chapters and articles were photocopied and handed around. Later, as the movement began to grow, home-based lending libraries were set up.[2] In 1977, a small mail-order book business was established that became, the following year, a full-fledged women's bookstore and center in Haifa, Kol Ha-Isha (woman's voice). The store imported feminist literature in large quantity, almost all in English. The stock of feminist literature in Hebrew, spine to spine, could be measured in inches. Two years later another women's center and bookstore (Tzena U'Rena) opened in Tel Aviv and, in 1981, a second branch of Kol Ha-Isha opened in Jerusalem. Because it was literature in English that helped spread the new feminist ideas among Israeli women, it is not surprising that the movement's leadership in the early days was dominated by "Anglo-Saxon" (English-speaking) Israelis, many of them relatively new immigrants who were part of a small wave of immigration that occurred during the late 1960s and early 1970s.

The American influence on the development of the Israeli women's movement throughout this period was evident organizationally as well as ideologically. Organizationally, the early Israeli feminists deliberately sought to replicate the American experience of consciousness-raising (CR) and established a loose structure that organized and nurtured small leaderless groups. These, in turn, spawned new groups by word of mouth. These groups met weekly for six months to a year. Often they became activist as well as discussion groups. Almost all the early feminist activists participated in CR groups. The model proved to be an effective way to build a movement.

The first of the second-wave Israeli feminists also adopted their initial tactics from the American women's movement. Following on the heels of 1960s radicalism in the U.S., the women's liberation movement was militant and confrontational. In Israel, too, the movement was deliberately confrontational, and for the same reason—to get media attention for feminist ideas. Throughout the 1970s, Israeli feminists held noisy demonstrations at rabbinical courts, political gatherings, and beauty pageants; they disrupted professional conferences and sessions of the Knesset. One of the movement's initial signature actions was a massive sit-in outside the chancellor's office of Haifa University. The sit-in went on for days until the university agreed to the women's demand for a day-care center for the children of students and faculty.[3]

With one notable exception, confrontation politics was almost entirely unknown in Israel in the 1960s and 1970s. The exception was the activism of the Black Panthers, a group of Mizrahi Jews, all young men from low-income neighborhoods in Haifa and Jerusalem; they demonstrated in low-income neighborhoods against economic and other discrimination against Jews from Arab countries. They deliberately adopted the name of the most militant of American black power groups of the sixties and seventies. After one of the Panthers' first demonstrations in Jerusalem, which ended in a confrontation with the police, Prime Minister Golda Meir dismissed them with a slap on the wrist, saying, "They're not nice boys." Now here were these not-so-nice girls, demonstrating in the streets, sometimes even coming into conflict with and getting arrested by the police. Even more than the messages of women's liberation, these tactics were both sensational and extremely controversial in the Israeli context. In an interview with Oriana Fallaci that first appeared in an early issue of *Ms.*, Golda Meir described feminists as "nuts."[4]

Early Israeli feminist theory, like that of the West, was what is now called "universalist." Feminists did not focus on the differences between women, but rather on the similarities, for such similarities were then the unknown. The goal was to analyze and understand the institutions of patriarchy and the systematic oppression of women. Uncovering the universalities among women was an important and necessary beginning in developing a coherent understanding of women's condition. If the conditions of restraint, discrimination, or oppression were experienced irrespective of class and ethnic differences, they had to have their roots in patriarchy. This ideology easily gave rise to what would later prove to be a too-facile concept of "sisterhood," an assumption that by standing together against patriarchal institutions, all women could find common ground.

Most Israeli feminists of the seventies shared the ideology of the radical elements of the U.S. women's movement. Radical Israeli feminists saw themselves as taking part in a militant revolutionary struggle, both for women's rights and for profound changes in the fabric of society. In Haifa, for example, the first organization created was called Women for a New Society (*Nashim l'ma'an chevrah m'khudeshet*); the acronym of this phrase, NILAK-HEM, means "we will struggle." In Jerusalem, the women's liberation movement was overtly Marxist. The very first group was formed within a political movement, Matzpen, which was associated internationally with the Socialist Workers Party (SWP). Among its earliest members were Leah Tzemel, later a lawyer prominent in defending the human rights of Palestinians, and the late Hagar Roublev, a founder of Women in Black and a leader of the Israeli women's peace movement. During the seventies in Israel, the expression "women's liberation" was eagerly embraced by feminists and carried the same force in direct translation that it does in English.

Finally, the movement's early choices of issues around which to organize reflected the experience of the West. As in the U.S., the first issues raised concerned reproductive rights and violence against women—issues that cut across class and ethnic lines and had sufficient shock value to attract media attention. Even the ways of organizing around these issues were learned from abroad: creation of rape crisis centers, reproductive and health services, battered women's shelters, hotlines, and Take Back the Night marches.

As in the U.S. and elsewhere, these strategic choices made sense for a fledgling movement. The early Israeli feminist movement needed to find issues with broad appeal to women, and it needed to disseminate an entirely new ideology and set of issues as widely as possible. It had no resources and little in the way of structure. Its activists were mostly young, in their twenties and thirties, with few or undeveloped professional skills and little influence. What fueled the movement was the shared experience of seeing the world from a radically altered perspective. Initially, much of that energy stemmed from and was fueled by anger. The early feminists were looking to do battle, and militancy was an apt expression of that mood.

One of the subtexts of Zionist ideology is that women serve their country by bearing and raising children (at least four, Ben Gurion decreed), while men serve the Zionist enterprise by "defending the homeland" and engaging in "productive" labor. For these Zionists, productive labor stands in contrast to providing services, which is women's work and is largely unremunerated. Rein argues that the feminist critique forced Israelis to see what was so profoundly habitual that it had become invisible: Women were virtually absent from the public sphere and were bound in service to children, husbands, and aging parents. By the 1970s, the daughters and granddaughters of the strong women who had immigrated to the Holy Land to found the Jewish state had been, to use Rein's term, "cowed."[5] The Yom Kippur War cracked the façade of women's supposed equality.

Some Israeli women, who had heretofore shown no interest in the feminist message, organized events to air feminist views on the meaning of the Yom Kippur War for women. It was unprecedented entrée for the radical feminists of the early 1970s into a stratum of young professional women who were making their way up the ladder of influence in the mainstream. This was the beginning of mainstream discourse on feminism, which was much accelerated four years later when feminists succeeded in establishing a Women's Party to run in the 1977 Knesset election.

Another consequence of the war was that it dealt a blow to the dominant Labor Party, who lost three seats to a fledgling liberal party to its left, the Citizens Rights Movement; two of those seats went to Shulamit Aloni, long known as an advocate of women's rights, and Marcia Freedman, the author of this article, at that time a leader of the radical feminist movement in Haifa. Following the war, feminist issues were raised in the Knesset and in public discourse for the first time since the early 1950s, during the First Knesset.

The widespread public airing of feminist issues was accelerated with the establishment of the Women's Party in 1977. It is important to note here that the strategy of establishing an all-women political party to advance women's issues was distinctly Israeli. The opportunity to run a fairly well financed electoral campaign was presented by Freedman's incumbency, certain features of the Israeli electoral system, and a unique historical set of circumstances. But it was also distinctly Israeli in another respect. One of the Women's Party activists found a rare book written in 1948 describing the struggle for suffrage during the time of the Yishuv (the pre-state Jewish settlement in Palestine), ending in the formation of a Women's List to run in the election of the First Knesset. The Women's List succeeded in electing one member, Rachel Kagan.[6]

The 1977 Women's Party, too, was successful, but in a different way. It did not elect a single representative, but it put feminism squarely on the political map and raised consciousness on a scale unknown earlier. For the first time, the radical feminists in Israel, so many of them Anglo-Saxons, were reaching women in all of Israel's very diverse communities and were being heard.

The party published an official "Women's Party Platform for Elections to the Ninth Knesset," which contained planks on the status of housewives, single women, women wage earners, poor women, female soldiers, and incarcerated women. It addressed parenthood, education, women's images/stereotypes, women's health, sexuality, violence against women, prostitution, and children's rights. The platform reveals a radical feminist movement that understood that gender oppression and all other oppressions are linked. Its opening statement calls for "equality between the sexes and economic, political and social equality between all people, whether female or male. Accordingly, we demand an end to all discrimination and inequality that exists on the basis of gender, ethnic or national origin, age, ability or world view."[7]

The greatest electoral success of the Women's Party was that the votes it got (a third of what was needed for a first seat) were very evenly distributed geographically and demographically; there was not a single polling place in the country that did not report at least one and as many as five votes for NES, the party's ballot acronym, meaning "miracle." Though the party's candidates were all Ashkenazi (as were most parties' candidates), votes came from Beduin towns, Arab villages and neighborhoods, low-income neighborhoods, and Mizrahi Jewish neighborhoods and development towns, as well as from middle-class Ashkenazi communities and the army. Since the candidates were entirely unknown and little effort was made to make them famous, it was the message that was getting through. In essence, six thousand Israeli women had shown their support for a well-publicized radical feminist agenda.

One of the perquisites of running was free television and radio time. At the time, there was only one television station and two radio stations, all government owned. During campaign season, one hour of prime time a night for several weeks was given over to the programming provided by each of the parties in the race. Most people, used to being in front of their televisions anyway and often interested in what the parties had to say, watched and listened. It was possible to get a great deal of information out. In one of the Women's Party's most successful slots, Israeli documentary filmmaker Shuli Eshel followed a traditional middle-aged Mizrahi woman as she shopped in Jerusalem's open-air market, sampling, selecting, bargaining. At the beginning of the three-minute episode, Eshel asks, "What kind of work do you do?" The woman replies, "Nothing. I'm just a housewife." The camera follows her as she carries her heavy bundles home and up four flights of steps, enters her small kitchen, unpacks and puts away her purchases, and starts to clean and scale the fish she'd purchased for Shabbat dinner. Eshel says, "Let me ask you again. What do you do?" The woman answers, "I told you. I don't do anything. I'm just a housewife." At the time, 73 percent of Israeli women listed their occupation as housewife. Even the most privileged of Anglo-Saxon women recognized themselves in the visual truth of women's unpaid labor and low self-esteem. The first plank in the Women's Party platform called for recognition of housewives as working women and the home as a workplace; the establishment of a high-level commission of economists to find a just solution to paying wages for housework; pension rights, health insurance, workman's compensation, and paid sabbaticals for housewives; and training, child care, and stipends for housewives wanting to retrain for another occupation.

As Leah Simmons Levin notes, "The effect of the Women's Party on the

1977 election is visible in how it extended the activism of the women's movement, thrusting feminist issues into an electoral campaign, a significant
achievement in a political environment in which gender discrimination was
invisible. In doing so, issues such as childcare, prostitution and sexual assault
about which the women's movement had tried to raise awareness during the
1970s, reached the unprecedented level of national debate."[8]

There were those who wanted to turn the Women's Party into a permanent institution that would run again in 1981. But the majority opposed the
idea, not wanting to sacrifice the movement's radical edge by putting all its
efforts and resources into electoral politics. Instead, the Women's Party voted
to dissolve itself and many of its activists became founders of a network of
feminist organizations, centers, shelters, and rape crisis centers.

Having uncovered and made known the dirty secrets of domestic and
sexual violence against women, feminists in Israel pioneered in providing
services for survivors.[9] They developed feminist models of service provision
that politicized and empowered while also aiding women in establishing their
independence. At the first shelter, in Haifa, for example, the women living
there were given lessons in self-defense and participated in nightly
consciousness-raising facilitated by someone on the shelter's staff. Though
the shelters counseled women of all backgrounds, the majority of those who
were resident were Mizrahi Jewish women.

Dynamic and active women's centers and libraries/archives/bookstores
were established in Haifa, Tel Aviv, and Jerusalem. Once again, the movement
adopted an organizing model that seemed to work in the U.S. and western
Europe. These centers served as entry points into feminism for thousands of
Israeli women, albeit almost entirely Ashkenazi Jewish; they functioned as
meeting points for Israeli feminists and American and other feminists visiting
Israel; they offered safe meeting places for lesbian feminists; and they helped
facilitate lesbian feminist organizing.

The origins of lesbian feminism in Israel can be traced to the mid-1970s,
when the first lesbian hot line was established in Tel Aviv. In 1976, lesbian
feminists announced the establishment of their first organization, called
Aleph, at the first annual feminist conference, held that year in Be'er Sheva.
Of the one hundred or so women attending that conference, almost 30 percent identified as lesbians. As a result, the not-so-secret "secret" of the number of lesbians active in the women's movement was out of the bag, and
discussions took place in many venues about the dangers of the movement's
being stigmatized as "lesbian," about whether lesbians were "better feminists"
than straight women, and about whether the Israel women's movement could

or should publicly support lesbian and gay rights. None of these issues was resolved, but they were being joined in a semipublic way for the first time. Aleph came and went in short order, since no one was willing to be identified publicly with it (which meant to come out, of course, and in the 1970s and early 1980s there was not a single lesbian feminist who was willing to be out).

Nevertheless, women's centers provided safe spaces for lesbians and thus became places from which to begin organizing and coming together as a community. The feminist literature that was sold in the centers' bookstores included lesbian literature, prominently displayed. Not all of those involved in running the centers were lesbians, of course, but enough were for there to be a general policy that even though as individuals in the wider world they were not out of the closet, at least in this safe world they would be visible.

Beginning in the mid-1980s, Israel's grassroots feminist movement was joined by a welcome second wave of feminist activism, first among academics, then journalists, then lawyers and politicians.[10] The emergence of these influential women as self-identified feminists was a major turning point for Israeli feminism, leading to the eventual mainstreaming of many core women's issues by the early 1990s. In this development, the Israeli feminist movement follows the trajectory of Western-style feminism. This phase of second-wave feminism in Israel was as highly influenced by American feminism as was the earlier phase. The fact of its transmission through academics indicates that, once again, fluency in English, the language of scholarly discourse, played a dominant role in importing American/Western-style feminism into Israel. By the mid-1970s, women's studies was well established in the U.S., and a decade later women's studies programs had taken root at most Israeli institutions of higher learning—Haifa, Tel Aviv, Bar Ilan, Ben Gurion, and Hebrew Universities.

In addition, by the mid-1980s American Jewish feminists, many of whom were known in Israel, were attaining positions of power and influence in the United States. American feminism actually was beginning to change the conditions of (at least some) women's lives, a fact that was not lost on Israeli professional women. As feminism in the U.S. became more respectable, Israeli professionals embraced their own feminism publicly. Many of these influential American Jewish feminists were on hand in 1984 for the first public action carried out by the group of women who later became the leaders of mainstream Israeli feminism. The gathering, at the Van Leer Institute in Jerusalem, was initiated and sponsored by the women's division of the American Jewish Congress. Led by Alice Shalvi and Galia Golan, both Anglo-Saxons who were long-term immigrants, and flanked by their American sisters, the conferees spontaneously marched to the King David Hotel, where outgoing Prime Minister Yitzhak Shamir and incoming Prime Minister Shimon Peres were meeting.

The occasion marked the birth of contemporary liberal feminism in Israel, which dominated the movement from the mid-1980s through the 1990s. Though it was different in both its tone and its emphases than the radical movement that emerged in the 1970s, it was no less based on Western models and was perhaps even more influenced by them. During this period there was an influx of funding from U.S. sources (mostly Jewish) for feminist activism that favored a liberal feminist agenda on the American model— attempting to use the legislature, the courts, and government agencies to bring about change in women's lives.

Liberal feminist organizations were so successful in attracting both funders and the support of influential individuals that, with a few important exceptions, radical feminism was driven underground. By 1985, with the exception of Haifa, the women's centers were closed and all the bookstores had disappeared. During that period, again thanks to an influx of funding for rape crisis centers and battered women's shelters, a large and organized movement against violence against women was developed. But as the years went on the radical feminists who had pioneered these services gradually gave way to professionals in the field, whose major advocacy efforts centered around securing additional government funding to provide more and better services. Though public consciousness of the extent of violence against women in Israel continued to expand, the issues over time lost their feminist base and came to be merged with the general issue of violence in Israeli society, rather than focused specifically on gender-based violence. At the same time, the emphasis on services seems to have displaced demands that the government, including the criminal justice system, take steps to reduce the incidence of violence against women and put prevention strategies in place.

Liberal feminism in Israel, on the face of it, accomplished a great deal in terms of new legislation and precedent-setting court and administrative decisions. Though they have never been implemented, new laws were enacted that guaranteed equal pay for comparable work and women's advancement in the civil service. Sexual harassment has been criminalized; the number of women holding political office has doubled; and there have been significant gains in the courts that opened up areas of military service previously closed to women (most notably, fighter pilot training courses), that forced publicly held corporations to seek women to serve on their boards of directors, and, most recently, that gave women the right to pray as they wished at the Western Wall. In addition, the establishment of a family court system provided women with an alternative to rabbinical courts, at least for some aspects of divorce proceedings, and single-parent families (almost all headed by poor women) were officially recognized as needing support and some basic entitlements.

What was lost, however, were two critical components of Israeli radical feminism. Most liberal feminists in Israel felt that the early feminist critique of the division of labor within the family and of the social construction of gender was too radical for Israeli consumption. Arguably, bringing a Western feminist critique to bear on the Israeli version of masculinity, femininity, family life, and reproductive rights without taking into account the specifically Jewish/Zionist psychopolitical context in which it would be received, created a significant backlash to feminism during the 1970s. Nevertheless, dropping these issues entirely created a situation in which the most fundamental principles of the feminist critique of gender, family, and reproduction have been pretty much suppressed in Israeli feminist discourse since the mid-1980s. The great majority of women, including progressive, educated women as well as mothers of large, low-income families, remain trapped in service to their families, even though now almost half (46 percent) of all women also work outside the home.

In addition, while it is true that some women have broken through into boardrooms, most women who work outside the home still work in traditionally gendered fields (social work, education, health care, personal care, and clerical, domestic, and factory work). In a poll taken in the winter of 1999 by *Ma'ariv*, one of Israel's most popular dailies, 44 percent of Israeli women self-identified as feminists. Nevertheless, most Israeli women (including the feminists) do not challenge themselves or men to change their behavior, their beliefs, or their values. This is simply not a dominant part of Israeli feminist discourse. In this most important respect, the American/Western model of feminism failed to take hold.

The second component of radical feminism that liberal feminists lost sight of was the effort to choose issues that had a broad appeal across different social and economic strata of society. The radical feminism that characterized the Israeli women's movement between 1970 and 1985 was, as noted, based on American-style radical feminism; its activists were almost entirely Ashkenazi Jews, and it, too, suffered from ethnic blindness. But it did have an appreciation of class differences that at least blunted the edges of the (until recently) invisible racism that has afflicted the feminist movement in Israel from its very inception. It is not a coincidence that the first groups to pick up the challenges of multicultural feminism that were issued in the mid-1990s were the Haifa-based organizations that have had a continuous base in radical feminism since the inception of the movement in 1970.

Until the mid-1990s, the Israeli feminist movement remained largely a white European movement that borrowed its agendas and strategies from Western feminism. As a result, the movement has had little knowledge of or authentic connection to the majority of Israeli women, who are not Ashkenazi—Mizrahi, Palestinian, Beduin, and now Ethiopian women, women from the former Soviet Union, and foreign workers. Ashkenazi Jews may be the dominant voice in Israeli society, but a largely Western, white, middle-class feminism cannot possibly speak effectively for or to the mix of women in Israel. I believe that adopting an exclusively Western feminist model has contributed to blinding the Israeli women's movement to the fact that in many respects Israel is not a first world country. The Ashkenazi-dominated movement does not and cannot represent most Israeli women.

This blindness was brought home dramatically in 1994 when a group of Mizrahi feminist activists disrupted the annual national feminist conference in an attempt to raise the issue of Ashkenazi hegemony. Participant and political scientist Henriette Dahan-Kalev has described this event. According to her account, a small group of Mizrahi activists disrupted the plenary proceedings,

> us[ing] harsh language to talk about the humiliation they had
> suffered because of racism. Women described their childhood,
> how their Iraqi names were taken from them and Israeli names
> given them instead. They recounted their first meetings with Is-
> raelis and the way they and their mothers were treated. As one
> woman is quoted as saying, "The social norms according to
> which class relationships are organized made us believe that we
> should demand of our mothers that they stop speaking Arabic,
> Iranian, Turkish, Indian; we begged them to try to lose their
> Moroccan, Yemenite, Iraqi accents. We wanted them to start
> behaving like Israelis, for God's sake—that is, to be like an
> Ashkenazi!" (*Hila News*, July 1994).[11]

Ultimately, the Mizrahi feminists and their allies walked out of the conference in protest. The following year they organized a separatist Mizrahi feminist conference, which essentially concretized and personalized Mizrahi consciousness. From this conference a clear Mizrahi feminist presence emerged.

A few years later, a well-established Arab-Jewish feminist organization was thrown into crisis when the Palestinians left to organize separately. As Shahira Shalabi, one of the founders of the resultant Palestinian feminist organization, Kayan, explains, the tensions within the Arab-Jewish organization

> raised very hard questions about the nature of the coexistence
> we thought we had achieved and the reality of the oppression
> of Arab women within the organization. The reality is that in
> all mixed Arab-Jewish organizations, Arab women never had an
> equal voice that reflected their actual numbers. The allocation
> of resources within these organizations was never equal, and
> every ounce of gain was at the price of a protracted and ex-
> hausting struggle.[12]

In challenging Ashkenazi hegemony, the Mizrahi, Palestinian, and other feminists of color have challenged the Israeli women's movement to reexamine its Anglo-Saxon origins, its dominance by Ashkenazi women, and its middle- and upper-class agenda.

In Dahan-Kalev's assessment,

> The asymmetric relations between Ashkenazi and Mizrahi
> women emerge in two areas: career and self-fulfillment versus
> low wages and labor-intensive jobs, and dependence on welfare
> and public services versus middle-class autonomy. These areas
> have high ethnic correlation in Israel, and social mobility
> across the ethnic divide is difficult. Thus far, the struggle to
> break through professional barriers based on gender has fo-
> cused mainly on securing representation for women on boards
> of directors, appointment of women to diplomatic posts, and
> the acceptance of women into the combat pilots training
> course, initiatives which have an impact on only a minority of
> Israeli women. Indeed, they have only theoretically extended
> the right to career, self-fulfillment, and professional advance-
> ment for the vast majority of women. Rather, they have yielded
> fruits for women who already have a career and want to pro-
> gress further—a very thin cohort, even among Ashkenazi
> women.[13]

Shahira Shalabi criticizes the first-world assumptions of the women's movement:

> Non-Western women cannot identify with a feminism that is imported from the West and which does not speak to their daily needs and their daily struggles within their own societies and cultures. There is an enormous socio-economic gap between Jewish women in Israel and Arab women who are still struggling to have their daily needs met. There is no way that an Arab woman who lives in a village without running water, without its own high school and without a single pre-school can identify with the white feminism that characterizes the Jewish feminist organizations in Israel.[14]

In recent years, lesbian feminists, religious feminists, and right-wing feminists have all weighed in on the identity politics issue that currently marks the Israeli women's movement. The result has been that the Biannual National Feminist Conference held in October 1999 was divided into four half-day conferences, each planned separately by one of the four dominant groups—Palestinian, Ashkenazi, Mizrahi, and lesbian.

These events in the mid-1990s marked a new phase in second-wave feminism in Israel. Just as the American movement was challenged by women of color during the 1980s, so was the Israeli movement challenged in the 1990s, but with important differences. In Israel, these challenges resonated (and still do) with the often bitter conflict between ethnicities, nationalities, and religious communities. Mizrahi and Palestinian women, for example, together constitute a large majority of women of color, but they remain deeply divided by the Israeli-Palestinian conflict.

For most of the 1990s, the various responses to these challenges were disappointing to Mizrahi, Sephardic, and Palestinian feminists, who perceived them as tokenism. During this period, the Ashkenazi women who were the powers-that-be in the feminist movement still, for the most part, were unwilling to consider their identity as anything but "Israeli."

The situation remains tense, but as the twenty-first century begins, there are some interesting developments. In both Jerusalem and Haifa, Israel's women's centers are grappling in good faith with the challenges of equitable power sharing and coalition building. The resulting balance of ethnicities is unstable and periodically explosive, but nevertheless there is slow forward progress. In addition, the Mizrahi feminist movement has begun to come into its own, organizing independently though still cooperating with feminist organizations who have shown good faith on multicultural issues. Small but significant numbers of Ashkenazi women are looking at their Israeli-Ashkenazi heritage through the prism of identity politics for the first time. It is important to note that for the most part and for whatever reason, the women who are seeking to understand their Ashkenazi ethnic identity are not primarily Anglo-Saxons. Finally, there are increasing signs that liberal feminists have begun to understand that their feminist mission must be multicultural, though it is not yet clear that they will be able to take the next step—to move over and make room for what Israeli feminists have begun to call, with postmodern correctness, "the Other."

These developments provide an important opportunity for Israeli women to develop a feminist model (or models) that can be more successful in changing women's lives than Western-style feminism has been. If Ashkenazi feminism continues to be an active force and if it can join together with Palestinian, Mizrahi, and other feminisms, the result might be not only a more authentically Israeli movement, but also a more powerful one.

Notes

1. Natalie Rein, *Daughters of Rachel: Women in Israel* (London: Penguin Books, 1979), p. 105.

2. Ibid., pp. 114, 117.

3. See Barbara Swirsky, "Israeli Feminism New and Old," in *Calling the Equality Bluff: Women in Israel*, ed. by Barbara Swirski and Marilyn P. Safir (New York: Pergamon Press, 1991), pp. 294–98.

4. Republished in Oriana Fallaci, *Interview with History*, (Boston: Houghton Mifflin, 1976).

5. Rein, *Daughters of Rachel*, p. 109.

6. Sarah Azaryahu, *The Union of Hebrew Women in Eretz Ysrael*, first published in 1948 and reissued in Hebrew and English by the Women's Aid Fund of Haifa in 1980; foreword and English translation by Marcia Freedman.

7. Published by the Women's Party in March 1977, p. 2.

8. Leah Simmons Levin, "Setting the Agenda: The Success of the 1977 Israel Women's Party," *Israel Studies* 4, no. 2, 1999.

9. Barbara Swirski, "Jews Don't Batter Their Wives: Another Myth Bites the Dust," in *Calling the Equality Bluff*, pp. 319–27.

10. See Marilyn P. Safir, et al., "The Interface of Feminism and Women's Studies in Israel," *Women's Studies Quarterly* 3 and 4 (1994): 116–31.

11. See Henriette Dahan-Kalev, "Mizrahi Feminism: The Unheard Voice," in this volume.

12. Shahira Shalabi, "Palestinian, Israeli, Woman, Feminist: Questions of Identity," *Jerusalem Women's Voices* 1, no. 2 (spring 1998): 3. Published (in English) by Kol Ha-Isha, the Jerusalem Women's Center.

13. Henriette Dahan-Kalev, "Tensions in Israeli Feminism: The Mizrahi Ashkenazi Rift," *Women's Studies International Forum* (2001): 1–16.

14. Shalabi, "Palestinian, Israeli, Woman, Feminist," p. 3.

Women and Religion in Israel

Naomi Graetz

In the twenty-first century it is worthwhile examining what if any have been the effects of feminism on Jewish religious life. It is most interesting to see what has happened in Israeli society as more and more women are redefining their relationship to God, to official expressions of religion, and to the patriarchal customs and laws of traditional Judaism.

Patriarchy was not invented by the Israelite religion. The creation story of Genesis 2–3, in which Eve is created from Adam's rib after Adam himself has been created, and in which Eve is eventually blamed for having tempted Adam to sin, seems to express patriarchy. However, in Genesis 1 there is an equally famous passage which states that God created man(kind) in his (our) image to rule over the earth. "God created man in his image, male and female he created them" (Gen. 1:27).[1] Clearly the Bible is not monolithic. There is an egalitarian tradition as well as a tradition that emphasizes man's preeminence and justifies his rule over women.

Not only was patriarchy not invented by the Israelite religion, it was also not invented by the Jewish religion.[2] The fact is that all religions of Western society are rooted in patriarchalism, not just the Jewish one.

Even though Jewish law is often protective of women, it discriminates against and patronizes them. Together with other cultures of its time, it emphasizes the role of women as wives and mothers. Thus a patriarchal stance has been dominant in Judaism. In Israel, Judaism is influenced by other patriarchal systems of Israeli society, notably that of Islam. The critique of patriarchy that has become widely accepted among religious Jewish fem-

17

inists in the United States has taken its time penetrating the religious milieu of Israeli society. This is partially because feminist concerns have mostly focused on political and social change rather than on religious change, and partially because of the traditional nature of Israeli society as a whole. Whereas Jews are often in the vanguard of activism in the West, in Israel, Jews often fight each other over these issues, for religion in Israel is closely connected with politics.

Israel is neither a theocracy nor a completely secular state. For instance, under the Rabbinical Courts Jurisdiction (Marriage and Divorce) Law, 1953, the rabbinical courts have exclusive jurisdiction in matters of marriage and divorce of Jews in Israel who are nationals or residents of the state. There is no separation between church and state in Israel; rather, there are state-recognized religions. The state recognizes that there are religious communities in addition to the Jewish one, such as Muslim, Druze, Bahai, and the many Christian communities; and there are authorized clergy for each of these communities. An example is the Druze Religious Courts Law, 1962, which established for the first time in Israel a Druze Religious Court that has exclusive jurisdiction in matters of marriage and divorce of Druze in Israel who are nationals or residents of the state. Thus Judaism is one of many religions. Despite its de jure recognition of other religions, the government has not given state recognition to Conservative, Reform, and Liberal Judaism, recognizing only the Orthodox branch of Judaism as the official state religion of Israel.[3]

The educational system consists of four main tracks: state education (*mamlachti*), state religious education (*mamlachti dati*), independent religious education (*chinuch atzma'i*), and independent schools (*zerem atzma'i*). Although in *mamlachti* schools, Jewish studies are given a national, cultural interpretation, without any emphasis on religious observance or belief, within this system there are the "Tali" schools, which devote more time to Jewish sources and traditions than is required in a state school.

The atmosphere in *mamlachti dati* schools is one of Torah observance, and teachers, principals, and supervisors are themselves observant. Students are expected to dress and behave according to Jewish law, and prayers are part of the school day. At the elementary level are schools in which boys and girls study together, and those in which classes are separate. *Chinuch Atzma'i* schools place a greater emphasis on religious studies and observance than do the state religious schools. General studies are offered as well. *Zerem atzma'i* schools include schools that are recognized by the Ministry of Education and those that are unofficial and unrecognized. Almost all high schools have the legal status of independent, recognized schools. Unofficial schools include the Cheder and Talmudei Torah, run by various religious groups. These schools follow their own curricula and use their own pedagogical methods, with no ministry supervision.

According to the regulations of the Knesset, the religious courts and the communal rabbis are appointed by a local community and sanctioned by the Chief Rabbinate. They are recognized as the official rabbis and serve as the religious representatives of the community in its relations with the governmental district authorities. The local rabbinates serve as courts of first instance, and their offices work with the committees of the local communities. Local rabbis are very often appointed on the basis of political connections, with regard neither for their abilities nor for the needs of the neighborhoods they serve. They do not reflect the popular will of their communities, yet these rabbis completely control religious affairs concerning synagogues, mikvas, marriage, supervision of burials, and kashrut (Jewish dietary laws).

Every local authority is required to appoint a religious council consisting of religious individuals who will provide all public religious facilities for the local population. Forty-five percent of the members are nominated by the minister, 45 percent by the local authority, and 10 percent by the local rabbinate. Fortunately, there are some communities that are blessed with rabbis who have talents and abilities and who genuinely care for the entire community, not only its religious members. Often, though, the local population is in conflict with the local rabbi and rabbinical council.[4]

Local religious councils have refused, with impunity, to honor the High Court rulings to seat Reform and Conservative representatives who were elected to the council. Women's advancement internally within the Orthodox movement is also considered threatening and therefore to be slowed down or eliminated. These women recognize that "it is a failure of understanding for religious leadership to base their own legitimacy and authority on the claim that no alternative practice has the right to exist."[5] They understand that these leaders are using political leverage to advance their goals, one of which is to prevent women from gaining equal rights.

It is clear that change does not take place in a vacuum. The particular context of change in the twenty-first century in the religious world, as it impacts on women and Judaism in Israel, is the cross-fertilization of ideas and practices between Israeli and American Jewish women. From the very beginning there has been international and interdenominational cooperation on such issues as seeking solutions to the problems of *agunot* (plural of *aguna*, the woman chained to her husband). According to Rochelle Furstenberg, a well-known journalist who writes about women and Judaism on the Israeli scene and who is an Orthodox woman, with a son-in-law who is a Masorti (Conservative) rabbi:

> The contribution of American immigrants to Israeli femi-
> nism is reflected in the high percentage of Americans in Re-
> form, Conservative, and Reconstructionist synagogues, which
> promote egalitarian modes of worship for Israelis. The first Is-
> raeli Reform woman rabbi, Na'amah Kelman, is of American
> background. In the Orthodox world, synagogues like the pre-
> dominantly English-speaking Yedidya have attempted to create
> more feminist-friendly services. The young American women
> who began flooding into Israel for Jewish study in the early
> '70s contributed to the flourishing of high-level Jewish educa-
> tion for both Israeli and American women. Women's prayer
> groups are another instance of cross-fertilization.[6]

In this article, I have chosen to focus on two major areas to show how religion in Israel affects women. The first area concerns prayer, theology, and ritual. The second has to do with women's religious learning and study. Obviously there will be some overlap. Fortunately or unfortunately (depending on one's vantage point), the status of women vis-à-vis religion in Israel is in constant flux. Hopefully the following will serve as an overview of the problems and the progress.

Prayer, theology, rituals

Prayer is a major activity for observant Jews. It is the most important way of connecting with God and as such is required of both men and women. However, women's role in prayer is secondary. Unlike men, women are exempt from prayer at specific times. The role model for women's prayer is Hannah, the mother of Samuel (I Sam.: 2), who prayed silently, with only her lips moving.[7] Although women are obligated to pray both because they need God's mercy and because they must give thanks, in practice their prayer is different from men's and performed at different times. There is the concept of a time-bound positive mitzvah (commandment). In Maimonides's commentary on the Shulkhan Arukh (literally "the prepared table," the name of the most authoritative code of Jewish law),[8] he writes: "[W]omen have been accustomed not to pray in a set manner since immediately in the morning, around the time of washing, they say some kind of request [as a prayer] and according to scriptural law that is sufficient. And it is possible that the rabbis also did not obligate them for more than that."[9] The ramifications of women not being obligated are many. Since they are not obligated to pray at specific times, they are not counted in a minyan (a gathering of ten adults; minyans are required before certain prayers can be said). This leads to a sense of second-class citizenship in the Orthodox world.[10]

In addition to prayers, there are public weekly readings of the Torah, the sacred scriptures of the Jews in the synagogue. On the one hand, since it has to be read at specific times, one would think that women do not have to hear it. On the other hand, in the Bible it states that everyone—men, women and children, even the strangers in the communities—are obligated to hear the word of God (Deut. 31: 9–12). Thus we have a conflict between a biblical source and a rabbinic source. It is obvious that if they are not required to hear the reading of the Torah, they will not be allowed to read the Torah for the entire congregation. This issue of women getting an *aliyah* (going up to the Torah to read or to recite a blessing over the Torah) is a major source of controversy in the Orthodox world. It has mostly been resolved in the Conservative synagogues in Israel and is not an issue among the Reform, who allow women the right to read Torah.

Conservative and Reform Judaism believe in the equality of men and women and have produced responsa and rituals to address religious needs in this area. In a study done by the ad hoc Committee on the Status of Women in the Masorti (Conservative) movement, Amy Lederhendler pointed to the significance of pluralism as a guiding principle within that movement. This study showed that at the time 41 percent of congregations in Israel had women serving as presidents and 59 percent had women on the ritual committees. In most Masorti synagogues woman are allowed to read the Torah publicly, be counted as part of the minyan, and sit together with men.[11] They are called to the Torah to recite blessings, recite kiddush (the prayer over wine), serve as cantors (leaders of services). They serve as rabbis and halakic authorities. In addition, they are encouraged to wear a tallit (prayer shawl) and tefillin (phylacteries). Since Conservative women and men pray together, they have not been part of the struggle of the "Women of the Wall." The Conservative movement has won its struggle to have their own space there, achieving a court ruling that gives them their own official area of prayer at Robinson's Arch, near the Southern Wall.

The idea of men and women praying together is foreign to religious and to many secular Israelis. The ultra-Orthodox consider this to be an abominable act. To them, there is no equal role for women in Judaism and anyone who grants it cannot be accepted as a religious Jew.

As explained earlier, the Orthodox view is that since women are not obligated to pray, they cannot publicly lead the services. Although some sources show that women are permitted to do so, and have done so in history, the prevalent custom forbids this, because a woman's physical presence and her voice have the potential to be sexually distracting. Women are seated separately in the synagogue so that they cannot be seen, but there remains the problem of their voices being provocative: *kol be-ishah ervah*. Women's voices are to be silenced; their voices are better not heard. Women's opinions are silenced or considered worthless. Women are seductresses or temptresses and their voices can cause men to sin. Women whose voices are heard are considered to be immodest. An example of this attitude is found in the *Ethics of the Fathers* (1:5) where it is said, "Anyone who converses excessively with a woman causes evil to himself." Perhaps this attitude toward women is behind the offensive prayer that men recite every morning, *Baruch atah adonai elohenu melekh ha-olam shelo asani ishah* ("Blessed art Thou O Lord our God, who did not make me a woman").

K'vod hatzibbur (the honor of the community) is one of the excuses for why women should not be doing such things as reading from the Torah in public. When a woman reads publicly, it implies that there are no men capable of reading—thus casting aspersions on the community's (men's) honor. This was the mindset for many years, until recently.

Possibly because of the influence of feminism and progress on these issues in the other movements, and because of a deeply felt spiritual need to express themselves as Jews in prayer, many women in the Orthodox community are beginning to pray in groups of women only. They do not call themselves a minyan, but rather a *tefillah* (prayer) group, despite the fact that there have been responsa permitting women to act as a minyan if it is a women-only group.[12] They are internationally affiliated into the Women's Tefillah Network and have a very active e-mail support group. The model that was set up with the help of American rabbis was that of permitting some prayers, but not permitting prayers which require a minyan.

In theory, these issues are not problematic in the Reform and Conservative communities. Tabory found in 1980 that the members of both movements in Israel had liberal attitudes about what women could and could not do in the synagogues. He found that Reform members were more liberal than the Conservative, but also that although congregants felt that women should be entitled to perform functions reserved for men in Orthodox congregations, a large number of women were not implementing these rights.[13]

Another issue that is problematic for women in Israel is of the Orthodox exclusion of women from public recitation of kaddish, the mourner's prayer for a deceased relative during a funeral, wreaking much emotional havoc. To have the right to mourn as an adult member of the Jewish community is to have the right to acknowledge personal loss as communal loss. It is to see oneself as a full participant of the Jewish community and, by extension, of the whole Jewish people. But there is something more. Being "allowed" to mourn is not just the other side of being allowed to celebrate. Being allowed to mourn publicly is being allowed to be vulnerable in the community. When Jews stand up to say kaddish and are then answered with the community's "Amen," they are being given the message that there is room in the community—indeed sacred space—for their pain and loss as well as for their victories.[14]

The problem of gendered God-language

There is another problem concerning prayer for women. This has to do with both the nature of the Hebrew language and the traditional metaphors referring to God as male. The default gender in Hebrew is male; moreover, there are no neutral forms of gender in Hebrew. From the traditional Orthodox standpoint, there are halakic limits on changing liturgy. There is what is called the *matbeia she-tav'u chachamim*, which are the fixed templates (or formulae) of prayer set by the sages. There are some offensive blessings in Orthodox prayer books, as we saw above. It is difficult to filter out gender bias in prayers. Moreover, Jewish men and women, steeped in tradition, no matter how liberal their orientation, find it hard to alter the hallowed liturgy.

Jewish feminists very often ask, "Can a traditional liturgy, created exclusively by men and replete with masculine imagery for God, express the religious sensibilities of women?" The answer seems to be, at best, only partially.

Jews with strong feminist inclinations have a problem relating to anthropomorphic descriptions of God, supernaturalism, hierarchy, the issue of the chosen people, gender inequalities, class discrimination, and animal sacrifice. Their awareness of feminist prayer texts and their solutions to many of these problematic issues increase their uneasiness with traditional prayer.[15] The answer given by Dr. Tamar Ross of Bar Ilan University at the second JOFA conference in 1999 is not very satisfactory to the feminist addressing gender inequities of prayer. She said that women should accept the fact that the language used to describe God is "experiential, not ontological." The attempt to describe God with male imagery is not the reality of God who is gender-less.

The average Israeli man or woman who reads Hebrew is often illiterate when it comes to the language of prayer. Most secular Israelis are uncom-fortable in synagogues in Israel and women, in particular, have been made to feel unwelcome or irrelevant in the "normal" Israeli synagogue. Part of the problem, of course, has to do with the gendered nature of the Hebrew language.

There have been attempts to deal with this problem in Israel. In America, many of the changes were introduced via translation and were not real emen-dations of the sacred language of Hebrew. One example of an Orthodox prayer book created specially for women is *Or va-Derekh le-bat Yisrael* put out by Rabbi Ovadia Yosef.[16] An example of a siddur that attempts to deal with some of these problems is the new Masorti siddur, *Va'ani Tefillati*, which is egalitarian in regard to religious practice. Yet one can argue that only "cosmetic" changes such as adding the names of the Matriarchs are tolerated, and not more serious ones such as devising gender-neutral metaphors for the Godhead.[17] Tikva Frymer-Kensky has pointed out the problem:

> The God of Biblical Israel is grammatically male: all the ver-bal forms, adjectives and pronouns are masculine. God in the Bible is also sociologically male: the husband, the father, the king. . . . This cumulative impact of male-centered language and imagery is profoundly alienating to women. . . . The fact that these images are used for God . . . reinvests these male images with . . . status and power. Women are completely left out of both the imagery and the power loop.[18]

There is a need to introduce female or gender-neutral God-language into the siddur. God's name, however, is not the only problem. What about the im-agery: the all-powerful, loving God who protects the weak (female) people of Israel?[19]

Not only the language but also the content of the siddur is problematic for feminists. In the daily *Amidah*, for example, most of the topics addressed reflect men's concerns as if they were the norm. From this point of view, it might be easier to write an alternative prayer than to change the God-language, because a new prayer would fill in what is missing, rather than replace a hallowed existing form. Many prayers have already been composed to address women's concerns, which are often related to women's biology and may not necessarily mesh with "universal" or "human" concerns.[20]

Rachel Adler points out that although Judaism and its prayer books have changed, women are still required to "temporarily abandon the selves they really are in order to pray in the words of the community, [to] fundamentally disorient themselves in order to orient their hearts."[21] She proposes new texts and modes of prayer that may break the rules or undermine the texts we use.

Much has already been done and is being done in the creation of new prayers and poetry that address women's concerns about menstruation, the onset of menarche, breast cancer, abortion, childbirth, sending sons off to war. To be sure, some issues that men have are not addressed either, like prostate cancer or problems of premature ejaculation.

More perhaps has been done in creating new midrash, or retellings of biblical stories. Some has been done by secular Israelis and incorporated into the liturgy. The most common additions have to do with including the mothers (*imahot*) with the forefathers (*avot*) in order to create parity. Thus, we see in the new siddur of the Masorti movement, the addition of Sarah, Rebecca, Rachel, and Leah. Or the Reform blessing after the meal, which includes women in the blessing (*haverai ve haverotai ne-varech*—friends [masc.] and friends [fem.], let us pray); and includes the four mothers as well, with an explanation. The Masorti siddur is "user friendly"—it includes women and recognizes their contributions to Jewish life and history, but it does so in a manner that expresses the dispute around this position. For example, the word *ve-imoteinu* (and our foremothers), wherever it appears next to *avoteinu* (our forefathers) in the obligatory prayers (and it does not always appear), is placed in brackets, making it evident that this is an optional alternative to the male norm. Because of the controversy in the Conservative movement on these issues, some Masorti rabbis refuse to allow prayer leaders to use this siddur in their services.[22] Because of its variances with the traditional language, they feel that the siddur is not halakically acceptable as a vehicle to fulfill the mitzvah of prayer.

The inclusion of women in religious life, on the other hand, is much less in dispute. This is exemplified in the Masorti siddur by the ceremony for the birth of a daughter (*Zeved habat*), the assignment of significant roles to women in the circumcision ceremony, the revision of the customary prayer for rain to include mention of both forefathers and foremothers, and the equivalent prayers for *benot* and *benei mitzvah*. The picture that is used to show the correct placement of the head phylactery is that of a woman.[23] And despite the controversy about the insertion of foremothers in the central *Amidah* prayer, they are inserted before the forefathers in the Grace after Meals.

Leah Shakdiel of Yeruham has a bank of creative prayers that she uses in her women's tefillah group, including variants for the the mourner's prayer that sidestep the problem of a minyan for women.

Karni Goldsmith has created a new feminist haggadah (1999) (book containing Passover seder ritual) for use in the Conservative movement. This haggadah was sent out to all the Conservative synagogues in Israel. Much of its content was translations and adaptations from American haggadahs, and its pictures were very provocative to the intended audience because of its overtly feminist message. The haggadah was supposed to be co-sponsored by Schechter Institute and other Masorti institutions, but because of its controversial nature some of these organizations removed their names from sponsorship.

Life Cycle Ceremonies

When we come to the issue of ritual and ceremonies, there seems to be less controversy. Ceremonies honoring the birth of girls are becoming more common in all denominations. However, there are those who argue that by creating new rituals we are desecrating God's name. Thus in the Orthodox world all the new ceremonies are looked upon as threatening.[24]

In the days of the Mishnah and Talmud, trees were occasionally planted in honor of a child's birth (*erez* for a boy, *oren* for a girl).[25] In 1954, the ceremony of *zeved habat* began to be popular. The Mizrahi groups use the expression *zeved habat*—*zeved* signifying plentitude, goodness, and gift. In this ceremony, which includes a festive dinner, a name is given for the girl and a blessing for the mother's health is offered. The Ashkenazi groups call this event *simchat habat* (the happiness of having a girl). Some even call it a *brita* (the feminine form of *brit*)—which is a misnomer. Traditionally, the first Sabbath after the daughter is born, the father is honored by reciting a blessing over the Torah. In Conservative and Reform synagogues, both parents often go up together and there is a ritual reading in honor of both parents.

More recently, there are "covenant" ceremonies for girls (without circumcision), done at home or in a hall. The assumption is that everyone is a member of the covenant (man, woman, child) and therefore has to be accepted into the people through a ceremony. Since this is a quasi-religious ceremony, it has resulted in much creativity on the part of those who do it.

The sources that the creators of these ceremonies use have to do with the four Mothers and Miriam, Deborah, Hanna. Sometimes a new midrash or theological explanation is created specially for the daughter's name.[26]

New rituals have been created for the bat mitzvah.[27] In the Conservative and Reform movements, boys and girls do the same things and have the same responsibilities. In the Orthodox communities, the celebration of the bat mitzvah is more of a private affair. Occasionally it is celebrated in the late afternoon service on Shabbat (Sabbath) in the synagogue. However, in the women's tefillah groups, the bat mitzvah girl might do everything that the boy does, including reading her portion of the Torah, reading the haftorah, leading the prayers, giving a speech.

Since so many women have not had a bat mitzvah experience as part of their growing up, more and more women are celebrating their bat mitzvah as adults.[28] The bat mitzvah consists of group or individual study followed by a group or individual bat mitzvah in the synagogue. An example of such an event was reported in the local newspaper in Beersheba. There was a picture on the front page with a woman holding the Torah and it was captioned "Women in Omer go up to the Torah." The subtitles referred to this happening as a "revolution"—ten women had a mass bat mitzvah and went up to the Torah for the first time. The response of the Orthodox rabbi was scorn: "tomorrow they will ask to be circumcised."[29]

Other rituals are connected with marriage. For instance, women are no longer passive under the huppah (the marriage canopy). Today, women, and not only men, hold up the poles. Females often read the ketubah, the marriage contract, during the ceremony. Often the bride recites a verse to express her words of love, or gives the groom a ring. While these activities are totally accepted in the Reform and Conservative movements, when they are done in a wedding performed by an Orthodox rabbi, even if the couple is secular, he makes it clear that these acts are not part of the ritual—and can only be done at the conclusion of the ceremony. Often, the Orthodox rabbi leaves once his part is over and then the couples can do the creative things they want.

Other rituals have to do with death. A major area of controversy in Israel is the woman's right to say kaddish, the mourner's prayer, for an immediate member of her family. In the Orthodox tradition, the men recite kaddish and women are often shunted aside. As stated earlier, part of the problem is that women are not counted as one of the ten men who are needed for a religious quorum (minyan). Today, many women (of all denominations) have taken it upon themselves to say kaddish. They find that it helps them move on with their grief in the framework of their community. Many women have described their experiences saying kaddish, in their own homes, in the local synagogues, and at the cemetery, on the day of the funeral. Often the first time a woman attends a synagogue is to say kaddish for a relative.

When a non-Israeli goes into a synagogue in Israel, the first thing he or she will notice is that all prayers are in Hebrew. Obvious as this may seem, it undercuts one of the important contributions of the modern Orthodox, Conservative, and Reform movements' innovations: namely, to speak and even have prayers or readings in the language of the home country. So what are the differences between the denominations in Judaism? The liturgies on the surface seem very similar. What is obviously different has to do with where the men and women sit and if there is a *mehitzah* (partition), and how high it is. Most of the Conservative and Reform congregations are egalitarian in their seating. In the Orthodox synagogue, seating for the congregation ranges from women in an upstairs balcony to women behind a curtain (some of which are not see-through), to men and women in side-by-side aisles with no room divider, to men and women in side-by-side aisles with a room divider of varying heights. (Ironically, the absence of a *mehitzah* in an Orthodox synagogue is a sign to women that they are not welcome.) The type of *mehitzah* sends a message (albeit tacit) as to women's place in the synagogue. One could speculate that the existence of women's prayer groups is a reaction to this message.

Innovation in prayer

A particularly well-known Orthodox egalitarian model of prayer was developed at Kehilat Yedidyah synagogue in Jerusalem, founded by Dr. Deborah Weissman, who tries to integrate halakah and feminism. Yedidyah has a pluralistic policy in regard to women reciting blessings. The Torah is either taken out or returned to the ark by women, little girls lead the congregation in post-prayer hymns, women make kiddush, men are called up to the Torah with the names of both their father and mother, and some women wear tallit and tefillin. They learn to carry the Torah and read from it. Women give sermons that men hear. The *mehitzah* in both places is a room divider that does not totally block vision.[30]

At the second JOFA conference in 1999 in New York City, Weissman expounded the synagogue's stance in four points: man and woman were created equal; halakah is a dynamic process, subject to history and sociology; feminism is a value *in itself*; and halakah will catch up with religious pioneers. A unique and controversial factor in this congregation is its decision-making process. They do not have one rabbinic authority. When there is a halakic issue, they ask questions to a group of ten rabbis, and then decide what to incorporate.

One of the more established facts of Orthodox woman's synagogue life is the assembly of a minyan of women for the reading of the Scroll of Esther (the megillah) on the holiday of Purim. Although there are debates in the Orthodox world as to whether women can constitute a minyan for this purpose, it is clear from the sources that "all—including women—are required in the reading of the *megillah*." However, there are rabbinic opinions that a man may not fulfill his *own* obligation to read the megillah by hearing a women read it.[31] Although the issue of a woman's voice (*kol ishah*) is sometimes heard as an objection to women reading publicly, in this case this objection is usually not heard. (Those who object usually do not give soundly based halakic reasons for this, but rather state it is "custom" for women not to read, or the fear embarrassing men.) Thus women gather together to read the megillah communally in all settings.[32]

The most interesting innovation for women has grown out of the the Rosh Hodesh, the first day of a new month. Study groups and prayer groups meet to observe the first day of the month, most notably the Women of the Wall Group (WoW). Sered describes how Middle Eastern women observe Rosh Hodesh. The festival of the new moon is a woman's holiday. On the day before the holiday, Mizrahi women visit cemeteries of their families and shrines such as Rachel's Tomb in Bethlehem. They do not launder or sew on this day and the older women light special candles for the dead, one for each relative, if possible.

This innovation seems to cut across all groups: Conservative, Orthodox, Reform. This celebration is an adaptation of Jewish tradition, since traditionally Rosh Hodesh was a Jewish woman's day of rest. These celebrations are ritualistic, social, and often scholarly. In Israel the groups tend to meet for study sessions. There is one in my community in Omer; Leah Shakdiel has been leading a Rosh Hodesh prayer service in Yeruham for many years, often with an invited speaker; in Jerusalem there is a group of women who have been meeting regularly to study texts and exchange personal comments around a theme.

Many of these women are part of the WoW group that goes to the Western Wall and has gained much notoriety in the process. Women's halakic prayer groups were what gave impetus to the Women of the Wall. During a 1988 conference entitled "The Empowerment of Jewish Women," sponsored jointly by the American Jewish Congress, the World Jewish Congress, and

Israel Women's Network, a group prepared for a women's service with a Torah reading at the Western Wall. This idea of Jewish women praying together at the Wall excited the group and after hours of consensus seeking, about seventy women walked with a Torah scroll to the wall, where they were pounced upon by reporters and hostile ultra-Orthodox women. The service itself was very moving, but the political ramifications of such a group are also very interesting.

What is most noteworthy is that even from the beginning, the group's leaders were interdenominational, consisting of Reconstructionist (Rabbi Deborah Brin and Shulamit Magnes), Reform (Rabbi Helene Ferris), Orthodox (Marion Krug, Rivkah Haut), and Conservative (Francine Klagsbrun). The service itself was halakic, in accordance with Orthodox practice. This meant that certain prayers were not said, the kaddish in particular. Although the Israeli women were less interested in praying at the Wall at the time, today the WoW group is truly international and many Israeli religious women are regular supporters of the group and pray together once a month on Rosh Hodesh. They sing at the Wall and then climb up to an area hidden from view and read the Torah.

Shulamit Magnus points out that this group "comprises women from every conceivable strand of Jewish life, radical feminists to Orthodox and everything in between, have bonded around a shared experience of affirmation: women's group prayer, with Torah reading, at the Western Wall." She points out that this bonding was not the original intention of the group, but that it is the most important aspect of the group's existence and has enabled them to take on the Israeli religious establishment.[33]

Women's learning and study

Before beginning a discussion of women's study, it is necessary to point out that literacy should not be taken for granted. The anthropologist Susan Sered, in her many studies of Middle Eastern women, has noted that very often these women are unable to read in any language. Ashkenazi Jewish women were unable to pray, learn, or read in the holy language, Hebrew, but able only to read in Yiddish. Jewish women in Yemen were forbidden to read because it was against the religion.[34] Yet they are in awe of the Hebrew alphabet, which represents learning for them. Often they will kiss and bless the holy letters or objects, like the mezuzah, that contain Hebrew letters.

In the non-Orthodox religious communities, women's education is usually not problematic. It has long been the norm for boys and girls—as well as for men and women—to study together, just as it is in secular communities.

Thus, the content of women's learning is usually no different than that of men's, although often boys are more advantaged in terms of length of learning time. Since the non-Orthodox streams in Israel are mostly influenced by Western norms, egalitarianism is a sine qua non of the Reform and Conservative movements, except on the once-thorny issue of women as rabbis, which has now been resolved. On the elementary school level there is the network of Tali schools, set up in different parts of the country. Immigrants, who were associated with the *masorti* movement, feeling that secular Israeli education did not provide their children with a sufficiently Jewish environment, created the first Tali school. These schools offer a non-Orthodox education option that is less hostile to the Jewish tradition than are the standard schools. These schools are coed and completely egalitarian and offer the entire secular curriculum, with an added emphasis on Judaic studies.

There are two coed *batei midrash* (pl. of *beit midrash*, religious school that teaches Jewish texts) in Jerusalem run by the Conservative movement. One is that of the Conservative *yeshiva* on Agron Street, which is mostly for Americans and is run by the United Synagogue. Here students study for the sake of learning, since there are no tests or requirements. The other is Shechter Institute, connected with both the Masorti movement of Israel and the Jewish Theological Seminary of America, which offers master's and doctoral programs in Jewish studies, rabbinics, and Jewish education. It is also possible to get the master's degree in Judaic studies with a specialty in gender studies. Its school attracts a spectrum of Jews, the majority of whom are Israelis involved in Jewish education. The *beit midrash* also operates the Tali Education Fund, which provides Jewish studies enrichment material to Israel's public schools, educational outreach programs in Eastern Europe and the former Soviet Union, and absorption programs for new immigrants to Israel.

The Reform movement has its own schools, a *beit midrash*: a liberal yeshiva, at Beit Shmuel, in Jerusalem; and Beit Daniel, which is the Reform synagogue and community center in Tel Aviv.

Another egalitarian institution is Pardes, directed by Rabbi Danny Landes and located in Talpiot in Jerusalem. It offers a classic education in texts for men and women and is open to all students. It considers itself a halakic institution and manages diplomatically to avoid controversy in addressing egalitarian concerns. There are no tests or grades at Pardes and students study forty hours a week. There are part- and full-time programs; studies may start in English, but then move on to Hebrew.

Another Orthodox institute is Yakar, located in Katamon in Jerusalem and founded by Rabbi Michael Rosen from England in 1992. There is a women's *beit midrash* program here, run by Mimi Feigelson, who is an expert in Hassidut and studied with Rabbi Shlomo Carlebach for many years. Yakar's philosophy is "tradition and creativity," and they explore texts thematically on such topics as death and dying. Women who study there are from all ages and backgrounds; there is no dress code—which means women do not have to cover their hair, and may wear pants.

Recently there has been a great change in the concept of Orthodox women studying sacred texts. It is not only that they are studying more but that they are studying texts that were previously off limits to them, either because it was not the custom for women to study these texts or because they did not have the requisite skills to do so.[35] The perception until lately was that women were lightheaded and therefore unable to understand the breadth and depth of a page of Talmud. There were even those who said that women should not study sacred texts: that "whoever teaches his daughter to study Torah, it is as if he is teaching her *tiflut* [vanity, foolishness, slyness]."[36] However, it was always understood that there were exceptions to this rule, as in the case of Beruriah of Talmudic fame and many others. Moreover, despite this negative attitude toward teaching women sacred texts, it was clear that women needed to know the laws applying to themselves.[37] Already in the nineteenth century, the dangers of women being ignorant of their own sacred texts were becoming apparent and the Hafetz Hayyim wrote that women who only got a secular education and remained ignorant of the oral law were alienated from Judaism and in danger of being lost to the Jewish community.[38] Thus it became incumbent on parents to see that their daughters got a Jewish education. The question then became, what kind of education? Should it be watered down for their needs? Were they capable of acquiring the sophisticated skills necessary for studying Talmud?

Women's study of sacred texts, in the ultra-Orthodox world, was only institutionalized eighty-five years ago, in 1917, when the first *beit ya'akov* school, an Orthodox school for women, was established in Poland by Sarah Schenirer (d. 1935). The first *beit ya'akov* in Palestine was established in 1936 by Rabbi Meir Sharansky. The graduates of this school system do not serve in the army, nor do they even do voluntary nonmilitary national service (*sherut leumi*). In general, the values inculcated in *beit ya'akov* girls are that modern culture is best avoided.[39]

The ambivalence toward women's study is perhaps best expressed in the haredi (ultra-Orthodox) community that Tamar El Or has extensively covered.[40] In general the haredi communities in Israel (and the West) respond to values of modernism by retreating into tighter groups, by segregating

themselves physically, and by building walls of custom to defend their existing practices. They have their own institutions, yet are involved in politics
in order to get their (some would argue, disproportionate) share of funding.
The role of women in such communities is essentialist; they marry young,
do not practice birth control, have large families, and see their role as wives
to support their husbands in learning. Despite the elevated status of learning
and prayer in the haredi community, Debra Kaufman has shown in her study
of American returnees to Orthodoxy (*ba'alot teshuva*), these women are
taught that they have better qualities than those of men, namely a capacity
for nurturing and a higher level of spirituality. These qualities justify their
segregation by sex and their exemption from the commandments to study
and pray. Ironically this attitude leads to a belief that women's culture is the
source for transformation of humanity, a view shared by radical feminists.
Yet the Orthodox women accept the rules set up by patriarchy, unlike feminists who want autonomy.[41]

Women's study is inimical to the haredi community, since girls and
women should be doing housework chores, yet the community has to deal
with it. Today it is a very important part of their lives. It is very often justified
by giving the women "practical"[42] knowledge that helps them perform their
daily roles as women, wives, and mothers. El Or describes the importance
of women's going to classes to study Jewish law, the Bible, or Jewish philosophy. She says this is not a marginal activity, but very central. They do not
study Talmudic texts but they do value the study of these texts, insofar as
they very often support their husbands, who study all day. As for themselves
they study in makeshift places with the rabbi's wife. Study is a paradoxical
activity for these women. On the one hand, they live their lives in a way that
upholds their community; on the other hand, they are refashioning their
community's definition of their status. El Or quotes one of the women as
saying,

> 'We are learning in order to know what to ask and not to
> know what to answer': (1) to emphasize . . . that in this place,
> in this class, everyone subscribes to the reality in which it is
> not women's role to think, and (2) to approach the world of
> thinking and inquiry, notwithstanding reason 1.[43]

There are those who feel that it is a mistake to allow women to study and
that doors have been opened that were better left shut.

Despite this ambivalent attitude toward women's study, more and more
institutions are opening that give women a chance to study *torah le-shma*

(study for the sake of learning, not necessarily to obtain a degree), and it is no longer strange that women want to and can study Talmud as intensively as men. As religious women gain degrees in higher secular education and become equal members of the workforce, they are also entering the halls of higher Jewish education. The fact that women are doctors and lawyers makes it obvious that they have the same ability as men to study. In addition, it has become clear to women that there is a direct correlation between knowledge of sacred texts and empowerment. It will be interesting to see whether women choose to study text in the same way that men do, or if they choose their own way of knowing and owning the text.

Even in the modern Orthodox world there are discussions about whether there should be different methodologies for teaching girls and women. There is the source book method as opposed to the primary text method. The former method is popularly used for girls but is not considered to be the "real thing"—it is considered superficial and limited. Traditional Talmud study consists of studying whole books—primary texts—not a compendium. Using the source book method is almost unheard of in the yeshiva world. Rabbis consider this to be a debasement of Torah study, by allowing girls to study this way the Orthodox world is making a statement that it is "only girls" studying, and their study does not count. Therefore many of the more modern schools emphasize equality of study. The problem with this method is that it is slower, and by concentrating on one book, one may miss out on a critical mass of knowledge.

Perhaps the best-known teacher to use the source book method in teaching Bible was Nechama Leibowitz, born in 1905. She pioneered a unique method of literary analysis of biblical text by creating Bible sheets—a juxtaposition of texts and commentaries meant to provoke thought. She would ask questions on these sheets and suggest that the answers could be found by looking at other commentaries on the sheets. By showing students the contradictions in the different texts, she hoped that they would see that there is a totality to the Bible. She was a gifted educator, who taught and influenced generations of educators. She was known for her modest Orthodox lifestyle and her avoidance of the women's movement. Yet despite Leibowitz's total acceptance in the "men's world," Rabbi Shlomo Riskin, who invited her to teach students in his yeshiva in 1987, was scolded by ultra-Orthodox rabbis for inviting a women to teach in a yeshiva. It was even proposed by them that she should teach the class behind a curtain.[44]

One of the first institutes that made sources in Bible, Midrash, and Talmud available to contemporary women was the Judith Lieberman Institute,

founded in 1980 and headed by Chana Safrai. In 1985 the institute branched
out into a new area: namely, enabling women from outlying cities to take
advantage of their programs. Classes were held weekly, four on Tuesdays and
two on Wednesdays. Some women stayed overnight, while others commuted.
The purpose was for the teacher to "self-destruct," i.e., to enable the student
to reach so advanced a level that she would no longer need a teacher. High-
level instructors, both male and female, gave the classes. The women came
from religious kibbutzim, Tel Aviv, Jerusalem, and Beersheba. Safrai started
the institute with three students at Ramot Shapiro outside of Jerusalem and
saw it branch into study groups all over the country. This institute, which
no longer exists, served as a model for subsequent study institutions.

The first academic course about Jewish women (entitled "Jewish Women:
Traditions and Transitions") was offered at the School for Overseas Students
at Hebrew University in 1985 and taught by Deborah Weissman, who is now
heading Kerem, a teacher training institute for Jewish education. She holds
that although rabbinic leaders have at times been guilty of misogyny (e.g.,
Rabbi Eliezer, Maimonides, Abarbanel, and Rabbi Kook), it would be a mistake to reject the entirety of what they taught. Weissman is an example of
an independent Orthodox feminist who moves comfortably between the different streams of Judaism in Israel and between academia and para-academic
settings, such as Kerem.

In the Orthodox world, the desire to study stems from the commandment
"*ve-shinnantem bam*"[45] (you should study the sacred texts and make them
yours and pass them on to your children). Much of the learning goes on in
the *beit midrash*. The function of the *beit midrash* is to enable the participants
to study texts without the "interference" of intermediaries such as teachers
or secondary sources. It is hands-on study, often in pairs (*hevruta*), of authentic primary sources. The result is to empower the learners, who in this
case are women. The education includes learning liturgical skills, like reading
from the Scroll of Esther on the holiday of Purim, as well as learning about
all the laws that apply to them, specifically those that determine what they
have to do and what they may not do.

About twenty years ago, Midreshet Lindenbaum was founded as a post–
high school program for women from abroad. It evolved from the Bruria
beit midrash, which was founded by Rabbi Chaim Brovender in 1976 and
was later integrated into the Ohr Torah Institution, founded by Rabbi
Shlomo Riskin in 1986. Since then it has evolved into a college for Jewish
studies that includes a women's *beit midrash* teacher training program. It
plans to develop into an accredited women's college and graduate school that

will focus on schools of secular law, psychiatric social work, conflict mediation, and Jewish law, among other majors. In 1990, Rabbi Riskin created the Monica Dennis Goldberg Program for Women's Advocates (*To'anot Batei Din*—literally, pleaders) in the rabbinical courts, the first and only school preparing candidates to pass the advocate test. The Advocates Program, directed by Nurit Fried, is a three-year intensive course and some of their sixty women graduates are already working within the court system. Their students often hold degrees in law, education, and social work; they study Jewish law texts in depth, focusing on laws of personal status. They are also trained in marriage and personal counseling. Until this program existed, the rabbinical courts were male-dominated and only secular female lawyers could plead for their clients. The courses empower women to understand the halakic texts they need to advise and protect their clients before the rabbinic courts, specifically in cases of divorce, where women are at a disadvantage. Three female graduates of the course have been chosen to sit on the newly formed Council of Rabbinical Court Advocates.

Another outgrowth of the Midreshet Lindenbaum program is Ohr Torah Stone's yad ha Ishah, the Max Morrison Legal Aid Center and Hotline for Women in Jerusalem, established in 1997 and directed by Jerusalem lawyer Susan Weiss, who lectures at the Advocates Program. This center provides legal aid to Israeli women who need help in obtaining a religious divorce decree. In their first year of operation, the center succeeded in getting religious divorces for many women who previously could not afford legal representation. The attitude of the director is that there is more freedom of movement within halakah than is generally acknowledged, and that it is necessary to push halakah to its limits in order to pressure rabbis to interpret the laws more broadly and alleviate the problems encountered by women in Jewish law. The advocates' goal is not to change halakah, but to seek creative solutions within it.

The first graduate of the course to gain prominence was Rachel Levmore. She was the first woman to serve on the directorate of Israel's rabbinical courts. She received her license as a rabbinic pleader in 1995, after a two-year course in which she had to show mastery of Jewish texts concerning marriage and divorce. Levmore is the assistant director in the administration of the rabbinical courts; she reviews the files of problematic divorce cases, in particular those having to do with *agunot*, wives whose husbands refuse to give them a get, a religious divorce.

Another institute is Nishmat, the Jerusalem Center for Advanced Jewish Study for Women, founded by its dean, Chana Henkin, in 1989. Henkin was previously the assistant principal of the state religious high school in Beit She'an; she received the Agrest Prize of the Israel Ministry of Education and the Samuel Belkin Award of Yeshiva University. Nishmat is located in the religious section of Bayit Vagan in Jerusalem and rents space from a synagogue. It has a *beit midrash* atmosphere, which means that there are tables for partnership study and an emphasis on independent study. There are also classes in Bible, philosophy, and prayer. Its focus is not only excellence in textual skills, but also spiritual growth. Most of the students are in their early twenties, between college and graduate school.

In 1997, Nishmat established the Keren Ariel Women's Halachic Institute to train yoatzot halakah, women halakic consultants, under the direction of Rabbi Yaacov Varhaftig, dean of the Institute, and Rabbi Yehuda Herzl Henkin. Yoatzot halakah are certified by a panel of Orthodox rabbis to be resources for women who have questions regarding Taharat Hamishpachah (an area of Jewish law that relates to marriage, sexuality, and women's health). This position was devised to assist women who are more comfortable discussing personal issues with other women. One of the women who has taken the course, Deena Zimmerman, is a pediatrician and certified lactation consultant. Zimmerman is a professor of clinical pediatrics and studied family purity issues (*niddah*). It is necessary to have women medical doctors with halakic expertise so that religious women can feel free to come to them for intimate advice on gynecological problems such as in vitro conception and amniocentesis.

The graduates are careful not to call themselves *poskot* (fem. pl. of *posek*). A *posek* is one who has halakic authority, one who earns the respect of his male colleagues over a long period and is known for his erudition. These *yoatzot* do not replace rabbis; they coordinate their decisions with them. They are halakic experts but not halakic decisors, since they do not make final decisions, and in complicated cases will consult with male rabbis. Their hotline is under the supervision of the Nishmat rabbis, with whom the yoatzot consult for the rabbinic ruling (piskah). Chana Henkin, who created the course, claims that this is not a feminist enterprise, since feminism is perceived both as antifamily and antireligious. The graduates are being accepted with very little fanfare and even the ultra-Orthodox rabbinic community seems to welcome them. They have opened a hot line for halakic questions and a website that invites one to "ask the yoatzot."[47] As of the year 2000 there were about sixteen women enrolled in the two-year program. The plan is to open a full class every two years, with five to seven pairs of study partners. All applicants go through a rigorous screening process. Only those who fit the very high criteria are accepted. The classes are deliberately kept small because of the intensity of the study and the supervision that each student receives.[48]

Another example of a place where women may study Jewish texts intensively is MaTaN, the Sadie Rennert Women's Institute for Torah Studies, directed by Malka Bina. She was a cofounder of Michlelet Bruria and founded MaTaN in 1988 with a group of students who became the board of directors and backbone of the institute. Among the notable teachers at the institute is Dr. Avivah Gottlieb Zornberg, who teaches the weekly portion and is the author of a widely acclaimed book about Genesis. Among MaTaN's outreach programs are programs for Ethiopian and Russian immigrants. It has branches in Raanana, Hasharon, Beersheva, Caesarea, and Tel Aviv. Its graduates teach in high schools and post–high school programs in Israel and the United States. MaTaN considers itself to be a catalyst, encouraging women from all walks of life to advance their Judaic studies, and considers this education to be one of the factors that will contribute to the quality of Jewish learning and living.

In a discussion such as this, it is easy to overlook Pelech, an experimental high school where observant girls are encouraged to ask questions and are taught tolerance, Zionism, democracy, and evolution. It was founded in 1975 by Alice Shalvi, who, together with other Orthodox feminists of that time, felt that there was no quality education for girls. When Pelech was founded, it was the exception to mediocre Jewish education for girls. Its first principal was Dr. Beverly Gribetz,[49] a Talmudic scholar; hiring her was in itself a statement, for the message was clear: no watered-down texts for Pelech girls. Malka Puterkovski has been the head instructor and program coordinator of Talmud and Halakah for the past ten years. Her great interest is introducing women with no previous learning experience to the world of Talmud. It is too soon to tell what the impact of such feminist Orthodox education will have on Israeli society, but some of the graduates are already making their impact in the professional world by offering alternative role models of what it means to be religious.

In contrast to Pelech, which is a totally Israeli institution, there is the feminist yeshiva in Jerusalem, Bat Kol, which runs a six-week program in the summer, bringing together women from all over the world and from all denominations to study Talmud and Torah. Its rabbis are Rochelle Robins and Sarra Levine. All the students are women, but there are some male lecturers. Most of the students are Canadian and American (classes are held in English); many are lawyers, academics, cantors, and artists. The purpose of the yeshiva is to combine intensive six-to-ten-hours-a-day study with artistic evening activities. The atmosphere is extremely open and the texts studied have a wide range of subject matter, including such taboo topics as sexuality, homosexuality, and rape. It is difficult to imagine that such a yeshiva, despite its location in Jerusalem, will have an impact on Israelis, since at the moment its target audience is English speakers.

Alternative army service for religious girls

Religious women do not have to serve in the Israeli Defense Force. All they have to do to avoid service is declare that they are religious and bring proof from their school or rabbi. Many religious women, however, do national service (*sherut leumi*) for one or two years, which has nothing to do with the army. These women work in schools, educational projects, hospitals, and mental institutions. It is a real educational experience for the religious woman who serves in the army or who does national service. Often it is the first time that she is exposed to the outside world and to men on a colleagial basis.

Many religious women wish to serve in the army and some of them also wish to serve in a religious framework. The Conservative movement has its own *nachal* unit (army settlement group), which is for both women and men. In a nachal group, the women undergo basic training and then work on a border kibbutz. The men serve extra time in the army and also work in the kibbutz. Orthodox women usually choose one of two programs. One of these is *tarbut toranit*, which works primarily in disadvantaged communities and with immigrants. The second is a tour guide program called Eretz Moreshet. There is some overlap between *sherut leumi* and *tarbut toranit*.

There are women who are in special *hesder* yeshiva programs, which are essentially *nachal* groups that study instead of working on a kibbutz. They are groups that combine study of texts and national army service. There are two institutes that offer these *hesder* programs for Torah study. One is at the *midrasha* of the religious kibbutz of Ein HaNatziv, located in the Beit Shean valley. In this program the women teach new immigrants, dropouts, and soldiers with adjustment problems, or run the *gadna* bases for high school kids (a week in a paramilitary setting for eleventh and twelfth graders). The other program is located at Midreshet Bruriah (Lindenbaum) and their students are confined to teaching jobs. Their army service too consists of teaching disadvantaged soldiers, and the women are issued special ankle-length uniform skirts, so that there will be no violation of their modesty.

Women Rabbis and Role Models

In 1989, women in the Conservative movement in Israel formed an ad hoc committee in order to put pressure on its home institution, the Beit Hamidrash, to allow women to be rabbis. Some of the women on this committee went to the United States to study and/or be ordained. Some of them waited it out and were ordained as Conservative rabbis in Israel. Each such happening was a cause for great fanfare, which may be strange to the outsider, since the Conservative movement in the U.S. had been ordaining women rabbis since 1985. In contrast, the Reform movement was already ordaining women rabbis in Israel and so some of the women lost patience and went to the Reform rabbinical school in Israel and became Reform rabbis.

From a handful of women rabbis, there are now more than twenty, some of whom are serving in pulpits, others in educational positions. They are all role models, both in their own communities and as representatives to the outside community, both secular and religious. (see appendix, following, for a representative list.) There are also religious role models who are neither rabbis nor rabbis' wives. It is important to note, before concluding, that we do not find rabbis or Judaic scholars among Middle Eastern Jewish women. But as Susan Sered has pointed out, these women are "extraordinarily religiously active."[50] She discusses the importance of old women who visit cemeteries and holy tombs to pray and ask for mercy, give money for holy causes, purchase blessings, and intercede with saints. They are the spiritual guardians of their descendants and the unborn. In Sered's words, they have domesticated religion. Since they cannot read, their religious participation consists of seeing the Torah ceremoniously lifted after the conclusion of the Torah reading, lighting candles, planting trees, and observing the Festival of the New Moon. In addition, much of the feminist cross-fertilization in Israel with American Jewish women has been through conferences and publications both in Israel and abroad. (see appendix.)

Conclusion

We have seen how women are adversely affected by the monopoly of the Orthodox establishment in Israel. In particular, we have looked at women's disabilities concerning prayer, theology, and ritual. We have also surveyed the resurgence and blossoming of women's religious learning and study and their participation in prayer. Women's increased knowledge base has empowered us to innovate and continue, following Jewish tradition, to reinterpret our ancient texts, while allowing us to fight for legal changes in women's status. We have benefited much from these ventures, as have the entire Jewish people. It is beyond the scope of this article to do more than survey the changes taking place, changes that will continue to increase, since the status of women in relation to religion in Israel is in constant flux. Hopefully, women's status vis-à-vis the religious establishment will eventually ensure an end to the patriarchal order that could not have been the intention of our Maker.

Appendix 1.
Sample listing of rabbis, rabbis' wives, and other role models

A. Conservative rabbis
1. Rabbi Einat Ramon, former spokesperson of the Masorti movement.
2. Rabbi Monique Susskind Goldberg, researcher at Shechter Institute.
3. Rabbi Gilah Dror, former pulpit rabbi in Beersheba for ten years, past president of the Rabbinical Assembly in Israel, first woman officer of the World Organization of the Rabbinical Assembly.

B. Reform rabbis
1. Rabbi Kinneret Shiryon, first woman rabbi in Israel, director of Kehillat Yozma in Modi'in, teaches for the Israel Union for Progressive Judaism.
2. Rabbi Na'amah Kelman, the first woman rabbi ordained at Hebrew Union College–Jewish Institute of Religion (HUC-JIR) in Jerusalem.
3. Rabbi Maya Leibovich, the first Israeli woman ordained as a rabbi at HUC-JIR, rabbi of Kehillat Mevasseret Zion, coeditor of a book on women in Judaism from biblical times until today.

C. Reconstructionist rabbi
   Rabbi Amy Klein serves as the Israel representative of the Reconstructionist Rabbinical College. The synagogue Mevakshei Derech (Seekers of the Path), in keeping with its principles, does not have a rabbi.

D. Rabbis' wives serving as religious role models
1. Rebbetizin Leah Kook lectures to haredi women, in evangelical-style talks in a weekly class. Her selflessness is legendary, and extends to the point of lending her children to childless friends.[51]
3. Rabbanit Zohara, the wife of a neighborhood rabbi in Jerusalem, described in Susan Sered's book. She knows each woman by name and "takes care of 1200 families." She sees it as her job to police women's morality and dress. Her status derives both from her being married to a rabbi and from her own strong personality and commitment to ultra-Orthodox Judaism. This despite her lack of any formal education.[44]

E. Other religious role models who are neither rabbis nor rabbis' wives

1. Professor Alice Shalvi, the founder and retired chair of the Israel Women's Network, was the first woman rector and the interim president of Schecter Institute, the Seminary of Judaic Studies in Jerusalem. It was the first time that a Jewish theological institution had appointed a woman as its academic head. Shalvi is considered Israel's most outspoken Conservative Jewish feminist, known for persistently challenging Israel's male-dominated establishment in her quest for equal opportunity, equal reward, and equal status for women. In the short time she has been involved in the Conservative movement, she has strengthened the Women in Judaism program at Schechter, encouraged the formation of the new Center for Women in Jewish Law, started the journal *Nashim*, and was the force behind the first annual Women's Study Day. After her retirement from being the rector of Schechter's, she became a very active chair of its board.

2. Leah Shakdiel of Yeruham is in many ways more radical than others in philosophy, yet she is staunchly Orthodox. Shakdiel first gained national prominence in February 1986, when she attempted to take her rightful seat on the local religious council.[53] Shakdiel is a practical activist and an innovative and independent thinker. She is a master teacher who commands a vast breadth of knowledge and is not bound by rules or loyalties. Her fight to stay in the religious council turned her into a symbol of the feminist cause when her case was debated in the Knesset. Her backers included the Association for Civil Rights in Israel, the New Israel Fund, and women's groups, all of which helped to finance her legal fight. Shakdiel took her case to the Israel Supreme Court and won.

3. Anat Hoffman is the model of an activist. She is a committed religious Jew who sat on the Jerusalem City Council and has often behaved in what some consider to be a provocative manner. As a politician she has taken on small-scale projects to make a point. Two instances: she was behind a move to have more streets named after women, and she got the all-female staff of the municipality to change its anwering message to a female voice using a female verb. Hoffman is an anomaly on the political scene—she is a member of the left-wing secular Meretz Party, a founder of the far-left Women in Black, a board member of Israel's Woman's Network, an active member of the Women of the Wall, and a staunch supporter of the Reform and Conservative Movements.[54] She herself is frustrated that the secular left has allowed Judaism to be usurped by the ultra-Orthodox and is equally annoyed with her friends in Meretz who have little, if any, understanding about the spiritual needs of women.

4. Naomi Ragen is a best-selling novelist whose subject matter is ultra-Orthodox women and the communities they live in. Her three novels, *Jephte's Daughter, Sotah*, and *The Rape of Tamar*, have been translated into Hebrew and have been on Israel's best-seller list for almost two years. She was a journalist with a biweekly column in the *Jerusalem Post* and she appears often on talk shows. She sees

herself as a modern-day prophet whose job is to castigate the "fat cats" of ultra-Orthodoxy. In many of her columns she writes about the attempts to silence and the silencing of women. She writes, "[O]ne cannot help but wonder at the fat-cat arrogance and lack of respect shown by these men, party functionaries in saintly guise.... [who] show a shocking disregard for the feelings not only of Women of the Wall, but of Jewish women in general." Although it is not for her, she has sympathy for women who have created new rituals for themselves, who don tefillin or wear a tallit.[55] As an Orthodox woman, she was the first to acknowledge that there are serious problems in the ultra-Orthodox community concerning marriage, divorce, and the *aguna* problem. She has her own website and many of her memorable columns appear on it. Her most recent creative work is the play *Minyan Nashim* (literally, a quorum of ten women), which was performed at Habimah National Theater. It is about a haredi mother who lives in Mea She'arim and has been denied access to her twelve children. The play is based on a true story and is meant to showcase injustice against women in that world.[56]

5. Tova Ilan was one of the founders of Kibbutz Ein Zurim, of which she is still a member. She studied education and rehabilitative teaching at the Hebrew University, and has been very active in the field of education. She was principal of a regional high school, where she contributed greatly to social integration. In 1988 she left the National Religious Party and was a founder of Meimad, an orthodox religious party whose agenda includes tolerance and dialogue. She works through philosophical, educational, and political channels to heal the rifts in Israeli society. Since 1987, Ilan has been the executive director of the Yaacov Herzog Center for Jewish Studies, located at Kibbutz Ein Zurim, in the south of Israel. One of its projects is running classes for minimally educated women, which is in keeping with one of its goals to support weaker sectors of the local population. Tova Ilan has won the Saul Lieberman Prize in Jewish Education and the Agrest Prize for Jewish Culture. In 1999 she received the Avi Chai Award for her work in encouraging dialogue between religious and secular groups in Israel. In 2000 she was the recipient of the Israel Prize.

6. Tzvia Greenfield is the director of Mifne (Turning Point) Institute, an organization that teaches democracy to ultra-orthodox women. She is the author of *Heim M'fahadim*[57], a no-holds-barred critique of religious political parties and a Hebrew bestseller. Greenfield is an ultra-Orthodox (haredi) woman who unflinchingly examines the haredi collective and is a well-known peace activist. In her book she analyzes the last thirty years and in particular the haredi and right-wing Orthodox world prior to Rabin's assassination. She is a frequent radio and television talk-show guest.

Appendix 2
Conferences and Publications

A. Conferences

  1. First International Conference on Halakah and the Jewish Woman, organized by Pnina Peli and Chana Safrai in December 1986. This conference brought together rabbis, scholars, and lay people from all over the world. Its purpose was to raise people's consciousness regarding the importance of women's issues in halakah. The speakers included a varied and distinguished list of feminists, rabbis, lawyers, academics, leaders of women's organizations, etc.

  2. In 1999, the international conference, "A Woman and Her Jewish Life," held in Jerusalem, was organized by Kolech, the religious women's forum founded by Chana Kehat. Unlike the conference organized in 1986, in which half the program and keynote speakers were male and not necessarily Orthodox, this conference was meant primarily for Orthodox women. There were mass learn-ins in which women scholars (primarily Orthodox) taught sacred texts, unmediated by male rabbis. Many of the teachers were the products of the modern Orthodox institutions described above. The conference received much coverage in the media, in part due to the organizing skills of Kolech. Kolech is perhaps the only Orthodox group that openly describes itself as feminist and acknowledges that a revolution is taking place in the women's study community. The purpose of the forum is to raise the status of women in the Jewish religious-Israeli society and enforce halakic initiatives for solving women's problems. Its two major areas of activities in Israel are legal aid and social welfare. Kolech was established in 1998 with the purpose of working with other women's organizations, recognizing that the religious woman has her own needs based on the inferior position that she suffers in Jewish law. It also publishes a newsletter on the weekly Torah portion, distributed to synagogues throughout Israel.

  3. In June 2000 the first Women's Study Day in Shechter was held, sponsored by the Masorti stream and the Women's League for Conservative Judaism in Israel. About two hundred women from Masorti congregations from all over Israel took off from work for a serious day of study. The women studied Bible, Talmud, rituals, and Torah skills. Women leaders in all the congregations were recognized, and women rabbis and cantorial students led two prayer services. Participants focused on several problems, including *agunot* and wifebeating. Study sessions were in Hebrew, English, Spanish, and Russian. An extremely inclusive board from all over the country planned the study day and other such days have since taken place throughout Israel.

B. Publications

  1. Two journals. In 1998, the first issue of *Nashim* appeared, cosponsored by the Schechter Institute of Jewish Studies in Jerusalem and the International Research

Institute on Jewish Women at Brandeis University. Guest editorship is alternated between Israeli and U.S. scholars on a regular basis. In 1999, the first issue of *Bikurim: The Torah Journal of Midreshet Lindenbaum* appeared. The volume includes articles by the class of 1997 and students studying in 1999. It is available online at http://www.lind.org.il/bikurim.htm.

2. *Jewish Legal Writings by Women* is edited by Micah D. Halpern and Chana Safrai. Safrai is currently at the Department of Jewish Thought at the Hebrew University in Jerusalem and the Shalom Hartman Institute. She has written as well as edited numerous books and articles in the areas of rabbinic literature and women's studies. The seventeen articles reflect a new era in which Jewish women display expertise and knowledge of Jewish law. The topics are varied, including the subjects of women donning tefillin, artificial insemination, breast-feeding, marriage of minors, cosmetics, hair distractions to men worshipping, menstruation and the pill, women saying kaddish, and the bat mitzvah in Jewish law.

3. *Barukh She'asani Ishah? (Bless God for creating me woman?)*, sponsored by the Reform Movement in Israel and published by a popular Israeli press in 1999, is another example of the significant change taking place in Israeli religious society. The book is a collection of articles containing personal stories, sociological studies, a critique of women's status in religion. It includes writers of all religious streams and exposes its readers to different approaches to women and religion in Israel.

4. *Silence Is Deadly: Judaism Confronts Wifebeating* (1998), by Naomi Graetz, addresses the specific problem of wifebeating and the fact that Jewish law can revictimize the wife who is beaten by her husband by not forcing the husband to give her a Jewish bill of divorce.

5. Haviva Ner-David wrote *Life on the Fringes: A Feminist Journey toward Traditional Rabbinic Ordination* (1999).[58] She lives in Israel and is hoping to be the first ordained Orthodox woman rabbi. She argues that the biggest obstacle is not halakic but social.

6. Ruth Ravitsky's edited book, *Women Reading from Genesis* (1999),[59] is the first anthology of commentaries written by Israeli women in Hebrew, mostly Orthodox women, about the Bible. The anthology includes both comments and retellings of stories about women in the Bible from a woman's point of view.

7. Yael Levine Katz, an Orthodox researcher in Jerusalem, has written an extraliturgical text on Tisha b'Av (The ninth day of the month of Av is the date for the commemoration of the destruction of both temples). *Tehinnat ha-Nashim le-Vinyan ha-Mikdash (Women's prayers for rebuilding the temple)* (1996),[60] is a new midrash, based on hundreds of Talmudic and midrashic sources. Though it is written in the form of traditional midrash-aggadah, it is a new creation and new elements have been introduced. She argues that the building of the temple was based on the merit of biblical and postbiblical women. In an article that Katz wrote describing

this text, she asks if this text is feminist, and doesn't exactly answer the question.[61] This text was sent out to rabbis in Israel and was approved as an additional reading for Tisha b'Av services in various Orthodox synagogues in Israel. It was used both in mixed learning programs and in women-only programs.

8. *Torah of the Mothers: Contemporary Jewish Women Read Classical Jewish Texts*, edited by Ora Wiskind Elper and Susan Handelman, is a collection of essays by a variety of women scholars. "The book is not designed to present topics that relate to women and Judaism or to promote a feminist agenda, but rather to showcase the contribution of women to contemporary Torah scholarship."[62] What is between the lines and not apparent to the casual reader is that the essays included in this book are all written by Orthodox Jewish women. The book begins by revering tradition and in particular five influential teachers who were major influences on all the authors. The book includes readings of biblical texts, rabbinic texts, and texts that examine historical and eschatological views of exile and redemption.

9. One of the most interesting publications to come out recently is the joint venture of the International Jewish Women's Human Rights Watch and the Conservative Movement's Center for Women in Jewish Law at the Schechter Institute of Jewish Studies. Sharon Shenhav is director of the International Jewish Women's Human Rights Watch, which documents the human rights violations of Jewish women, it plans to create a central database of women who are *agunot* in their community and to publicize these cases as infringements of Jewish women's rights. Because of Shenhav's pessimism about Orthodox women's effecting change, she has formed a coalition with Rabbi David Golinkin, the head of the Center for Women in Jewish Law.[63] The center is publishing both a book about the *aguna* dilemma in the twentieth century, reviewing all the halakic solutions that have been suggested, and biannual pamphlets examining court cases that have not been resolved.[64] Two women rabbis, Monique Susskind Goldberg and Diana Vila, were two of the research fellows involved in the research. They are hoping to influence decision makers in the legal community, the lay public, and the Orthodox hierarchy in Israel. The goal of the series is to "pressure the rabbinical courts to publish their decisions in a timely and orderly fashion, much as civil court decisions are published, and to encourage rabbinical courts to use the halakhic tools which are at their disposal in order to free modern-day *agunot*."[65]

Notes

1. See Phyllis A. Bird, "Male and Female He Created Them," *Harvard Theological Review* 74, no. 2 (1981): 129–59. See also Phyllis Trible, "Depatriarchalizing in Biblical Interpretation," *Journal of the American Academy of Religion* (March 1973): 30–48.

2. Israelite religion refers exclusively to the Biblical period. The Jewish religion (or

Judaism) is a more general term which stems from the Bible, but also includes the interpretive traditions of the Mishnah, Talmud, Codes, etc. Both Judith Plaskow and Susannah Heschel, whose identity with Judaism is as strong as their feminist beliefs, caution Christian feminists not to blame Judaism for the introduction of patriarchy to Western civilization. In their articles, they attempt to warn Christian feminists against falling into the trap of sloppy scholarship, of anti-Semitism (under the guise of antipatriarchalism), and of avoiding a confrontation with the darker side of their own religion. Unfortunately, examples abound of Christian feminists who have adopted a theology that claims that Christianity represents liberation for women, whereas Judaism represents oppression for women. According to the Jewish historian Shaye Cohen, this is an example of "the old Christian animosity toward Judaism [resurfacing] in a new form." See Plaskow, "Blaming the Jews for the Birth of Patriarchy," in *Nice Jewish Girls: A Lesbian Anthology*, ed. Evelyn Beck (Watertown, Mass.: Persephone Press, 1982), pp. 250–54, and Heschel, "Anti-Judaism in Christian Feminist Theology," *Tikkun* 5, no. 3 (1990): 25–28, 95–97. See for example, Marla Selvidge's comparison of Mark's liberation message with the oppressive message of the "androcentric" book of Leviticus about the restrictive purity laws concerning menstruation. "Mark 5:25–34 and Leviticus 15:19–20," *Journal of Biblical Literature* 103, no. 4 (1984): 623. See Cohen, "The Modern Study of Ancient Judaism," in *The State of Jewish Studies*, ed. Shaye Cohen and Edward L. Greenstein (Detroit: Wayne State University Press, 1990), p. 57. See also Susannah Heschel, who writes that German feminists consider "negative depictions of Judaism" to be "accepted as legitimate evaluations of it, rather than as part of a systemic misrepresentation endemic to Occidental culture." From "Configurations of Patriarchy Judaism, and Nazism in German Feminist Thought," in *Gender and Judaism*, ed. T. M. Rudavsky (New York: New York University Press, 1995), p. 146.

3. See "Israel, State of: Legal and Judicial System," in *Encyclopedia Judaica* (Shaker Heights, Ohio: Judaica Multimedia, 1997), for more details about state recognition of religion.

4. See "Israel, State of: Religious Life and Communities," in *Encyclopedia Judaica* (Shaker Heights, Ohio: Judaica Multimedia, 1997), for more details about local rabbis.

5. The quote is from an ad that appeared in the *Jewish Week* (16 June 2000). "JOFA [Jewish Orthodox Feminist Alliance] deplores the actions of those Knesset members who would seek to undo the Israeli Supreme Court decision by imposing a seven year prison sentence on women who choose to read from the Torah and engage in other ritual acts at the Kotel [the Western Wall]."

6. Rochelle Furstenberg, "Israeli Feminism Takes Account," *Jerusalem Post*, 24 May 2000.

7. In point of fact, Hannah serves a role model for all Jews who pray, since the Amidah, the silent prayer, is the principal prayer in the service and it is said silently by all while standing.

8. Written by Joseph Caro (1488–1575), it was first printed in Venice in 1565.

9. Abraham Gumbiner, "Magen Avraham: Commentary on the *Shulkan Arukh*," *Orah Hayyim* 106, no. 2, cited by Rachel Biale, *Women and Jewish Law* (New York: Schocken Books, 1984), p. 19.

10. To be fair, this issue has not been entirely resolved in the Conservative world, either, and there are still synagogues in Israel (e.g., Ra'anana) where women are not counted and are not allowed to lead prayers.

11. Amy Lederhendler, "Left, Right and Center: Women in the Masorti Movement," *The Messer of the Masorti Movement* (spring 1990): 5.

12. In an e-mail communication of the women's tefillah network, there was a reference to Rabbi Goren's responsum, written on the stationery of the chief rabbinate. Although he never retracted his responsum, he claimed that he was writing about a theoretical case and not about real women. It was a private communication and the Baltimore Women's Tefillah Group (WTG) publicized it (Rivka Haut, 25 June 2000). In another e-mail communication there is a reference to Rabbi Yoel Bin-Nun: that ten women who take upon themselves all the mitzvot (commandments) can constitute a minyan (Debby Weissman, 26 June 2000).

13. Some modern Orthodox rabbis are willing to mention the mother's name when naming a child in the synagogue and allow women to say the prayer of *birkhat ha-gomel* (said after an accident or childbirth) out loud in the synagogue. Ephraim Tabory, *A Sociological Study of the Reform and Conservative Movements in Israel* (Ph.D. diss., Bar Ilan University, 1980), p. 351.

14. "Bella's Bat Mitzvah," *Journey* (winter 2000): p. 12. *Journey* is a publication of Ma'yan, the Jewish Women's Project, a program of the Jewish Community Center in Manhattan. See also Esther M. Broner, *Mornings and Mournings: A Kaddish Journal* (New York: HarperCollins, 1994). For an Orthodox feminist discussion of the halakhic (Jewish law) issues regarding women and the recitation of Kaddish, see Rochelle L. Millen, "The Female Voice of Kaddish," in Jewish Legal Writings by Women (Jerusalem: Urim Publications, 1998).

15. Marcia Falk, in *Book of Blessings* (San Francisco: Harper, 1996) "solved" the problem of addressing prayers to a masculine God (*Barukh ata adonai*) who is ruler of the world (*melekh ha'olam*) by introducing the formula "Let us bless the source of life" (*nevarekh et ein ha-hayyim*). This has become the standard gender-inclusive blessing formula, though Falk has never referred to her work as a siddur (prayer book). For more on this topic, see Paula Hyman, "Looking to the Future: Conclusions," in *Daughters of the King: Women and the Synagogue*, ed. Susan Grossman and Rivka Haut (Philadelphia: Jewish Publication Society, 1992), p. 303.

16. Jerusalem: Yeshivat Or va-Derekh, 1988.

17. In a review I wrote about this siddur, I state "It is serious to me, as a feminist, that the God-language of the siddur is exclusively male, that God is addressed only in the masculine, and that the prayers often reflect male perspectives masquerading as universal concerns." See Naomi Graetz, "Review Essay: Siddur Va'ani Tefillati," *NASHIM: A Journal of Jewish Women's Studies and Gender Issues* 2 (March 1999): 161–72.

18. We could use *Shekhinah, Malkat Ha'olam* (the Queen of the world), *Malkat Hashamayim* (the Queen of Heaven), or *Rahamema* (the Merciful One). But are these really solutions? Frymer-Kensky notes out that although their "resonance is indeed biblical, [they are] quite negative. The historical use of these terms to refer to pagan gods gives them connotations far beyond the normal meanings of the words." "On Feminine God-Talk," *The Reconstructionist* 59:1 (Spring 1994): 48–49.

19. I have written extensively about this in my book *Silence Is Deadly: Judaism Confronts Wifebeating* (Northvale, N.J.: Jason Aronson, 1998).

20. Susan Grossman has suggested a "Meditation after a Miscarriage" and Tikva Frymer-Kensky a "Ritual for Affirming and Accepting Pregnancy." See Grossman and Haut, *Daughters of the King*. The Israeli poet Esther Raab wrote "A Woman's Song," a poem that is very much a prayer, using the formula *barukh she-asani isha* ("Blessed are You for making me a woman"). See Ellen M. Umansky and Diane Ashton, eds., *Four Centuries of Jewish Women's Spirituality: A Sourcebook* (Boston: Beacon Press, 1992).

21. Rachel Adler, *Engendering Judaism: An Inclusive Theology and Ethics* (Philadelphia: Jewish Publication Society, 1998), p. 65.

22. It is ironic that in the *beit midrash* (rabbinical school) of Shechter Institute, whose president is Rabbi David Golinkin, that the *shaliach ztibbur* (the one who leads services) is forbidden to use the controversial Masorti siddur. At the Women's Study Day sponsored by the institute, women were told to bring this siddur and it was used—but Golinkin was not present (at the time Alice Shalvi was rector and acting president).

23. I would like to thank David Ellenson for sharing with me in manuscript his forthcoming article, "A New Rite From Israel: Reflections on *Siddur Va'ani Tefillati* of the *masorti* (Conservative) Movement," which later appeared in *Studies in Contemporary Jewry: An Annual XV.* Published for the Avraham Harman Institute of Contemporary Jewry, Hebrew University of Jerusalem, by Oxford University Press, 1999. pp. 29–30. He wrote that the "move towards gender-inclusivity that marks the ethos of *Va'ani Tefillati* is most fully and obviously expressed . . . by a woman, garbed in a *kippah* [head-covering], wearing the head *tefillin.* . . . This picture delivers a powerful statement. It indicates that the *masorti* Movement has internalized a feminist critique contending that patriarchal cultures posit the male as normative. . . . The icon of the female wearing *tefillin* presents the argument that the female is no longer 'other.' From the standpoint of semiotics, this is the single most powerful example of innovation contained in the *siddur*."

24. According to Wolowelsky, the importance of the "welcoming ceremony" for daughters is not its ceremonial aspect, but the public attention. Joel Wolowelsky, *Women, Jewish Law and Modernity: New Opportunities in a Post-Feminist Age* (New York: K'tav Publishing House, 1997), pp. 44–45.

25. Gittin 57a.

26. Maya Lebowitz and Yoram Mazor, "Women's Participation in Life Cycle Events," in *Barukh She'asani Isha*? (Blessed the One who made me a woman? The woman in Judaism—from the Bible unto today; in Hebrew), ed. David Joel, Ariel, Maya Lebowitz, and Yoram Mazor (Tel Aviv: Yediyot Achronot, 1999). Put out by the Reform movement in Israel.

27. Bar mitzvah is for a boy when he becomes an adult member of the congregation; the Bat mitzvah is for a girl who does the same.

28. For more on this topic see Stuart Schoenfeld, "Ritual and Role Transition: Adult Bat Mitzvah as a Successful Rite of Passage," in *The Uses of Tradition: Jewish Community in the Modern Era*, ed. Jack Wertheimer (New York: Jewish Theological Seminary, 1992), pp. 349–376.

29. *Kol bi*, 8 June 1995.

30. For more about the Yedidya congregation, go to their site at http://yedidya. tripod.com/news.htm. There are other innovative Orthodox Kehillot (congregations). The newest one is Shira Hadasha ("New Song") which meets in the German Colony in Jerusalem. The driving force of the group is Tova Hartman-Halbertal. A unique feature here is that a minyan composed of ten men and ten women is necessary for prayers to begin. The ten men is the traditional quorum, whereas the ten women is the practice in this synagogue. For more details see, Elli Wohlgelernter, "The Simha of Torah—for Women," *Jerusalem Post*, September 27, 2002, B5. For another article about Jerusalem's feminist Orthodox congregation, which is winning passionate support for its envelope pushing, see Netty C. Gross, "A Year since the Revolution," *Jerusalem Report*, 10 February 2003, pp. 24–25.

31. Shulhan Arukh, Orah Hayyim 669:1.

32. Wolowelsky, *Women, Jewish Law and Modernity*, pp. 94–98.

33. Shulamit S. Magnus, "Re-Inventing Miriam's Well: Feminist Jewish Cere-monials." In *The Uses of Tradition*, p. 347. See also Phyllis Chesler and Rivka Haut, eds., *Women of the Wall: Claiming Sacred Ground* (Woodstock, Vt.: Jewish Lights Pub., 2002).

34. Lisa Gilad, *Ginger and Salt: Yemini Jewish Women in an Israeli Town* (Boulder, Colo.: Westview Press, 1989), and Rhonda Berger-Sofer, "Pious Women: A Study of Women's Roles in a Hassidic and Pious Community: Mea She'arim" (Ph.D. diss., Rutgers University, 1979).

35. Moses Maimonides, *Talmud Torah*, p. 13.

36. M. Sotah 3:4 or Sotah 20a.

37. Moses Isserless, commenting on the Shulkan Arukh (Yoreh Deah 246:6).

38. R. Israel Meir Ha-Kohen (known as Hafetz Hayyim after the title of his first work; Radun, Poland, 1838–1933). His best-known work is the six-volume *Mishnah Berurah* (1894–1907), a commentary on *Shulhan Arukh (Orah Hayyim)*, which is a reference book on halakic matters.

39. For more about the Haredi women's school system, see Deborah Weissman,

"Bais Ya'akov: A Historical Model for Jewish Feminists," in Elizabeth Kolten, ed., *The Jewish Woman: New Perspectives* (New York: Schocken Books, 1976), pp. 139–48. The article was based on her thesis, "Bais Ya'akov, A Women's Educational Movement in the Polish Jewish Community: A Case Study in Tradition and Modernity," NYU, 1977. See too Eetta Prince-Gibson, "Haredi girls can now study for cutting-edge careers and be traditional," in Jewish Bulletin Online, http://www.jewishsf.com/bk000811/supharedigirls.shtml.

40. Tamar El Or, *Educated and Ignorant: Ultraorthodox Jewish Women and Their World* (Boulder, Colo.: Lynne Rienner Publishers, 1994).

41. Debra Kaufman, *Rachel's Daughters: Newly Orthodox Women* (New Brunswick, N.J.: Rutgers University Press, 1991), pp. 149–154.

42. El Or distinguishes between practical classes and substance classes, which can only be taken with a rabbi's prescription.

43. Tamar El Or, "Ultraorthodox Jewish Women," in *Israeli Judaism* ed. Shlomo Deshen, Charles S. Liebman, and Moshe Shokeid (New Brunswick, N.J.: Transaction Publishers, 1995), pp. 149–69; quote at p. 166.

44. Naomi Ragen, "The Boulders in the River: A Thousand Years of Women's Achievements," from her website, www.naomiragen.com, September 23, 1999.

45. Deuteronomy 6:4–9 is part of the text of the *S'hma*, which is recited twice daily: "Hear, O Israel! The Lord is our God, the Lord alone. You shall love the Lord your God with all your heart and with all your soul and with all your might. Take to heart these instructions with which I charge you this day. Impress them upon your children. Recite them when you stay at home and when you are away, when you lie down and when you get up. Bind them as a sign on your hand and let them serve as a symbol on your forehead; inscribe them on the doorposts of your house and on your gates."

47. Chana Henkin, "Symposium on Women and Jewish Education," *Tradition* 28, no. 3 (spring, 1994): 33. For more information about Nishmat, see their website at www.nishmat.net.

48. To ask a question of one of the advisers and receive an answer authored by Dr. Zimmerman, see the website, http://www.yoatzot.org/about.php.

49. Gribetz is now a principal at Evelina De Rothschild High School in Jerusalem, a school whose entrance requirements are less rigorous than Pelech's. It is this school's policy to be as inclusive as possible and to raise as many religious women as possible to a high level of education, rather than be an elitist institution.

50. Susan Sered, *Women as Ritual Experts: The Religious Lives of Elderly Jewish Women in Jerusalem* (New York: Oxford University Press, 1992), pp. 17–33.

51. Rachel Ginsberg, "The Revival Rebbetzin," *Country Yossi Family Magazine* (November 1997); countryyossi.com.

52. Sered, *Women as Ritual Experts*, pp. 41–46.

53. Liora Moriel, "Lea Shakdiel—A Portrait of the Woman," *Jerusalem Post*, 19 September 1986.

54. Yossi Klein Halevi, "Up Against the Wall," *The Jerusalem Report*, 3 July 2000: 18–19.

55. Naomi Ragen, "Those Subversive Women's Voices," www.naomiragen.com, 30 June 2000.

56. For a review of this play, see Helen Kaye, "A Minyan of Women," in the *Jerusalem Post*, 19 July 2002.

57. Tzvia Greenfield, *Heim M'fahadim* (Cosmic fear: the religious right in Israel) (Tel Aviv: Yediot Abronot, 2001).

58. Needham, Mass.: JFL Books.

59. Tel Aviv: Yediot Aharonot.

60. Tel Aviv: Eked.

61. An article delivered at the Kolech conference in 1999 in Jerusalem, copy given to me by author (in Hebrew).

62. Book review in Torah Community Connections, www.torahcc.org/bookreviews/5761/mothersbr.htm.

63. Diane Friedgut. "Major Chance for Change: Jewish Women and the Law," *Women's League Outlook* 70, no.4 (summer 2000): 30.

64. From David Golinkin's introduction to "The *Aguna* Dilemma: Case Study Number One," *Jewish Law Watch* (January 2000): 3. The forthcoming book *Solutions to the Agunah Dilemma in the Twentieth Century*, written by the staff of the Schechter Institute of Jewish Studies, will be published (in Hebrew) by the Institute. Another recent publication of the Schechter Institute is David Golinkin's *The Status of Women in Jewish Law* (2001; in Hebrew with English summaries). This book contains the response about women published by the Va'ad Halacha (law committee) of the Masorti movement in Israel.

65. Ibid., p. 4.

Works Consulted

Adelman, Peninah. *Miriam's Well: Rituals for Jewish Women Around the Year*. Fresh Meadows, N.Y.: Biblio Press, 1986.

Adler, Rachel. *Engendering Judaism: An Inclusive Theology and Ethics*. Philadelphia: Jewish Publication Society, 1998.

Ariel, David Joel, Maya Leibowitz, and Yoram Mazor, eds. *Barukh She'asani Ishah?* (Blessed the One who made me a woman?: Women in Judaism—from the biblical times until today) (in Hebrew). Tel Aviv: Yediot Aharonot, 1999. Put out by the Reform movement in Israel.

Azmon, Yael, ed. *A View into the Lives of Women in Jewish Societies: Collected Essays* (in Hebrew). Jerusalem: Zalman Shazar Center for Jewish History, 1995.

Berger-Sofer, Rhonda. "Pious Women: A Study of Women's Roles in a Hassidic and Pious Community: Mea She'arim." Ph.D. diss., Rutgers University, 1979.

Biale, Rachel. *Women and Jewish Law*. New York: Shocken Books, 1984.

Bird, Phyllis A. "Male and Female He Created Them." *Harvard Theological Review* 74, no.2 (1981): 129–59.

Bogoch, Bryna and Rachelle Don Yechiya. *The Gender of Justice: Bias Against Women in Israeli Courts* (in Hebrew). Jerusalem: The Jerusalem Institute for Israel Studies, 1999.

Boyarin, Daniel. *Unheroic Conduct: The Rise of Heterosexuality and the Invention of the Jewish Man*. Berkeley: University of California, 1997.

Cantor, Aviva. *Jewish Women/Jewish Men: The Legacy of Patriarchy in Jewish Life*. New York: Harper Collins, 1995.

Chesler, Phyllis, and Rivka Haut (eds.). *Women of the Wall: Claiming Sacred Ground* (Woodstock, Vt.: Jewish Lights Publishing, 2002).

Chigier, Moshe. *Husband and Wife in Israeli Law*. Jerusalem: Harry Fischel Institute, 1985.

Cohen, Boaz. "Betrothal in Jewish and Roman Law." *Proceedings of the American Academy for Jewish Research* 18 (1948–49).

Cohen, Shaye. "The Modern Study of Ancient Judaism." In *The State of Jewish Studies*, edited by Shaye Cohen and Edward L. Greenstein. Detroit: Wayne State University Press, 1990.

Comet-Murciano, Aviva. *Jewish Denominational Approaches to Religious Feminism*. New York, Yeshiva University, 1992.

Danyluk, Angie. *Living Feminism and Orthodoxy: Orthodox Jewish Feminists*. Master's thesis, York University, Ontario, 1997.

Davidman, Lynn. *Tradition in a Rootless World: Women Turn to Orthodox Judaism*. Berkeley: University of California Press, 1991.

Dorff, Elliot N., and Arthur Rossett. *The Living Tree*. Albany, N.Y.: SUNY Press, 1988.

Edelman, Martin. *Courts, Politics, and Culture in Israel*. Charlottesville: The University Press of Virginia, 1994.

Elon, Menachem. *Mishpat Ivri* (Jewish law), (in Hebrew). 3 vols. Jerusalem: Magnes Press, 1973.

El Or, Tamar. *Educated and Ignorant: Ultra-orthodox Jewish Women and Their World*. Boulder, Colo.: Lynne Rienner, Publishers, 1994.

———. *Next Passover: Literacy and Identity of Young Religious Zionist Women* (in Hebrew). Tel Aviv: Am Oved Publishers, 1998.

———. "Ultraorthodox Jewish Women." In *Israeli Judaism*, edited by Shlomo Deshen, Charles S. Liebman, and Moshe Shokeid. New Brunswick, N.J.: Transaction Publishers, 1995, pp. 149–69.

Elper, Ora Wiskind, and Susan Handelman, eds. *Torah of the Mothers: Contemporary Jewish Women Read Classical Jewish Texts*. Jerusalem: Urim Publications, 2001.

Englard, Izhak. *Religious Law in the Israel Legal System*. Jerusalem: Alpha Press, 1975.

Falk, Marcia. *Book of Blessings*. San Francisco: Harper, 1996.

Friedgut, Diane. "Major Chance for Change: Jewish Women and the Law." *Women's League Outlook* 70, no.4 (summer 2000): 29–31.

Frymer-Kensky, Tikvah. "On Feminine God-Talk." *The Reconstructionist* 59, no.1 (spring 1994): 48–49.

Furstenberg, Rochelle. "Israeli Feminism Takes Account." *Jerusalem Post*, 24 May 2000.

Gilad, Lisa. *Ginger and Salt: Yemini Jewish Women in an Israeli Town*. Boulder, Colo.: Westview Press, 1989.

Graetz, Naomi. "Review Essay: Siddur Va'ani Tefillati." *NASHIM: A Journal of Jewish Women's Studies and Gender Issues* 2 (March 1999): 161–72.

————. *Silence is Deadly: Judaism Confronts Wifebeating*. Northwale, N.J.: Jason Aronson, 1998.

Grossman, Susan, and Rivkah Haut, eds. *Daughters of the King: Women and the Synagogue*. Philadelphia: The Jewish Publication Society, 1992.

Halpern, Micah D., and Chana Safrai, eds. *Jewish Legal Writings by Women*. Jerusalem: Urim Publications, 1998.

Hauptman, Judith. *Rereading the Rabbis: A Woman's Voice*. Boulder, Colo.: Westview Press, 1998.

Henkin, Chana. "Symposium on Women and Jewish Education," *Tradition* 28, no. 3 (spring, 1994): 31–33.

————. "Women and the issuing of halakhic rulings." In *Jewish Legal Writings by Women*, edited by D. Halpern and Chana Safrai. Jerusalem: Urim Publications, 1998: 278–87.

Heschel, Susannah. "Anti-Judaism in Christian Feminist Theology." *Tikkun* 5, no.3 (1990): 25–28, 95–97.

————. "Configurations of Patriarchy, Judaism, and Nazism in German Feminist Thought." In *Gender and Judaism*, edited by T. M. Rudavsky. New York: New York University Press, 1995, pp. 135–154.

Heschel, Susannah, ed. *On Being a Jewish Feminist: A Reader*. New York: Schocken Books, 1983.

Hyman, Meryl. *Who is a Jew? Conversations, Not Conclusions*. Woodstock, Vt.: Jewish Lights Publishing, 1998.

Hyman, Paula E. "Looking to the Future: Conclusions." In *Daughters of the King: Women and the Synagogue*, edited by Susan Grossman and Rivka Haut. Philadelphia: Jewish Publication Society, 1992.

Kaufman, Debra. *Rachel's Daughters: Newly Orthodox Women*. New Brunswick, N.J.: Rutgers University Press, 1991.

Lebowitz, Maya, and Yoram Mazor. "Women's Participation in Life Cycle Events." In *Barukh She'asani Ishah?*, pp. 169–77.

Lederhendler, Amy. "Left, Right and Center: Women in the *Masorti* Movement." *The Messer of the Masorti Movement* (spring 1990).

Magnus, Shulamit S. "Re-Inventing Miriam's Well: Feminist Jewish Ceremonials." In *The Uses of Tradition: Jewish Community in the Modern Era*, edited by Jack Wertheimer. New York: Jewish Theological Seminary, 1992, pp. 331–47.

Ner-David, Haviva. *Life on the Fringes: A Feminist Journey toward Traditional Rabbinic Ordination*. Needham, Mass.: JFL Books, 1999.

Paul, Shalom. *Studies in the Book of the Covenant in the Light of Biblical and Cuneiform Law*. Leiden,: Ger. Brill, 1970.

Plaskow, Judith. "Blaming the Jews for the Birth of Patriarchy." In *Nice Jewish Girls: A Lesbian Anthology*, edited by Evelyn Beck. Watertown, Mass.: Persephone Press, 1982.

———. *Standing Again at Sinai: Judaism from a Feminist Perspective*. San Francisco: Harper and Row, 1990.

Ravitsky, Ruth. *Reading from Genesis* (in Hebrew). Tel Aviv: Yediot Aharonot, 1999.

Sacks, Maurie, ed. *Active Voices: Women in Jewish Culture*. Chicago: University of Illinois, 1995.

Schoenfeld, Stuart. "Ritual and Role Transition: Adult Bat Mitzvah as a Successful Rite of Passage." In *The Uses of Tradition: Jewish Community in the Modern Era*, pp. 349–76.

Selvidge, Marla. "Mark 5:25–34 and Leviticus 15:19–20." *Journal of Biblical Literature* 103, no.4 (1984).

Sered, Susan S. "Women and religious change in Israel: Rebellion or Revolution." *Sociology of Religion* 58, no. 1 (1997): 1–24.

———. *Women as Ritual Experts: The Religious Lives of Elderly Jewish Women in Jerusalem*. New York: Oxford University Press, 1992.

Shifman, Pinhas. *Civil Marriage in Israel: The Case for Reform*. Series no. 62. Jerusalem: Jerusalem Institute for Israel Studies Research, 1995.

Siddur Va'ani Tefillati. Rabbinical Assembly in Israel, 1998.

Tabory, Ephraim. "A Sociological Study of the Reform and Conservative Movements in Israel." Ph.D. diss., Bar Ilan University, 1980.

———. "Rights and Rites: Women's Roles in Liberal Religious Movements in Israel." *Sex Roles* 11, nos.1–2 (1984): 155–66.

Trible, Phyllis. "Depatriarchalizing in Biblical Interpretation," *Journal of the American Academy of Religion* (March 1973): 30–48.

Umansky, Ellen M, and Diane Ashton, eds. *Four Centuries of Jewish Women's Spirituality: A Sourcebook*. Boston: Beacon Press, 1992.

Wegner, Judith Romney. "The Status of Women in Jewish and Islamic Marriage and Divorce Law." *Harvard Women's Law Journal* 5 (1982).

Wertheimer, Jack, ed. *The Uses of Tradition: Jewish Community in the Modern Era*. New York: Jewish Theological Seminary, 1992.

Wolowelsky, Joel. *Women, Jewish Law and Modernity: New Opportunities in a Post-Feminist Age*. New York: K'tav Publishing House, 1997.

Zolty, Shoshana P. *And all your Children Shall be Learned: Women and the Study Of Torah in Jewish Law and History*. (Northvale, N.J.: Jason Aronson, 1993.

Zornberg, Aviva. *The Beginning of Desire: Reflections on Genesis*. New York: Doubleday, 1995.

Women, Law, Religion, and Politics in Israel: A Human Rights Perspective

Marsha Freeman

The establishment of the State of Israel in 1948 represented a human rights triumph in a postwar political wasteland. Fifty years later, Israel's continued existence and the development of its society remain exemplary of both human rights principles and deep internal and external political divisions. Women's roles, rights, and status exemplify the complexity of Israel's accomplishments and failings as a twentieth-century democracy.

Israel is the only working democracy in the Middle East. It has taken in millions of immigrants from disparate backgrounds, their only commonality a thread of Jewish identity. It has the only truly industrialized, capitalist economy in the region. The human rights and political issues Israel now faces relate to its success as a diverse, industrialized democracy with a special history. It has the human and economic resources to become once again a beacon unto the region and unto the world, a place where divisions based on race, ethnicity, country of origin, religion, and above all, sex, can be successfully resolved. But to do so will require creativity and good will, which are much harder to come by than the mechanics of voting rights and economic development.

Israel's history as an embattled state increases both the stakes and the difficulty of addressing internal human rights issues. The argument that sur-

The author acknowledges with gratitude the inspiration and friendship of Alice Shalvi and Frances Raday, the research support of Kerri Kleven and Jeffrey Baldwin-Bott, and a special relationship with Regina Brener, who taught me that Hasidic Judaism and compassionate feminism need not be mutually exclusive.

vival supersedes rights carries a certain weight in a place that is entirely surrounded by sworn enemies. And the argument that national and/or ethnic identity supersedes the rights of individuals within the identified group also is weightier where nationhood itself is constantly threatened by neighbors and barely accepted by the rest of the world. But the strength of a people, and of a nation, is only as great as its willingness to underwrite justice for its individual members and citizens. A people that rests its self-definition on behavior that oppresses its own members is a people without a heart, and without a heart it ultimately cannot survive. And a nation that treats its own citizens unequally, allowing certain groups to remain privileged in direct contravention of human rights standards to which it has formally subscribed, ultimately risks destruction through the force of internal divisions. *Like all embattled states seeking a peaceful future, the Israeli government and its citizens must answer the question, "When the shooting stops, who are we? And until the shooting stops, how do we maintain our humanity toward each other?"*

Constitutional standards and legislation

Most countries begin to answer the question "Who are we?" by creating a constitution with stated national values and principles of governance. But Israel does not have a written constitution. The 1948 Declaration of Independence stated the essential premises upon which the legal system should develop, including a declaration of equality between the sexes.[1] As the Declaration did not have constitutional force, the legal foundations upon which legislation rests are a series of laws stating fundamental principles, which presumably reflect the principles of the Declaration. The first and, until 1992, the only legislation relating to human rights was the Women's Equal Rights Law of 1951. The government of Israel claims that this law has been given great symbolic significance in several Supreme Court cases,[2] but its usefulness is undercut by its failure to provide the Supreme Court with the power to override acts of the Knesset that conflict with it, and its exclusion of personal status law with respect to marriage and divorce.[3]

In the 1980s and 1990s a number of laws were enacted that address specific sex discrimination issues. The criminal laws were amended to eliminate evidentiary requirements that revictimized rape survivors who testified in court. The Prevention of Violence in the Family Act of 1992 provides for an exclusion order against a violent spouse. In 1988 an equal employment opportunities law was adopted. The Property Relations Between Spouses Act was amended in 1990 to extend the division of marital property (subject to division on divorce) to include shares in cooperatives and such formerly "nontransferable" property as goodwill and pension funds.

In 1992, two basic laws were adopted by Israel, providing a formal basis for further legislation. Human Dignity and Freedom, a basic law that purports to provide for fundamental human rights, does not specify a right to equality or to nondiscrimination on the basis of sex. According to Professor Frances Raday, the language of these laws was compromised to avoid a political confrontation on the issue of equality.[4]

A comprehensive law prohibiting sexual harassment, including in the military, was adopted in 1998. The Equal Pay (Male and Female) Law was passed in 1996. The Government Corporations Law was amended in 1993 to provide for representation by women on the boards of all state corporations,[5] and in 1995 the State Services Law was amended to provide for affirmative action in the civil service.

The equivocal nature of Israel's formal commitment to equality was underscored by its ratification of the United Nations Convention on the Elimination of All Forms of Discrimination against Women (the CEDAW Convention) in 1991. The government claims that the convention "clearly had influence on the legislation of the [1992] Basic Laws."[6] However, the limited language of the basic law Human Dignity and Freedom reflects the limitations placed on the convention ratification. Israel ratified with significant reservations that critically undermine its apparent commitment.[7] One reservation, to Convention Article 7(b), pertaining to women in public life, indicates that the government will not insist that women be appointed to sit on religious courts where the religious community prohibits women from holding such positions.

The second reservation concerns family law. The government entered a broad reservation to Convention Article 16, pertaining to marriage and family law, thereby refusing to adopt an obligation to eliminate discrimination "insofar as the Laws of personal status binding on the several religious communities in Israel do not conform with the provisions of that article." This essentially precludes examination of the inequalities in all the communal family law systems. Given that Israel does not have a civil family law, this reservation preserves essential inequality, with no possibility of advocating change to conform with international law.

In short, Israel has made a significant effort to address in legislation many of the equality issues that are implicit in the language of its Declaration of Independence and the basic law Human Dignity and Freedom. But no government has yet been willing to confront the religious communities as to the essential inequality of religious law. The state of justice within the family is emblematic of the state of justice within the larger society. The family is "the unit within which concepts of justice are first learned and in which socialization to equality, or inequality as the case may be, is imprinted on the human psyche. The idea of a just society without a just family is antithetical."[8]

Human Rights and Status of Women: indicators and realities

Political Participation

Historically the number of women in elective office is considerably lower than could be expected given their high level of education and the intensity of Israeli political life. Despite nominal equality in voting rights and high levels of voter turnout among women, female candidates for high office have been few, and fewer have been elected. Global and national studies indicate traditional portrayals of women in the media and poor coverage of women who run for electoral office.[9] From the establishment of the State of Israel to the mid-1990s, only six women had served as cabinet ministers,[10] and the election of Golda Meir as Prime Minister in 1969 proved to be an historical anomaly. While Likud governments have been less than hospitable to women's high-level participation, the election of Ehud Barak in 1997—with considerable support from women voters—was expected to produce a more balanced cabinet. However, Barak initially appointed only one woman to a cabinet ministry and appointed a second one only under pressure from female constituencies.

This experience underscores a basic cultural issue in Israeli politics and public life. Israeli activists have noted that Israel's history of being constantly on guard, if not at war, against surrounding enemies has resulted in the culture disproportionately valuing heroism and military experience as essential to public leadership. Women's heroism is of a different nature than raw physical courage and distinction in combat, and the culture does not have a construct for recognizing their leadership qualities. Ehud Barak's failure to see women as viable cabinet ministers—despite having been elected by centrist-left voters—underscores the military man's inability to consider women as leaders.

While women have made some headway at the municipal level, their numbers in the Knesset remain minimal, and they have never held leadership positions there. In the United States, women made their way into national politics after a generation of experience at state and local levels, and still the cultural and practical obstacles have prevented them from reaching a level of political visibility concomitant with their experience and their numbers. In Israel, progress is likely to be slowed by the failure of the peace process in addition to the cultural obstacles that women face everywhere else in the world.

Israeli women are even less visible in international fora than in national politics. They are sparse in the foreign service, and their point of view is rarely represented in delegations to international conferences. They have next to no role at all in the official peace negotiations with Arab nations, because Israeli representation is drawn from the ranks of senior army officers and top civil servants, neither of which includes women.[11]

Health and Reproductive Rights

Women's health status in Israel is generally comparable to that in other industrialized countries—that is, they nominally have equal access to health services. Two issues dominate discussion of inadequacies in women's health care: access to contraception, and adequate attention to causes and treatments of diseases specific to women. Both issues indicate cultural biases.

According to both the government and NGO reports, Israel's pronatalist policies with respect to the Jewish population have resulted in a very high level of support for high technology fertility treatments, such as advanced drug therapies and in vitro fertilization, and very low levels of support for ordinary means of contraception.[12] This creates hardships in that women are not adequately advised of contraceptive methods in the course of standard health care, and they must pay for contraceptives. While such pronatalist policies need not be seen as malicious, they have a significant effect on women's control over their reproductive destiny and reflect a cultural assumption that women's major contribution to the social economy is as mothers.

A recent comprehensive study of women's health concludes that more resources should be devoted to education and research on female cancers, particularly breast cancer, and that greater attention be paid to the incidence of heart disease in women. These issues are related to attitudes concerning the relative importance of "women's diseases" as well as to failure to understand how certain diseases present in women.[13]

Employment Equity

With respect to employment issues, Israel presents a prime example of the disparities in women's worlds between laws on the books and reality on the ground. Despite a series of enactments that specifically address issues of wage discrimination, differentials in retirement age, and equal employment opportunity, a very large wage disparity remains, and enforcement of the antidiscrimination laws is weak or nil. According to the Israel Women's Network and other NGOs, the Ministry of Labour and Welfare does not provide adequate oversight for implementation of the Equal Opportunity in Employment Law.[14] Lacking social support and financial means to bring lawsuits, few women seek the judicial remedies provided in the law.[15]

Women remain underrepresented in managerial levels in both the public and the private sectors.[16] While a 1987 law prohibits forcing women to retire earlier than men, employers prefer to send women rather than men to early retirement when the workforce is cut back. Women who have retired early rarely can find other jobs and remain unemployed. Moreover, they receive enlarged pensions only until age sixty, while men receive an enlarged pension until age 65.[17]

All of these issues reflect an essential lack of respect for women as essential to the workforce and an underestimation of their capabilities. This underestimation is established in the earliest years, in that stereotypical attitudes and lower expectations for girls permeate the educational setting.[18]

Status of Arab women

The situation of Palestinian women differs somewhat depending on whether they reside in Israel, the occupied territories, or the areas under the authority of the Palestinian Authority (PA). What all have in common is that they consistently suffer the double discrimination of being women in a highly patriarchal culture, exacerbated by the policies of the government of Israel. While Israeli Arab women nominally have rights with respect to the government (such as voting, health care, education) that those in the territories do not, all suffer in differing degrees from discriminatory policies. Women in the areas under the control of the Palestinian Authority also are in the anomalous position of living under a "government" that "belongs" to them but is not accountable for their rights as a recognized state would be.[19]

The situation of Palestinian women in Israel was documented extensively in a statement submitted by Palestinian experts and groups in 1997 to the UN Committee on the Elimination of Discrimination against Women.[20] The statement documented the results of discrimination in education, employment, and health care, both by the government against Palestinians and as a result of internal community norms. Health care in particular is a problem, and nowhere more than in the unrecognized villages, populated largely by Bedouins.[21]

According to Palestinian NGOs, Arab women experience an extraordinary level of gender stereotyping within their community. They are expected to place their family's interests ahead of their own and "are raised to follow and to depend on men."[22] Because of this community norm, honor killings go largely unpunished, since judges and police see them as a private matter within the community. In misplaced efforts to be culturally sensitive, judges "view the murderer as a victim of the same values and norms which perpetuate honor killing" and reduce charges to manslaughter. In the same vein, police send back home women who file complaints of violence against them, "respecting" the cultural norm that a Palestinian woman's place is in her home.[23]

The patriarchal nature of the culture is nowhere more clearly visible and enforced than in the law and practice of marriage and divorce. The Israeli penal code prohibition of polygamy is not enforced against Muslims who marry more than one woman; the law prohibiting marriage between minors under the age of seventeen is not enforced; and the question of forced marriage is not addressed.[24] The discussion that follows looks at the nature of personal status laws and religious courts relating to Arab women (Muslim and Christian).

Family Law and Status of Women

International discourse on family issues is founded on the premise that "the family is the basic unit of society."[25] It is the space in which citizens are produced—born, nurtured, educated, trained to be adult actors in society. It is the foundation of identity for individuals, cultures, and societies. The family is the basic point of reference for individuals in answering the question, "Who do I belong to?" And it is a basic point of reference for the state in determining who belongs to it for purposes of offering protection, determining duties, and delivering services.

Regardless of social or political system, the state therefore has a stake in defining family structure. It has a corollary stake in assigning rights and responsibilities to family members, as sanctioned definitions provide for order and predictability in social structures and in relationships between family and state. The components of the legal system relating to family structure, rights, and responsibilities are referred to generically as laws of personal status. Personal status laws include regulation of marriage, divorce, inheritance, and adoption. They also refer to rights between family members as to ownership and management of property during and after marriage.

The human rights issues in personal status law lie in the source of the definitions sanctioned by the state and in the level of legal recognition given to religious, cultural, or communal definitions that violate international human rights norms. In many states the definitions of family structure and responsibilities are contiguous with or give legal status to religious or customary prescriptions that discriminate against women.[26] Most sub-Saharan African and many Asian and Pacific countries recognize discriminatory religious and customary systems of marriage, divorce, and inheritance as applicable to particular communities.[27] Most countries that either are Islamic by self-definition or have an identified Muslim community recognize Islamic law (*Shar'ia*) as the source of personal status law applied to Muslims, although the variations and interpretations are numerous and complex. And many states that do not overtly recognize community-based personal status law have incorporated discriminatory religious or customary principles into a "civil" system. For example, although relatively few Latin Americans are observant Catholics, Catholic cultural norms are still so strong that abortion remains illegal or highly restricted in most Latin American countries, and Chile still does not provide for divorce.

In most respects, the law of personal status in Israel appears to meet the standards of contemporary democracy. Many of the aspects of marriage, divorce, and inheritance are regulated by a statutory system that treats women and men equally.

But the core of personal status law is the determination of what a family is, who belongs to it; and in that respect Israeli law and practice are essentially discriminatory and profoundly unjust. Determination of the state of marriage and the status of divorce is relegated entirely to the religious authorities. To be married in Israel, the parties must be married according to the law of their religious community. To be divorced, even if they were married elsewhere, they must follow the procedures prescribed by the law of their religious community. The statutory law does not provide for any form of civil marriage or divorce. In essence the law requires that people identify themselves as belonging to a religious community and behave according to religious law regardless of their level of commitment to religious identity and practice. A state that was born out of history's worst oppression and prides itself on upholding freedom of religion has established itself as a place in which citizens are coerced into "belonging" to a religion in order to exercise that most basic human right, formation of a family.[28] The ironies are compounded by the discriminatory nature of the religious law to which citizens are forced to conform.

The law of each religious community discriminates against women by rule, by practice, and by its own ethic. The three main religions of Israel—Judaism, Islam, and Christianity—are fundamentally patriarchal, and their institutions are designed to perpetuate that patriarchy. The marital law regime in each religion gives men greater power than women within the marital relationship and as to its legal dissolution. And the tribunals that adjudicate marital issues are by religious law and by custom entirely male.[29]

Jewish Law

Jewish marriage and divorce are regulated by sets of interrelated civil (statutory) and religious laws. Under the statutory law, civil courts have jurisdiction over almost all aspects of divorce, including property division, custody, and maintenance (spousal support). The laws pertaining to these issues are essentially similar to law in other industrialized democracies, and women's rights to an equal share of property upon divorce, to post-decree financial support (maintenance), and to custody of the children, are embodied in law and to a considerable extent in practice.[30] However, the civil courts do not have jurisdiction over the dissolution of a marriage. In Jewish law, a marriage is dissolved by issuance of a *get*, an agreement of divorce, which must be issued by a *bet din* (religious court).

The essential inequality of the religious divorce procedure is that a *get* cannot be issued without the signed consent of the husband, while a *bet din* can issue a *get* in certain situations without the consent of the wife. This places in male hands the ultimate power over whether a marriage legally continues, regardless of fault or other circumstances. Concomitantly, the husband also retains power over the wife's remarriage, as she cannot be married under Jewish law without being properly divorced. A husband, however, can obtain a special dispensation of the *bet din* to remarry even where the wife refuses to sign the *get*, while a wife cannot obtain such dispensation.[31]

The consequences of this inequality run deep and forever. If a married woman has a child by a man who is not her husband, that child is considered a *mamzer* (bastard) under Jewish law, is excluded from all benefits of the community, and cannot marry another Jew except another *mamzer*. The child of a man who is not married to the mother is not a *mamzer* by virtue of its father's marital status (although the mother's marital status will have an effect).[32]

In Jewish communities outside of Israel, where marriage under civil law is possible, Jews who do not care about their status under Jewish law may obtain a civil divorce, remarry, bear additional children, divorce again, ad infinitum, with little consequence in their daily lives. In Israel, however, the enshrinement of Jewish law and Jewish tribunals as the sole authority over marital status, places all Jewish women at the mercy of their husbands. Even in the most liberated of households, the imbalance of power casts its shadow. And in very traditional households it reinforces other inequalities in Jewish law of marriage.[33]

Under Israeli law the religious courts have concurrent jurisdiction with the civil courts over property division and other matters relating to the divorce. While the religious courts are supposed to follow the civil law with respect to these matters, they tend to favor men in their allocations of property and child custody. This sets up a "race to the courthouse" situation, since a man who is contemplating divorce can expect to obtain a better result if he begins a divorce in the religious court, filing the property claim with it, before the wife can file in civil court.[34]

Islamic Law

In its traditional forms Islamic family law, like Jewish law, is inherently unequal. Islam permits polygamy, allowing a man to have up to four wives; women are entitled to inherit from their parents only half of what their brothers inherit; and men can divorce their wives by pronouncing the *talaq* (a statement of divorcement) without grounds, while women must apply to a religious court and establish grounds for divorce.

Like Jewish and Christian women, with respect to most issues relating to "personal status" Israeli Muslim women are subject to the civil law, which provides for equality between spouses and other family members. The civil law of inheritance, for example, applies to members of all religious communities and deals with men and women on an equal basis.[35] Polygamy was officially prohibited in 1977, although some forms prevail by custom and without challenge by the government.[36] Marital property division is supposed to proceed according to civil law; many Muslim women sign away this right in the marriage contract, providing for property division according to *Shar'ia*, but the Supreme Court has held that such provisions are invalid.[37]

But the Islamic religious courts retain authority to determine marital status according to Islamic law, which reinforces fundamental inequality in the family. A man who wants to divorce his wife need only pronounce "I divorce thee" three times—and it is done. While the courts are supposed to impose procedural restraints on this process, they rarely question to the point of disallowing the divorce.[38] Women, on the other hand, have to establish abandonment, failure to support, or other grounds to obtain a divorce. And like the *bet din*, the Islamic *Shar'ia* courts are composed only of men.

Christian Law

While many fewer women in Israel profess Christianity than Judaism or Islam, they experience discrimination equal to that found in the other communities. Christian Palestinians are primarily Eastern rite, usually Armenian Orthodox. According to Palestinian activists, Orthodox religious authority is also highly patriarchal, and some women consider that they would fare better under Islamic law.[39] While the Catholic prohibition of divorce applies equally to men and women, as a practical matter it tends to work more hardship on women since it exacerbates the power imbalance in traditional marriages.[40] And while Christians do not deal with religious courts as do Jews and Muslims, they must deal with an exclusively male priesthood.

The Family Law Regime and Human Rights Implementation: Preserving Discrimination in the Name of Identity

According to basic international standards the reservation of certain aspects of family law to deeply patriarchal, discriminatory religious systems is a violation of women's human rights. The Israeli government's reservations to the CEDAW Convention indicate an admission that preservation of this legal regime represents an inability to live up to the human rights obligations articulated in Articles 7 (pertaining to participation in public life) and 16 (family law).[41] The imposition of discriminatory religious law also contravenes the provisions of CEDAW Convention Articles 5 (obligation to address discriminatory customs and traditions and to eliminate sex stereotyping) and 15 (obligation to provide for equal legal capacity).

History and Identity

The preservation of religious authority as to matters of personal status is rooted in the history of the state. The Millett system of maintaining communal autonomy over laws of personal status was instituted in Palestine by the Ottoman Empire. When the British took over, they simply continued the system. At independence, maintaining this autonomy became important to non-Jewish communities as a way of holding on to their identity in a state identified essentially as Jewish. And the Jewish community has an enormous stake in retaining separate laws as a matter of maintaining the "Jewishness" of the state. Even among secular Jews, the retention of Jewish law sanctioned by the state is a critical element of maintaining the Jewish identity of Israel.[42] The human rights problem lies in the rigidity with which Jewish law is reinforced.

Strictly speaking, the hegemony of Orthodoxy only applies to the very narrow question of marriage and divorce status. All other elements of what are generally considered to be personal status issues, such as custody and inheritance, are at least optionally covered by civil law. What is the special importance of marriage status, that it appears to be the one untouchable element of personal law?

The determination of marital status fundamentally defines who belongs to whom, and where control lies over family members and property. In most cultures marriage rites are critical in determining lineage, and lineage is critical in determining who is allowed access to resources, including use and inheritance of property.[43] In Judaism, marriage is not required to designate a child as Jewish, but the child's rights within the community are determined by the parents' marital status.

A more radical view of marriage is that it is fundamentally designed to control women's sexuality.[44] While sexuality is in many respects celebrated in Judaism, the traditional definition of adultery as sexual relations between a *married or unmarried* man, and a *married* woman, underscores the notion that women's sexuality can endanger the social order while men's sexuality can be indulged with fewer repercussions. Whether or not one accepts that premise, the "double standard" under which women's sexual behavior in most societies is much more restricted than that of men, indicates a pervasive concern over lineage. Men need to know that they are the only person who could be the father of a woman's child. Women need to be controlled so their children's lineage is clear.

Because of its history and the history of the Holocaust, the question of who belongs to whom is especially poignant in Israel. And this poignancy plays into the hands of those for whom religious identity is more political than spiritual.

Women and Identity Politics

Israel is not unique in the degree to which communal identity seems to be more about power than about community. Nor is it unique in the degree to which women's roles and control over women's lives are used to define communal identity. What is unique is the level to which communal identity colors the politics and limits the exercise of basic human rights in a country that is in most respects a modern, industrialized, fully functioning democratic state.[45]

Israel has in common with every communalist state the acceptance of the flawed premise that preservation of communal tradition or culture justifies violation of the rights of individuals within the community. This premise does violence not only to fundamental human rights principles but to the community itself. A community that holds itself together at the expense of its individual members rends its own social fabric. In the long term, such self-inflicted violence damages the community—spiritually, morally, and politically.

Invariably the individuals who are prevented in the name of community from exercising their human rights are people whose status historically has been constructed by the community to place them in less powerful positions. Most often those people are women. The allocation of rights and responsibilities in religious communities "is rooted not in objective bases for differentiation between the authority and functions assigned respectively to men and women in the family, but in the gender ideologies of the religious tradition itself"—a tradition defined by men.[46]

Women in traditionalist communities are trapped by a tautology of gender. Their roles are assigned and limited by male-defined family and community norms. They frequently are seen as vessels of the culture, their functions and limitations cited as critical to the historical and moral identity of the community. One common aspect of the cultural norm is denial of women's freedom to question or alter their role. A woman who questions risks ostracism or excommunication from the community.

Arguments that invoke fundamental fairness or human rights principles fail to impress the defenders of communal-based discrimination. A more practical approach is to ask what the cost is to the community of maintaining a discriminatory practice, and what will be the cost (or benefit) to the community of changing it. On an internal community level, for example, the question could be posed as to the cost to the community of holding an *agunah* to be bound to her marriage, in a status that denies the community itself its member's potential contribution: in a new relationship she could produce more Jewish children, and every household lost diminishes the community's strength.

On a larger level, the question should be posed as to the cost to the state of providing unequivocal support to a patriarchal system that has proven to be so debilitating—morally as well as practically—to half its citizens. Failure to provide other options concerning an issue as deeply significant as marital status reinforces discriminatory attitudes that pervade the culture.

Application of international human rights standards to support change should not be seen as an attack on the culture of Judaism, but as an invitation to grow. By definition, a culture that does not change is a dead culture. While Jewish law is claimed by the Orthodox to be the immutable word of G-d, as a practical matter even the Orthodox do not live as people did in biblical times, or even as their ancestors did in the shtetls of Europe. They interpret the law. They choose daily accommodations with modern life.

The operative term in the argument is "choice." Civil societies maintain themselves by choosing (voting for) governance that will establish reasonable limitations, and by self-imposed limitations on behavior, for the sake of maintaining a sense of public order and predictability. If individuals wish to live with greater limitations on movement and behavior, they should be free to do so. But no citizen of a modern democracy should have forced on her a set of limitations that are defined by a class of men who deem themselves answerable only to G-d and not to the modern state, with its obligations to support its citizens' human rights.

Freedom of religion and the right to nondiscrimination

Freedom of religion is stated as a fundamental human right in the Universal Declaration of Human Rights and other international instruments.[47] Arguably,[48] even a country that declares an official state religion does not violate its citizens' rights to freedom of religion if they are free to choose whether to adhere to the state religion, another religion, or no religion.[48] In modern democracies built on a human rights foundation, citizens have a right to decide whether they will engage in religious ritual and identity. The Israeli system denies that choice, in that, in order to marry within the country, citizens are required to live by certain religious laws whether or not they believe in them.

Elimination of the Orthodox hegemony as to definition of marital status would not deny freedom of religion to the Orthodox. It would give people a choice as to their religious practice.

All human rights analysis, in the end, is about the balancing of individual rights against the interest of the state in maintaining public order and welfare. Just as there is no absolute right to freedom of speech, as it must be balanced against the state's responsibility to protect its people from the harm that can be done by certain forms of speech, there is no absolute right to nondiscrimination or to freedom of religion. The state has a right to perform certain actions that may be discriminatory if the state interest is great enough.

Arguably the Israeli state's interest in maintaining Jewish identity could support the grant of a privileged position to religious authorities in defining certain standards of behavior. Allowing religious authorities to define the rules of Jewish marriage does not contravene international human rights norms. But allowing religious authorities to establish discriminatory religion-based rules of marriage for all persons who are identified as Jews, regardless of their personal beliefs, violates citizens' rights to freedom of religion as well as reinforces sex discrimination.

RECOMMENDATIONS

Israel is not the only country that requires its citizens to choose between marrying under a religious regime and foregoing formal marriage entirely. But it is the only democratic state in which the law does not provide a nonreligious alternative. Providing for civil marriage and divorce would allow Israelis to marry according to their conscience, in accordance with fundamental human rights principles.

The lack of provision for civil marriage prevents Israelis from marrying across religious lines. While many argue that interfaith marriage holds the seeds of destruction for the Jewish people, this argument is not as compelling with respect to Israel as it is with respect to the diaspora. Israelis of different communities have lived side by side for generations in varying states of cordiality and enmity. Those who want to remain entirely separate would always be able to do so. Allowing those who wish to cross those lines to legally commingle their futures, might well provide opportunities to develop somewhat better understanding of the "other"—which would be no small thing in Israel. And those few who would have the courage to do so are unlikely to dilute Jewish identity. Frequently such experience reinforces one's own identity.

More significantly in terms of numbers, secular Jews who wish to marry and divorce without the imposition of Orthodox strictures pose little danger to Jewish identity. Indeed, forcing them to marry and divorce according to laws that they do not truly respect and in which they do not believe, in the name of communal preservation, has led only to resentment and undermining of the potential for dedication to the religious, as differentiated from the ethnic, nature of Jewish identity.

Most significantly, civil marriage would provide a way for Israelis to commit to their future and to the future of their community with a free conscience, in the best traditions of Judaism and of the human rights context in which the State of Israel was founded.

Notes

1. "The State of Israel will maintain equal social and political rights for all citizens, irrespective of religion, race or sex." Declaration of Independence, 14 May 1948.

2. Initial and Second Periodic Reports of States Parties: Israel. United Nations Committee on the Elimination of Discrimination against Women, (8 April 1997), p. 22. Henceforth, "Report to CEDAW."

3. Frances Raday, "Constitutional Evolution in Israel and Equality Between Men and Women," in *Chartering Human Rights*, Proceedings of the Canada-Israel Law Conference, Faculty of Law Hebrew University, 20–23 December 1992 (Jerusalem: Hebrew University, 1998), p. 4.

4. Frances Raday, "Religion, Multiculturalism and Equality: The Israeli Case," *Israel Yearbook on Human Rights*, vol. 25 (1996), pp. 193–241, at 212. In its 1997 review of Israel's implementation of the Convention on the Elimination of All Forms of Discrimination against Women, the UN Committee on Elimination of Discrimination against Women noted that "the fact that no basic law embodies the principle of equality or prohibits discrimination hinder[s] the implementation of the Convention." *Concluding Comments and Recommendations for Israel*, CEDAW/C/1997/II/l.1/Add.7.

5. In *Israel Women's Network* v. *The Government of Israel* (1994), the Supreme Court voided appointments of three men to the board of directors in government corporations and held that affirmative action is required to ensure female representation in accordance with the law.

6. Report to CEDAW, p. 25.

7. A reservation is a statement, entered at the time of ratification, that a government will not be bound by obligations under a particular provision of the convention. Usually a reservation is entered when a government insists that culturally or historically it cannot change certain laws or enact new laws to comply with an obligation. Reservations can be withdrawn when laws and policies are changed, and in some cases this has occurred with respect to the CEDAW Convention.

8. Raday, "Chartering Human Rights," p. 16.

9. Report to CEDAW, pp. 52–56.

10. Report to CEDAW, p. 101.

11. *IWRAW (International Women's Rights Action Watch) to CEDAW Reports: Israel*, p. 24.

12. Report to CEDAW, pp. 204–207, 210; *IWRAW to CEDAW Reports*, pp. 28–29.

13. *Women's Health in Israel 1999: A Data Book*. Hadassah and Israel Women's

Network in cooperation with the Israel Center for Disease Control (New York: Hadassah Publications, 2000).

14. *IWRAW to CEDAW Reports: Israel*, pp. 27–28.

15. Ibid.

16. Ibid.

17. Ibid., pp. 25–26.

18. Ibid., p. 25.

19. This author has received inquiries, for example, from Palestinian activists seeking to determine the applicability of international human rights principles and the account-ability of the Palestinian Authority for such obligations. As a governing authority not con-stituted as an independent state, the PA's formal accountability is negligible, even under nonbinding instruments such as the Universal Declaration of Human Rights.

20. This statement was prepared by a coalition of Palestinian women in Israel and submitted as part of the *IWRAW to CEDAW Reports*.

21. *IWRAW to CEDAW Reports: Israel*, p. 52.

22. Ibid., p. 47.

23. *IWRAW to CEDAW Reports*, pp. 47–48.

24. *IWRAW to CEDAW Reports*, pp. 54–55.

25. See Universal Declaration of Human Rights, Art. 16; International Covenant on Civil and Political Rights, Art. 23; Raday, "Constitutional Evolution in Israel," p. 16. In 1986 the Commonwealth Lawyers Association focused its triennial meeting on this topic, airing for the practicing bar the relationship between the rights of women and the nature of traditional families in Commonwealth countries.

26. Because this discussion focuses on sex discrimination, it will not touch upon the other forms of discrimination related to family status that are sanctioned by the state. But it is important to note that the family also can be the locus of state-sanctioned discriminatory attitudes and practices that work against children or against members of certain racial, ethnic, or religious groups.

27. The literature on sex discrimination under customary and religious legal systems is enormous. For a simple exposition of the issues in African customary law, see M. Freeman, "Measuring Equality: Women's Legal Capacity in Five Commonwealth Coun-tries," *Berkeley Women's Law Journal* (spring 1990). For a cogent discussion of the issues in Islamic law, see A. Mayer, "Restrictions on the Rights and Freedoms of Women," chap. 4 in *Islam and Human Rights: Tradition and Politics* (Boulder, Colo.: Westview Press, 1991), pp. 109–42.

28. Universal Declaration of Human Rights, Art. 16: "Men and women of full age ... have the right to marry and to found a family. They are entitled to equal rights as to marriage, during marriage, and at its dissolution." While religious freedom is a prized human right (Universal Declaration of Human Rights, Art. 18), the oppression of women either directly in the name of religion or indirectly as a result of application of religious

law, can appear to place the right to religious freedom in direct contradiction of the right to nondiscrimination on the basis of sex (Universal Declaration of Human Rights, Art. 2: "Everyone is entitled to all the rights and freedoms set forth in this Declaration, without distinction of any kind, such as...sex....")

The political nature of religion in Israel is another discussion. Since its inception the citizenry and the state have struggled with the issue of identity as a Jewish state and the politics of religion. Thus far no political movement has succeeded in breaking the Orthodox stranglehold on the definitions and official practice of Judaism.

29. Israel reserved to Art. 7 of the Convention on the Elimination of All Forms of Discrimination against Women, which provides for equality in public life, to avoid challenging the tradition of male-only religious courts.

30. While the government of Israel failed to discuss these issues in its most recent report to the CEDAW Committee on grounds that its reservation to Art. 16 precluded any accountability, the NGOs submitted information on the marriage laws because of their impact on women. See discussion below, concerning inequities in the treatment of women by the religious courts. See fn. 19, above, and related text.

31. Frances Raday, "Israel—The Incorporation of Religious Patriarchy in a Modern State," 4 *International Review of Comparative Public Policy* 209 (1992): 212–13; *IWRAW to CEDAW Reports: Israel*. Based on a report provided by the Israel Women's Network: IWRAW. (1997), pp. 32–33.

32. Raday, "The Incorporation of Religious Patriarchy," p. 212.

33. Ibid., p. 213, noting these aspects of Jewish law in marriage.

34. *IWRAW to CEDAW Reports: Israel*. Based on a report provided by the Israel Women's Network: IWRAW (1997), pp. 32–33.

35. Raday, "Religion, Multiculturalism, and Equality," p. 232; *IWRAW to CEDAW Reports: Israel*, p. 54.

36. Ibid., p. 54.

37. *IWRAW to CEDAW Reports: Israel*; Report of The Working Group on the Status of Palestinian Women in Israel (1997), p. 55.

38. Raday, "Religion, Multiculturalism, and Equality," p. 232; *IWRAW to CEDAW Reports*, p. 55.

39. Private conversations with activists, Women's Legal Aid and Counseling Center, East Jerusalem, November 1999.

40. Raday suggests that the traditional Christian marriage vow of obedience made by the woman, but not by the man, establishes an inherently unequal relationship from its inception. "Religion, Multiculturalism, and Equality," pp. 232–233. The Catholic prohibition of divorce and the conduct of Eastern rite religious authorities multiply this effect.

41. See discussion above, pp. 57, 58.

42. See Raday, "Religion, Multiculturalism, and Equality," pp. 194–95. This situation pertains in many postcolonial states. The irony of reinforcing independent identity by fiercely holding on to a system condescendingly imposed by colonial authorities for purposes of control, is rarely noted in discussions of communalism and rights.

43. In Islam, for example, children always belong to the father's lineage. In some Islamic countries, if a woman has a child and is not married or cannot prove the marriage, the child is not only a "bastard" but is also rendered stateless, because citizenship is transmitted only by the father. Under African custom, in patrilineal ethnic groups, a child belongs to the mother's lineage if the marriage rites have not been completed and to the father's if they have; the consequences of being born "out of wedlock" are not as severe they have been traditionally in Western systems.

44. A British expert who lived in sub-Saharan Africa for twenty years and had worked on the groundbreaking (and never adopted) model law on marriage and divorce in Kenya noted this in a private conversation in 1987. In the succeeding years, this author has seen the premise reconfirmed all over the world.

45. The only industrialized countries that have entered reservations to CEDAW Art. 7 are those that are constitutional monarchies in which only males can hold the throne. No industrialized country has entered substantive reservations to Art. 16. The Israeli government should note that most of the substantive reservations to Art. 16 have been entered by Islamic states.

46. Donna Sullivan, "Gender Equality and Religious Freedom: Toward a Framework for Conflict Resolution," *NYU Journal of International Law and Policy*, no. 24 (1992): 795–856.

47. UDHR Art. 18; International Covenant on Civil and Political Rights, Art. 18.

48. The U.S. Constitutions prohibition of establishment of religion is not a universally held value. The critical question as to "establishment" is whether the tenets of a particular religion are promoted or in some way forced on all citizens.

Gender Equality in the Kibbutz— From Ideology to Reality

Michal Palgi

Equality and democracy are among the basic values of the kibbutz. To meet these values it has developed a unique social model, according to which the community provides all major household services. Meals are cooked in the communal kitchen and served there; clothes are cleaned, mended, and ironed in the communal laundry; and children are looked after in the children's houses. Thus, many of the traditional household chores are recognized as legitimate, full-time work. Women and men are economically independent of each other. All women belong to the workforce. Economic rewards are equal for all and are independent of the work or prestige of one's occupation. Women receive the same economic rewards as men, and a single parent receives the same for the children as a couple. Participation in the governing bodies of the kibbutz is open to all members.

This model is interesting to those concerned with equality between the sexes because kibbutz communities try to implement an ideology of equality by restructuring social institutions. Likewise, the kibbutz symbolizes the building of a new nation for Jews in Israel with hopes of a different occupational and social structure, a different organization and ideology, a different gender division of labor. The kibbutz ideology is not aimed specifically at gender equality but at equality among people in general. Yet gender equality has been given much attention throughout the history of kibbutz communities because "the problem of the woman member" (meaning her inferior status) has not been solved by the structural changes.[1] Recently, due to ideological, social, and economic changes, the kibbutz communities have decided on far-reaching changes, that are seemingly gender-neutral, but have and will continue to have significant impact on gender equality and on women's lives especially. Again "the problem of the woman member" is raised.

The most radical changes that have been introduced in some kibbutz communities have to do with the work sphere, in the hope that these will make the kibbutz more efficient in dealing with its economic crisis. Men holding central positions in their kibbutz communities suggested most of the changes; some were suggested by outside organizational experts. Women in the kibbutz communities suggested none of the changes, yet they are the ones most affected. Acker, Smith, and this author discuss how organizational processes, which are stated in an abstract gender-neutral fashion, are gender based.[2] In view of this, the following questions are examined here: Where has the kibbutz succeeded in achieving gender equality and where has it failed? What are the reasons for success and failure? How have the recent changes in the kibbutz affected gender equality? The answers to these questions are given through an analytical description of women's positions in different kibbutz spheres and the changes that have occurred in them.

Kibbutz Women and Higher Education

In the beginning kibbutz members did not think higher education was important. Many of them had some higher education and some had completed high school. They tried to change the typical occupational structure of the diaspora Jews and create a nation where the Jews were divided equally among all professions. Thus in the early 1970s the right to higher education belonged mainly to persons whose education was perceived to contribute to the direct needs of the kibbutz—for example, educators for all ages; these types of studies were called "functional studies." Mainly women went to study education and as a result there were more women with higher education in the kibbutz than men. Men for the most part took short agricultural courses. Today every kibbutz member is entitled to further his or her studies in any field and in any academic institution. Statistics show that 35 percent of all men and 37 percent of all women aged sixty-five and under have obtained an academic degree (undergraduate or graduate). Among those aged thirty-one to forty, the percentage of men with an academic degree reaches forty-one and the percentage of women, forty-nine.[3] The gap between women and men narrows within the younger age group, and more men are now acquiring academic education. There are differences in the areas of study: the majority of the women turn to the social sciences, philosophy, the arts, and

the service professions, while most of the men study economics, pure sciences, and technical professions.

Recent changes in the kibbutz have also affected the education of women,
especially the young ones. The community no longer automatically finances
higher education of young people in the kibbutz. In earlier times youngsters
had first to become kibbutz members (through candidacy and referendum
processes), and then wait their turn for studies financed by the kibbutz.
Today they do not have to become members, but they do have to finance a
big part of the cost of their studies themselves. They do this by working
either in the kibbutz or outside the kibbutz. Their parents, who live on
kibbutz budgets, cannot support them. The lower value of women's work in
the Israeli market makes it much more difficult for young women than for
young men to obtain the money needed. Because of these changes in the
kibbutz, gender inequalities that exist outside the kibbutz end up penetrating
the kibbutz.

Kibbutz Women and Work

The organization of work

All women on the kibbutz belong to the workforce. Most of them, about 55
percent, work in education and consumption services.[4] These jobs provide
services to the community, and those who have them are not perceived as
earning money for the community. About 67 percent of the men produce
goods that are sold outside the kibbutz or work on salaried jobs; they
therefore earn money. Although in most kibbutzim no one has a private
income, everyone knows who earns the money and who does not. Women
work in places that usually do not add income to the kibbutz; on the con-
trary, they spend the income. The argument that women work in places that
invest in the future of the kibbutz (education, health) is not raised too often.
Kibbutz women usually work in small teams and give service to other human
beings. Work time is inflexible, as the needs of human beings (especially
young children, but also hungry grown-ups) have to be answered on time;
these characteristics result in relatively high work strain.[5] Men also work in
small teams but the objects they work with are nonhuman and often do not
need constant care. Formally, women have shorter working hours than men,
an arrangement that could be considered a unique privilege for women, but
which legitimizes their responsibilities at home (they get shorter working
hours in acknowledgement of the work they do in their households). This
arrangement has also reduced women's appeal to potential kibbutz employers

in nontraditional jobs. Moreover, kibbutz jobs that do not offer shorter hours do not appeal to many women, especially as jobs in such service work as education have their rewards. In several studies women and men report similar opportunities for self-realization: that is, doing interesting work, learning new things, and being able to use their ideas and initiative in their jobs.[6] A high percentage of women also report much job satisfaction.[7] At the same time, women recognize that the prestige of their occupations is lower than the prestige of male occupations.[8] Additionally, for a greater percentage of the women's occupations less training is required, even though they have a higher level of training than men (32 percent of the women work in a job that requires less than six months' training, while only 21 percent of the men work in such jobs).[9]

Some change has occurred during the last decade in the occupational systems of the kibbutz.[10] The percentages of agricultural and education workers have fallen, while the percentages of administrative and clerical workers are on the rise. The increase in the percentage of women in industry stems from both the inclusion of "female trades" (such as sewing and tourism) in this category, and the expansion of clerical work in the industrial plants. The decrease in the number of women in education is due to the abandonment of this field by female members and the introduction of outside child-care workers, or the integration of several kibbutz education systems into a regional one, which saves labor force. These changes have been possible mainly through two decisions made by the kibbutz and one made by the Israeli Ministry of Education.

The first decision made by the kibbutzim was to cut back the staff in education and to streamline the workforce in the consumption services. This was done by raising the number of children in the care of each educator and by opening the education centers and services to people outside the kibbutz (74 percent of kibbutzim reported doing so by the end of 2001).[11] The goal is to turn the women's workplaces into profitable centers that will need fewer workers, and the kibbutz women will be free to choose careers or to move to the "income-generating sector."

The second decision was to surrender the principle of self-employment. Until recently this principle was used mainly to restrict the incorporation of paid workers in child care; in the production branches it was more lax. Kibbutz members believed that those who internalized the kibbutz ideology and whom the kibbutz trusted should educate the children. This is the reason why in earlier times educators were chosen very carefully and enjoyed very great respect. The situation has changed in the last two decades. Many women paid a heavy toll for maintaining the principle of self-employment: they were prevented from working where they really wanted. This fundamental obstacle was recently removed, and it is widely recognized that every man and woman has the right to occupational fields of their own choice, even when it is necessary to hire an employee for a position not filled through internal staffing.[12] As a result, more salaried workers are employed today in production and services, including education in a parallel trend, more kibbutz members are turning to outside employment. This trend has not yet changed the apportionment of work between the sexes in the kibbutz employment system, although there is some expansion of opportunities for women in nontraditional positions.

The lowering of the market fences in the kibbutz has exposed women to the salary injustices prevalent in Israeli society. They are paid according to their profession, and female professions usually have inferior salaries. This would not affect kibbutz women so much if changes to differential recompense for work had not been introduced in some kibbutzim, as is discussed in the following section of this chapter.

The third decision, which was made by the Israeli Ministry of Education, was to support financially only elementary schools above a certain size. Kibbutz schools did not qualify for support. Therefore the kibbutzim decided to merge the elementary schools in each region into one regional school. This change, which was forced on the kibbutzim, has left many women with no jobs, some of them at an age when job seeking is quite difficult. On the other hand, it has opened new opportunities and job enrichment to those women who work in the bigger elementary schools.

Rewards for work

Until recently all kibbutz members received identical allowances without regard to the amount, type, or quality of their work. Various changes in this area have been implemented in many kibbutzim, vitiating equality among members' allowances and creating differences in their standard of living. One change has been to link the number of extra hours a member puts in to the allowance received (implemented in 36 percent of kibbutzim, according to Getz). Another is for a special bonus for those who undertake disagreeable tasks. A third concerns a differential wage to members according to their work, or at least the introduction of a differential component in the allowance according to the contribution to the kibbutz; this proposal has been implemented in 41 percent of kibbutzim.[13] Analysis of gender income distribution shows that kibbutz women earn less than men and their previous equal economic status no longer exists in kibbutzim that have implemented these changes. This is particularly true for single mothers and older women, but also for most other women.[14]

In sum, kibbutz communities have a clear gender division of labor that places women in a subordinate position. The gender division of labor constitutes an implicit gender contract that defines what jobs men perform and what jobs women perform. Men do jobs that are considered essential for survival while women do jobs that are seen as helpful for survival. These gender divisions persisted even at times when, according to change theories, they should have ameliorated: times of technological changes and rapid economic growth. Even then, women's status, prestige, and power remained static.

Managerial and Political Position of Kibbutz Women

In the past, kibbutz economy was managed through direct democracy and equality. The different kibbutz units (economic and social) convened about once a week to discuss with all the workers topics concerning them and their workplace. Decisions were made democratically through the workers' assembly. Long-range decisions, such as investment, had to be approved by the kibbutz assembly. Managers were elected by the workers (plant managers by the kibbutz assembly) and they were rotated every few years. When the kibbutzim went into economic difficulties, many of them decided that the kibbutz managerial system was to blame, and therefore had to change. They believed that the change should be into a more contractual and market relationship between the kibbutz and its members, between the different kibbutz units and kibbutz employees. Also, less democracy and less equality would enhance smooth running of the kibbutz and the motivation of the more accomplished members.

Women in the kibbutz have always occupied more marginal positions than men. Few women hold central offices, especially economic.[15] This was reflected also in their own evaluations. When women were canvassed about the centrality of their positions in the kibbutz compared with those of their spouses, they placed themselves at the periphery and their spouses in the center. The same response pattern emerged when they were asked about their parents. Men placed themselves at the center when asked the same questions.[16] In recent years some women have entered into positions that control kibbutz budgets, yet their ratio among managers in the economic sector has not increased. It has increased in the service and education sectors, but this "does not count." It is not considered as "real" management in the eyes of kibbutz members, as these areas are not "production" and do not provide much income to the kibbutz.

Women's underrepresentation in managerial and economic offices can be explained by their lack of experience in the production sphere, but also by the recent decision to eliminate arbitrary rotation among successful kibbutz managers. Until recently, each manager was elected for a term not exceeding five years. The rotation mechanism prevented the creation of a powerful economic elite. When the economic crisis began, there were those who believed that the cause of the crisis lay in the constant random rotation of the managers. As most of the managers in the economic sector of the kibbutz are men, the elimination of their arbitrary rotation is blocking the way for new managers, especially women, who aspire to management positions.

Another aspect of the change in kibbutz organizational democracy is the transfer of decision making to experts. This is justified by the argument that it is appropriate that decision making be transferred into the hands of a smaller group of experts (77 percent of kibbutzim have boards of directors in industry; 43 percent have boards of directors in agriculture; in 44 percent of kibbutzim there is an economic directorate instead of a central committee), and that there should be an elected directorate instead of the kibbutz general assembly (30 percent of all kibbutzim decided on this change).[17] In fact, committees of experts had operated even in the past, but it is now proposed to grant these experts authority for decision making, instead of using them in the advisory capacity they enjoyed previously. These proposals originated in the widespread belief that the average kibbutz member is no longer capable of keeping up with the complexities of modern technology and economics. In addition, a position has been maintained in various debates that the failure of the kibbutz originated in nonexpert participation in decision making. The proposal to cancel the general assembly, the main decision-making body, was founded on these apprehensions, and on the realization that the number of participants in these meetings had decreased. The result of this proposal was to give much power to elected councils and reduce the power of the assembly by convening it less frequently, only for matters concerning basic principles of the kibbutz.

These changes in the democratic practices of the kibbutz affect women, especially as few of them specialize in economics and management. Even in the general assembly, where discussions often do not need this type of expertise, women participate less than men. Most kibbutzim have perceived this problem, and have decided on a quota of women in these bodies. The problem is that this quota is not always available, or sometimes the quota is small ("at least one woman"), or it consists of the few token women in each kibbutz who have some economic or managerial experience. All these processes in the kibbutz require less involvement by the majority of the members in decision-making bodies and in processes going on in the kibbutz. The most affected population is women, who do not always have representatives in these bodies who are gender-aware.

Another change that increases members' inability to control and follow processes in the kibbutz and that affects the direct democracy that used to prevail in the kibbutz is the separation between the "economy" and the "community." This is signified by the creation of two separate, semi-autonomous entities in the kibbutz: the economic/production and the consumption/communal (74 percent of kibbutzim decided on this change).[18] The economic/ production corporations have autonomy to operate within the boundaries set by the kibbutz's main decision-making bodies, and so does the consumption/communal entity. The implications of this separation are twofold: control of the production branches is increasingly slipping away from kibbutz members, and these branches are also becoming separated from the service branches and central committees. The separation at once restricts the amount of qualitative information flowing to the kibbutz community, lessens the latter's ability to influence, and weakens overall community control. The severing of the connection between the production sector and general community (the opportunity to participate in information and decision making) is likely to exacerbate both the alienation of members from their work and their reticence to invest in their jobs. Due to the particular lack of qualifications in the economic arena among women in the kibbutz, their vulnerability is greater, hence their feeling of frustration and helplessness. In addition, a paradoxical situation might arise where the economic sector is very well off while the community sector has few resources. This might lead to a lower standard of living in communities that own flourishing enterprises. Those responsible to the "community" sector of the kibbutz are women, and those responsible to the "economic" sector are men; the separation between the two sectors can easily be considered the separation between the "spenders" (women) and the "earners" (men).

Kibbutz Women and Their Families

The kibbutz family has undergone major changes since 1910 when the first kibbutz, Degania, was formed. With these changes, the role and opportunities

of women within the kibbutz have changed also. Below is a short summary
of the history of the kibbutz family and its connection to the position of
women in the community.

The first kibbutzim (1910s–1920s) crystallized the structure their families
should have. This included the pattern of children's collective sleeping. The
children were to have their own children's houses where they would lead
autonomous lives. According to this arrangement parents had quite a minimal role: they had a couple of hours in the afternoon to spend with the
children; the kibbutz educators took care of them the rest of the time. Some
psychologists suggest that in these arrangements was a latent message to the
parents, and in particularly to the mothers, that the kibbutz did not trust
their ability to educate and socialize their children according to kibbutz values.[19] The consequence was the revolt of women in later days against the
educational system. The kibbutz communities were small and homogeneous
with very few women and children—the family was only second in importance, the community came first. The kibbutz was considered every member's
family. As such, the "family" decided whether women could or could not
have a child. In some kibbutzim it was decided that because of economic,
health, and security conditions at a particular time it was not possible for
women to have children; those who did get pregnant had to sway the kibbutz
or leave.

From the start, only women took care of kibbutz children. Already in
Degania when the first child was born, the mother, not the community, had
to look after him. Later, when more children were born, women, not men,
took turns caring for them. The pattern of women as educators was set from
the start of the kibbutz.[20]

In the 1930s and 1940s the percentage of women and children in the
kibbutzim grew, and nuclear families became more common. Small rooms
were allocated to families, but not on a permanent basis. They often had to
move from one room to another. National and collective goals continued to
be more important than the family. Absorption of newcomers to the kibbutzim made the kibbutzim less homogeneous and a bit bigger, making the
nuclear family an "emotional refuge" in lieu of the "kibbutz."

The next two decades (1950s–1960s) were characterized by a change in
the centrality of the family and by a sharper gender division of labor in
kibbutz occupations. At that time the national importance of the kibbutz
diminished, as did the national duties it had to fulfill. As a result it channeled
its resources into agricultural development and into improving its members'
living standard. The fall in the number of immigrants to Israel and to the

kibbutz made the family the most important source for recruitment of new members. The kibbutz became a family-oriented society. The role of the family was mainly expressive; all the other roles a family plays were still carried out by the kibbutz, but this was slowly changing.

In the 1970s and 1980s the family came to dominate kibbutz life. Many kibbutzim had large, extended families that supported their members and often affected decision making. The extended families were run and kept united by women. Such familial ceremonies as women's ten o'clock work break to visit the young children (which was called "the love hour"), and the four o'clock coffee get-together (which later became a meal) every Saturday afternoon—or in some families every afternoon—became common. Many kibbutzim changed the children's sleeping arrangements; children began sleeping in their parents' houses instead of in the kibbutz children's houses. The instigators of these changes were the women. They did not always await the decision of the kibbutz for this change but often decided to act without permission.[21]

At this stage the division of labor within the family was more egalitarian than at work.[22] Even so, it was the women's responsibility to see that household chores were done and that the children were taken care of. They did more cleaning and cooking than men. Women got one hour a day as worktime credit for looking after the household.[23] In kibbutzim where the children slept in their parents' houses the families, instead of the child-care workers, were responsible for feeding and bathing the children. This transferred more chores from the public domain to the private house. In the kibbutz communities, women worked close to home in education and consumption, and their workday at the children's house started with the arrival of the children. Men usually worked away from the center of the kibbutz, in agriculture and industry, where the workday started very early. As a result, when the children slept in their parents' houses the mothers usually woke them, looked after their clothes, and cared for their health. The father's work started too early, and took him too far away for him to be an equal partner in these chores.[24]

The higher divorce rate, marriage at an older age, and the lowering of the birth rate that were in evidence at the end of the 1980s began the next phase in the status of the family in the kibbutz. The extreme collectivism at the beginning of the kibbutz had placed the family in the periphery; the ebbing of collectivism and the rise of individualism has again placed it at the periphery. In the intermediate phase between extreme collectivism and extreme individualism the family had flourished—its role had become "instrumental" and not only a "mental refuge."

Several changes occurred at the end of the 1980s and in the 1990s that affected the roles of the family in the kibbutz and gender equality. The first change was the shift of several tasks that were formerly communal responsibilities to the jurisdiction of the family. The process had begun prior to the economic crisis in the mid-1980s, perhaps as a result of ideological changes in the kibbutz, but it accelerated during the crisis. Examples include: a transition from children sleeping in the communal children's houses to sleeping in their parents' houses in all kibbutzim; some transferred breakfast and/or supper from the communal dining room to the family house (already implemented in 67 percent of kibbutzim);[25] some decided that the work of laundering and ironing clothing should be done in the family house rather than by a communal laundry service. It was hoped that in this way various female kibbutz members would be freed from their work and could assume income-earning tasks. In some cases this strategy worked, while in others women (especially the older ones) were left with few employment options since their skills were no longer needed. This privatization process in the kibbutzim "normalized" the kibbutz family, turning it into a "regular" household providing most of its own consumption functions and services. Findings indicate that, for women, this privatization resulted in a greater investment of work hours in the private sector and in the family house, and a curtailment of hours in the communal sector and in career development.[26] The abolition of extensive branches of such communal services as the dining room, laundry, etc., placed new stumbling blocks instead of the old in the path of a woman aspiring to a career of her choice.

National Organization of Female Kibbutz Members

Leading women requested that departments devoted to the promotion of gender equality be established within the framework of the national organization of the kibbutz movements. This request was met with surprise and opposition. The kibbutz leadership believed that the kibbutz was well advanced on issues of gender equality and did not need a special department for this purpose. But a few years later, the two largest kibbutz movements, the United Kibbutz Movement (Takam) and the Kibbutz Artzi Movement, decided to establish departments devoted to the promotion of gender equality. The decision was consolidated and put into practice as a result of social activism by female kibbutz members at the grassroots level, and after prolonged debates in which the protagonists were the administrators of the organization. The women at the heads of these sections adopted a clearly feminist approach, backed up by a united support group of forty female kibbutz members.

The radical strategy of the "equality departments" was set in motion at three transitional levels: the individual, the kibbutz, and the kibbutz movements. The equality departments organized workshops for consciousness-raising and assertiveness training. They proposed, for the kibbutzim, monthly lectures and symposia on gender equality; they also produced written material and videos. In addition, the equality section put out a newsletter called *HaMashveh* (The equalizer). To initiate change from the top down, these sections made efforts to supply information to various departments at the kibbutz movements concerning expressions of gender inequality in kibbutz life, and they proposed solutions for such problems. The major female activists conducted a fierce struggle to increase the percentage of women who worked in senior positions and who had central duties in the kibbutzim and in the kibbutz movements.

The equality departments expressed vigorous opposition to the "double messages," (on one hand stating that women can enter any job in the kibbutz or the movement, while on the other putting barriers in their way such as rules of rotation that applied only to women or saying that there are no women with appropriate skills) and personally supported women who wanted to pursue nontraditional occupations. A scholarship fund was established for women studying management. The political mission was to develop and bring forward women qualified for community and political positions, even those not inclined to adopt feminist views.

Popular understanding in the kibbutz movement in its earlier years, as well as in the world feminist movement in the first half of the last century, had defined gender equality as the inclusion of women in all-male occupations and tasks. By contrast, the new wave stood for the interchange of women and men among occupations traditionally defined as appropriate only to one sex or the other. On this ideological basis the departments recommended the inclusion of men in the education of young children. In the Kibbutz Artzi Movement a decision was made that the staff of the children's houses must consist of at least 5 percent male workers.[27]

Thanks to this approach, the barrier preventing the entry of males into caregiver tasks has been broken down, though not fast enough and not so as to provide men such jobs as professions or as steady work.

Yet the equality departments have not succeeded in changing negative attitudes toward feminist organizations. The use of the term "feminism" continues to arouse negative verbal reactions. Feminist action has not succeeded in convincing kibbutz members—women and men alike—about the sources of inequality. On only one point has understanding been reached: all agree that the potential of women in the work sphere is certainly far more restricted than that of men.

The economic crisis, which continued into the 1990s, brought about cutbacks and structural changes in the kibbutz movements; among the first departments affected by the cutbacks were those devoted to gender equality. Now, at the beginning of the twenty-first century, the two big kibbutz movements have amalgamated. This new situation has opened opportunities to reestablish the equality departments. Leading kibbutz feminists are now planning the activities of this renewed venture.

Conclusions

The kibbutz experiment elicits questions and solutions that are fertile ground for the development of feminist theories and practice. Some of the issues it has addressed successfully are the feminization of poverty, the economic independence of women, formal political equality, collective child rearing, and the role of community in family life.

The kibbutz, in its traditional form, has achieved much in promoting women's equality, even though supporters of gender equality are appalled at its partial achievements. At face value, the major successes of the kibbutz seem almost ideal. Women can be candidates for all offices in the kibbutz and have the same right as men to participate in kibbutz political life. Most women belong to the kibbutz workforce. Their personal economic situation is equal to that of men, from the viewpoint of the individual budgetary allowances they receive, pension plans entitlement, general insurance, and occupational safety. Their clothing and shoe allowances even exceed that of the male members. The socioeconomic situation of a single female parent is similar to that of a single male parent; neither faces any danger of poverty or inability to support her or his dependents. The heads of single-parent families receive allowances that are even greater than those received by other female or male members, as the financial expenses of the household and the family fall on the budget of one adult and not two. Today these facts hold true for over half of the kibbutzim; slightly different conditions prevail in the rest of the kibbutzim, which have implemented a bonus system in members' budget allowances according to their work and/or duties or to a salary system.

Three processes or trends that affect gender equality in the kibbutz are apparent. First, as a result of a growing division of labor, almost all workers in child care, laundry, and kitchen services are women, while most of the agricultural and industrial workers are men. Does sex-role division necessarily lead to inequality between the sexes? Equal opportunities to enter all jobs and offices in the kibbutz exist, but there is always social pressure on women and men to enter the jobs that are perceived to be the responsibility of their gender. This leads to strong pressure on women to continue working in nurturing and service jobs and to a vicious circle that reinforces the sexual division of labor. These jobs used to carry almost the same prestige as any other nonmanagerial jobs of the same skill level, but this is no longer so, since many of the kibbutzim evaluate work according to its market value instead of its social value. The most prestigious jobs now are in top management or top-earning arenas and are usually held by men.

The gender division of labor has some additional by-products: it reinforces stereotypic attitudes about the abilities of women, it limits the scope of occupational aspirations of women and girls, it channels women to specific occupational sectors, it excludes women from some occupations—frequently occupations that promise such rewards as power, prestige, and money. When changes occur in a sector where women work they become vulnerable, because they are perceived by themselves as well as by others to have single-trend skills. This makes them less flexible in a job search and lowers the range of jobs they deem suitable for themselves. In addition, they are perceived, as a result of their concentration in occupational fields not needing much economic knowledge, to be unfit for occupational and political positions that control the economy of the kibbutz.

Regarding the second process affecting gender equality, the family has become increasingly important in kibbutz communities, as manifested in the high rate of childbirth and marriage. This process has taken the form of organizational changes in the kibbutz. Children sleep in their parents' houses in all kibbutzim, while formerly they slept in children's houses, where they received care and schooling. Many household chores that were previously done by the community are now done in members' private houses (meals, laundry).

Does the growing importance of the family lead to inequality? Studies dealing with the division of labor within the family household before the children moved to sleep in their parents' houses found that there was little sexual division of labor. Later studies have found that women's time performing household chores has increased, but not men's. It seems that, paradoxically, while the kibbutz was more collective women were freer from household chores but bound in their choice of job by collective needs. Now that the kibbutz is more individualistic women are free to pursue their own careers but are bound by family duties. Their freedom does not depend now on the kibbutz but on the relationship and role division with their spouses.

A third dramatic process occurred in the mid-1980s. The kibbutz communities suffered from the economic crisis in Israel. Measures to overcome such crises have often affected gender equality by limiting the opportunities of people (mostly women) in nonmanagerial and noneconomic positions to assume managerial positions and to participate in economic decision making. Recent studies indicate that the economic crisis has produced more gender inequality, but also more inequality among women. When gender inequality increases, within-gender inequalities also increase. In kibbutzim that link the size of salary one earns to the size of kibbutz budget one gets, there is a growing gender budget gap as well as widening differences among women. Often women who have given up promising careers to respond to the needs of the kibbutz find themselves in the low-earning bracket. At the same time, young women or women who were not prepared to forfeit their own vocational aspirations in favor of kibbutz needs are in a much higher budget bracket.[28]

Still, the relief of women from the binding duty to work in education or the services has opened new horizons for them. Some choose work in traditional occupations, but others (quite a few) enter nontraditional careers. Again, a paradoxical situation occurs. When the kibbutz was more collective, democratic, and egalitarian, women were restricted in choosing their vocational fate. Since the kibbutz has become more individualistic, less egalitarian, and less democratic, women have been freer in their choices. Because women as a group were responsible for the smooth running of education and the services, the withdrawal of any woman from this responsibility is tacitly considered a breach of an unwritten contract. The feminist question that faces the few who decide not to meet kibbutz expectations is whether they should give up their freedom to choose their desired career so that their sister women will not have to carry the burden alone. Luckily, with the introduction of paid labor into education this dilemma has been resolved, although for some women it is too late.

What will be the ultimate result of these changes in the kibbutz with respect to women's status? The changes will have conflicting effects. The positive results—the opening up of the outside job market to the kibbutz—will expand the variety of women's occupations and will allow them to achieve more in professional and economic fields; these achievements will improve their social status. However, it is to be remembered that this trend also exposes women to the social discrimination that exists in Israeli society. It is almost self-evident to say that when the kibbutz loses its unique characteristics, women will lose the advantages that the old kibbutz bestowed upon them: economic equality, equivalent social security, and legal equality. The status of women in the kibbutz will approximate the status of women in Israeli society, with its advantages and its drawbacks.

In conclusion, the change of the kibbutz from a society where the dominant relationships are based on cooperation and equality to a society that puts a stronger emphasis on market relationships has a negative impact on gender equality, although some women have benefited from the change. With respect to feminist theory, it is possible to learn from the kibbutz experience that technological and economic changes do not improve gender equality in society; this can be accomplished only if such mechanisms are consciously targeted to this task. Such attempts will not take place in a period of economic crisis, when most extreme organizational and social changes are decided, as long as gender equality is not seen as essential to the existence of the kibbutz.

Notes

1. Lionel Tiger and Joseph Shepher, *Women in the Kibbutz* (New York: Harcourt Brace Jovanovich, 1975); Melford E. Spiro, *Gender and Culture: Kibbutz Women Revisited* (New York: Shocken Books, 1979); Michal Palgi, et al., eds., *Sexual Equality: The Israeli Kibbutz Tests the Theories* (Norwood, Pa.: Norwood Editions, 1983); Michal Palgi, "Women in the Changing Kibbutz Economy," *Economic and Industrial Democracy* 15 (1994): 15–73; Michal Palgi, "Women in the Changing World of the Kibbutz," *Women in Judaism, A Multidisciplinary Journal* 1 (1997): 1–9, Gila Adar; "Women in the Changing Kibbutz," in *Crisis in the Israeli Kibbutz*, ed. U. Leviathan, H. Oliver, and J. Quarter (Westport, Conn.: Praeger, 1998), pp. 111–18.

2. Joan Acker, "Making Gender Visible," in *Feminism and Sociological Theory*, ed. R. A. Wallace. (London: Sage Publications, 1989), pp. 65–81; Joan Acker, "Hierarchies, Jobs, Bodies: A Theory of Gendered Organizations," *Gender and Society 4*, no. 2 (1990): 139–58; Dorothy Smith, *The Everyday World as Problematic: A Feminist Sociology* (Boston: Northeastern University Press, 1988); Palgi, "Women in the Changing Kibbutz Economy."

3. Michal Palgi, *Public Opinion Survey in the Kibbutzim* (in Hebrew) (Haifa: Institute for Kibbutz Research, University of Haifa, 2001.)

4. Ibid.

5. Michal Palgi, "Nurses in the Kibbutz: Survey Findings and a Suggestion for a Theoretical Framework for Research on the Role of Nurses in the Kibbutz" (in Hebrew), *HaKibbutz* 6–7 (1979): 303–13; Palgi, "Women in the Changing Kibbutz Economy"; Palgi, "Women in the Changing World of the Kibbutz"; Amia Lieblich, *Kibbutz Maqom* (in Hebrew) (Jerusalem: Shocken, 1981); Rosanna Hertz and Wayne Baker, "Women's and Men's Work in an Israeli Kibbutz: Gender and Allocation of Labor," in *Sexual Equality*, pp. 154–73.

6. Palgi, et al, *Sexual Equality*.

7. Palgi, *Public Opinion Survey in the Kibbutzim*.

8. Gila Adar and Hanna Lewis, *Female Kibbutz Members: A Survey of Women in Communal Functions* (in Hebrew) (Efal: Yad Tabenkin and Institute for Kibbutz Research, University of Haifa, 1988).

9. Palgi, *Public Opinion Survey in the Kibbutzim*.

10. Palgi, "Women in the Changing World of the Kibbutz."

11. Shlomo Getz, *Changes in the Kibbutz* (in Hebrew) (Haifa: Institute for Kibbutz Research, University of Haifa, 2002).

12. Uriel Leviatan, *Findings from Follow-Up Surveys* (in Hebrew) (Haifa: Institute for Kibbutz Research, University of Haifa, 1995).

13. Getz, *Changes in the Kibbutz* (2002).

14. Dani Meiri, "Gender Division in Earning—A Case Study" (in Hebrew), unpublished seminar paper, Emek Yezreel College, 2000.

15. Adar and Lewis, "Female Kibbutz Members"; Martha Mednick, "Social Change and Sex-Role Inertia: The Case of the Kibbutz," in *Women and Achievement: Social and Motivational Analyses*, ed. by M. T. S. Mednick, S. S. Tangri, and L. W. Hoffman (New York: Wiley and Sons, 1975), pp. 85–103; Paula Rayman, *The Kibbutz Community and Nation Building* (Princeton, N.J.: Princeton University Press 1981); Aviva Zamir, *Through the Glass Ceiling—Women in Managerial Positions in the Kibbutz* (in Hebrew) (Efal, Israel: Yad Tabenkin, 1999); Palgi, *Public Opinion Survey*.

16. Mednick, "Social Change and Sex-Role Inertia."

17. Shlomo Getz, *Changes in the Kibbutz* (in Hebrew) (Haifa: Institute for Kibbutz Research, University of Haifa, 2000.)

18. Getz, *Changes in the Kibbutz* (2002).

19. Yair Palgi (with A. Raviv), "The perception of family-environmental characteristics in Kibbutzim: A comparison between the two sleeping arrangements," in *Kibbutz Members Study Kibbutz Children*, ed. Z. Lavi (New York: Greenwood Press, 1990).

20. Michal Palgi, "Motherhood in the Kibbutz," in *Calling the Equality Bluff: Women in Israel*, ed. B. Swirsky and M. Safir (New York: Pergamon Press, 1991), pp. 261–69.

21. Joseph Shepher, *The Effect of the System of Children's Sleeping Arrangements on the Social Structure of the Kibbutz* (in Hebrew). Tel Aviv: Union of Kevutzot and Kibbutzim, 1967; Palgi, "Motherhood in the Kibbutz".

22. Fritz Selier, "Family and Family Tasks in a Communal Society," in *Integrated Co-operatives in the Industrial Society: the Example of the Kibbutz*, ed. K. Bartolke, T. Bergmann, and L. Liegle (Assen, The Netherlands: Van Gorcum, 1980), pp. 77–85; Eliette Orchan, "Research on Equality Between the Sexes and the Division of Housework in Today's Kibbutz" (in Hebrew), seminar paper, University of Tel Aviv. 1990.

23. Kibbutz Artzi Convention, 1966.

24. Eliezer Ben-Rafael and Sasha Weitman, "The Reconstruction of the Family in the Kibbutz," *European Journal of Sociology* 21 (1984): 1–27; Eliezer Ben-Rafael and Sasha Weitman, "Women and the Reconstruction of the Family in the Kibbutz" (in Hebrew). *Megamot* 29, no. 3 (1986): 306–20.

25. Getz, *Changes in the Kibbutz*.

26. Palgi, "Women in the Changing Kibbutz Economy."

27. Palgi, "Women in the Changing World of the Kibbutz."

28. Amia Lieblich, *Transformations of a Community* (in Hebrew) (Jerusalem: Schocken, 2000).

Bibliography

Acker, Joan. "Hierarchies, Jobs, Bodies: A Theory of Gendered Organizations." *Gender and Society* 4, no. 2 (1990): 139–158.

———. "Making Gender Visible." In *Feminism and Sociological Theory*, edited by R. A. Wallace, pp. 65–81. London: Sage Publications, 1989.

Adar, Gila. "Women in the Changing Kibbutz." In *Crisis in the Israeli Kibbutz*, edited by U. Leviathan, H. Oliver, and J. Quarter, pp. 111–18. Westport, Conn.: Praeger, 1998.

Adar, Gila, and Hanna Lewis. "Female Kibbutz Members: A Survey of Women in Communal Functions" (in Hebrew). Yad Tabenkin and Institute for Kibbutz Research, University of Haifa. 1988.

Ben-Rafael, Eliezer, and Sasha Weitman. "The Reconstruction of the Family in the Kibbutz." *European Journal of Sociology* 21: (1984): 1–27.

———. "Women and the Reconstruction of the Family in the Kibbutz" (in Hebrew). *Megamot* 29, no. 3 (1986): 306–320.

Getz, Shlomo. *Changes in the Kibbutz* (in Hebrew). Haifa: Institute for Kibbutz Research, University of Haifa, 2000.

——— *Changes in the Kibbutz* (in Hebrew). Haifa: Institute for Kibbutz Research, University of Haifa, 2002.

Hertz, Rosanna, and Wayne Baker. "Women's and Men's Work in an Israeli Kibbutz: Gender and Allocation of Labor." In *Sexual Equality: The Israeli Kibbutz Tests the Theories*, edited by M. Palgi, et al., pp. 154–173. Norwood, Pa.: Norwood Editions, 1983.

Leviatan, Uriel. *Findings from Follow-Up Surveys* (in Hebrew). Haifa: Institute for Kibbutz Research, University of Haifa, 1995.

Lieblich, Amia. *Kibbutz Maqom* (in Hebrew). Jerusalem: Schocken, 1981.

———. *Transformations of a Community* (in Hebrew). Jerusalem: Schocken, 2000.

Mednick, Martha. "Social Change and Sex-Role Inertia: The Case of the Kibbutz." In *Women and Achievement: Social and Motivational Analyses*. edited by Martha T. S. Mednick, Sandra S. Tangri, and Lois W. Hoffman. pp. 85–103. New York: John Wiley and Sons, 1975.

Mednick, Martha T. S., Sandra S. Tangri, and Lois W. Hoffman, eds. *Women and Achievement: Social and Motivational Analyses*. (New York: John Wiley and Sons, 1975).

Meiri, Dani. "Gender Division in Earning—A Case Study" (in Hebrew). Unpublished seminar paper, Emek Yezreel College, 2000.

Orchan, Eliette. "Research on Equality Between the Sexes and the Division of Housework in Today's Kibbutz" (in Hebrew). Seminar paper, University of Tel Aviv, 1990.

Palgi, Michal. "Motherhood in the Kibbutz." In *Calling the Equality Bluff: Women in Israel*, edited by B. Swirsky and M. Safir, pp. 261–69. New York: Pergamon Press 1991.

———"Nurses in the Kibbutz: Survey Findings and a Suggestion for a Theoretical Framework for Research on the Role of Nurses in the Kibbutz" (in Hebrew). *HaKibbutz* 6–7 (1979): pp. 303–313.

———. *Public Opinion Survey in the Kibbutzim* (in Hebrew). Haifa: Institute for Kibbutz Research, University of Haifa, 2001.

———. "Women in the Changing Kibbutz Economy." *Economic and Industrial Democracy* 15:(1994): 15–73.

———. "Women in the Changing World of the Kibbutz." *Women in Judaism, A Multidisciplinary Journal* 1 (1997): 1–9.

Palgi, Michal et al. eds. *Sexual Equality: The Israeli Kibbutz Tests the Theories*. Norwood, Pa.: Norwood Editions, 1983.

Palgi, Yair (with Raviv, A.). "The perception of family-environmental characteristics in Kibbutzim: A comparison between the two sleeping arrangements." In *Kibbutz Members Study Kibbutz Children*. Edited by Z. Lavi. New York: Greenwood Press, 1990.

Rayman, Paula. *The Kibbutz Community and Nation Building*. Princeton, N.J.: Princeton University Press, 1981.

Rosner, Menachem. "High Tech in Kibbutz Industry: Structural Factors and Social Implications." In *The Social Implications of Robotics and Advanced Industrial Automation*, edited by D. Millin and B. Raab, pp. 81–85. Amsterdam: North-Holland/Elsevier, 1989.

———. "Organizations Between Community and Market: The Case of the Kibbutz." *Economic and Industrial Democracy* 14 (1993): 369–97.

Selier, Fritz. "Family and Family Tasks in a Communal Society." In *Integrated Cooperatives in the Industrial Society: the Example of the Kibbutz*, edited by K. Bartolke, T. Bergmann, and L. Liegle, pp. 77–85. Assen, The Netherlands: Van Gorcum, 1980.

Shepher, Joseph. *The Effect of the System of Children's Sleeping Arrangements on the Social Structure of the Kibbutz* (in Hebrew). Tel Aviv: Union of Kevutzot and Kibbutzim, 1967.

Smith, Dorothy. *The Everyday World as Problematic: A Feminist Sociology*. Boston: Northeastern University Press, 1988.

Spiro, Melford E. *Gender and Culture: Kibbutz Women Revisited*. New York: Schocken Books, 1979.

Tiger, Lionel, and Joseph Shepher. *Women in the Kibbutz*. New York: Harcourt Brace Jovanovich, 1975.

Zamir, Aviva. *Through the Glass Ceiling—Women in Managerial Positions in the Kibbutz* (in Hebrew). Efal, Israel: Yad Tabenkin, 1999.

Mizrahi Feminism: The Unheard Voice

Henriette Dahan-Kalev

Introduction

During the 1950s, following the establishment of the State of Israel in 1948, there were two great waves of immigration into the new country. In one wave, the most well documented, more than 335,000 survivors of European Jewry joined the 650,000 Jewish pioneers who had founded the country, most of whom, too, were of European origin (Ashkenazi Jews). The other great wave of immigration during the 1950s brought 1,600,000 Jews whose families had lived for centuries as part of the Arab world (Mizrahi Jews). These Jews came from Morocco and other countries of North Africa, the Middle East, and East Asia. Their native languages, their dress, their foods, and many of their customs were Oriental, mostly Arab. Unlike most of European Jewry in the twentieth century, these Oriental Jews were traditionally observant, though their religious practice had evolved independently of European Judaism and was different in many respects. What distinguished Oriental Jews from Israelis of European origin was that they lived at peace with their traditional religious practice, while the European Zionists discarded it. Whereas European Zionists cut themselves off from the European Diaspora, religion, and tradition, the Oriental immigrants to Israel had no reason to feel in conflict with their culture and history of origin. It was only when they came to Israel and confronted the prejudice of Europeans against their culture that they developed a deeply conflicted identity.

By the 1970s, Oriental Jews in Israel already constituted a deprived second- and third-generation lower class. During these years the ethnic divide along socioeconomic parameters could no longer be ignored, and the terms Mizrahi and Ashkenazi became central to public discourse in Israel.

Reflecting the wider society, the women's movement in Israel, during all of its thirty-year history, has been overwhelmingly dominated by Ashkenazi women. From the beginning, Mizrahi feminists were marginal and few in number, and, despite their presence, the Mizrahi voice in the Israeli women's movement was not heard. In the mid-1990s, however, the Mizrahi feminist voice broke suddenly and angrily onto the scene, disrupting the tenth Annual Feminist Conference, to the great dismay of most Ashkenazi women. The following year, Mizrahi women held their own conference, which became a milestone in the development of feminist consciousness in Israel.

In this article I shall present an analysis of the Mizrahi feminist experience. More broadly, I shall consider these issues in the framework of theories of oppression and exclusion and their implications for feminism.

Mizrahi feminism has its origins in three decades of discrimination experienced by Mizrahi women active in the Israeli women's movement, both in the larger society and in the movement. The Mizrahi challenge to Israeli feminism raises the question of the legitimacy of Israeli feminism to represent women in all sectors of Israeli society. Mizrahi women have raised questions about the extent to which the range of needs and interests of concern to the movement represent those of all groups of women. Ultimately, Mizrahi feminists have expressed doubts about the concept of sisterhood as practiced by their Ashkenazi colleagues and have demanded that feminist groups and organizations review their values and ideology, and acknowledge that they represent only limited sections of Israeli society. Unlike the Ashkenazi women who were mostly of the middle class and hence could enjoy many resources, Mizrahi women who were mainly of the lower class have never had such means.

Theory

In feminist literature, oppressive relationships are described as functioning through hidden systems that do not need explicitly discriminatory laws in order to function efficiently.[1] Even in a democracy, where a commitment to equality and pluralism prevails, such hidden systems exist. The exclusion, marginalization, and invisibility of "weaker" populations are simply "understood" and need not be maintained by tyrannical means. As Young explains:

> Oppression designates the disadvantage and injustice some people suffer not because tyrannical power coerces them, but be-

cause of the everyday practice of a well-intentioned liberal society. . . . The tyranny of a ruling group over another, as in South
Africa, must certainly be called oppressive. But oppression also
refers to systematic constraints on groups that are not necessarily the result of intentions of a tyrant. . . . It names, as Marilyn
Frye puts it, "an enclosing structure of forces and barriers
which tends to the immobilization and reduction of a group or
category of people." . . . [It is] the exercise of power as the effect of often liberal and "humane" practices of education, bu-
reaucratic administration, production and distribution of con-
sumer goods, medicine, and so on.[2]

Thus, under a political umbrella of commitment to equality and human
rights, some populations find themselves exposed to racism and humiliation
because they belong to a particular race, religion, ethnic group, class, or
gender. One of the most difficult problems in analyzing this phenomenon is
its invisibility. The attempt to expose the exclusion, marginalization, and
denial mechanisms of oppression is almost an attempt to prove the existence
of nothingness; the theoretical difficulty is to unveil the hidden contradiction
of tacit oppression in a presumed reality of nonoppression. In a democratic
reality like that which prevails in Israel, commitment to human rights can
coexist with discrimination and racism thanks to social practices of denial.
These practices are constructed within intergroup relationships, and they are
intensified in social and political settings.

The Feminist Agenda in Israel and the
Absence of Mizrahi Women's Issues

Though there are many issues on the predominantly Ashkenazi Israeli feminist agenda that nominally cross socioeconomic lines (and therefore, to some
extent, the ethnic divide), few recent issues have galvanized the attention and
resources of the majority of Israeli feminists as that of women's right to be
combat pilots. It took a Supreme Court decision, handed down in April 1994,
to open air force pilot training courses to women. The case became a feminist
cause célèbre.

It is not surprising that this particular issue attracted so much attention
and support—it is, after all, a demand that patriarchy can understand. It
resonates with the Zionist ethos of self-defense and the primacy of the military. Winning the case was an important symbol, to be sure. Yet very few
women would ever directly benefit from the outcome. The choice of lending

so many resources to support this case was never weighed against putting the same resources behind a case that would affect large numbers of low-income women, most of them Mizrahi. This is a good example of the ethnic blindness discussed earlier; here it functions to filter out such "irrelevant" issues as the concerns of Mizrahi women.

Israeli feminism does not differentiate between the concerns of Ashkenazi and Mizrahi women. Women's issues are considered to affect all women equally. The personal, political, and cultural experiences of Mizrahi women—all the differentiating socioeconomic characteristics that have placed them in an inferior relationship to Ashkenazi women—are most often ignored, if not denied. The struggle to open up new career paths for women such as being a fighter pilot, the issues of domestic violence and equal representation on the boards of publicly held corporations—these battles have all been assumed to be of equal concern to all women, no matter their background.

Placing the Mizrahi Issue on the Israeli Feminist Agenda

During the 1970s and 1980s, the feminist agenda did not often include the "Mizrahi issue" in spite of the fact that ethnic conflict in the wider society was generally recognized and already on the agenda of public discourse. It was raised within the feminist context for the first time, at the Fourth Annual Feminist Conference in 1984, which included a workshop entitled "The World of Mizrahi Women." There were few Mizrahi women among the presenters at this conference, and most of them were women who had "made it"—women who had university degrees, were pursuing careers, and had moved into the middle class. In this sense they had more in common with Ashkenazi middle-class women than with the vast majority of Mizrahi women, who were mainly lower class and whose concerns were about raising children in large families, low income from manual jobs, and lack of affiliation with a labor union that could protect them from being exploited. They had no opportunities to compare their own education or develop their professional skills.

It was another decade before Mizrahi feminist activists again organized a presence within the annual conference, and this proved to be explosive. During 1994 and 1995 the deeply problematic relationships between Ashkenazi and Mizrahi feminists that had been heating up for some time, boiled to the surface.

After many failed attempts to raise the Mizrahi issue at feminist gatherings, during a planned part of the conference agenda a few Mizrahi activists disrupted the 1994 annual conference by raising the issue unexpectedly from the floor, and they chose the most well attended plenary session of the conference to do so.[3] Speaking from the floor, surrounded by Ashkenazi faces, they spoke of the racism they had experienced throughout their lives—from childhood through adolescence and since becoming feminist activists.

When members of the audience attempted to bring the session back to its planned agenda, a few Mizrahi women took the stage to pursue their point. They expressed themselves with rage and hostility, speaking from the gut, where these emotions had lain dormant for a long time, nourished by the seeming indifference of their supposedly feminist sisters. They used harsh language to describe the humiliation they had suffered because of racism. Women described their childhood experiences, how, for instance, their Iraqi names were taken away and Israeli names given to them instead. They recounted their first meetings with Israelis and the way they and their mothers were treated. As one woman put it, "The social norms according to which class relationships are organized made us believe that we should demand of our mothers that they stop speaking Arabic, Iranian, Turkish, Indian; we begged them to try to lose their Moroccan, Yemenite, Iraqi accents. We wanted them to start behaving like Israelis, for God's sake—that is, to be like an Ashkenazi!"[4]

For the Mizrahi women, the atmosphere was charged with humiliation and rage. Speaking at the 1994 conference, this is how one Mizrahi feminist remembered her years of activism during the 1980s:

> I remember that once I asked the chair of the [feminist] movement why they [the activists] do not go to lower-class neighborhoods? "What do you want me to talk with them about?" she asked me in wonder. I was hurt.[5]

From the margins of the organizations to which they had been relegated, Mizrahi activists like Mira Eliezer had tried to raise the ethnic issue, but every time they made an attempt, they discovered anew that the feminist commitment to "sisterhood and solidarity" dissolved. The 1994 conference was just one more example of silencing. Though some of the Ashkenazi women present at the conference supported the Mizrahi demand that the conference discuss their issues of discrimination based on ethnic background, most others objected, and the participants were unable to reach an agreement. Outraged, the Mizrahi women walked out. As a result, some Mizrahi activists left the movement very disappointed, and those who had the strength to stay have, over the years, increased their pressure on the Ashkenazi leadership to recognize the issues and begin to work on them.

Ethnic conflict within the feminist movement was the catalyst for Mizrahi women to see themselves as a group and has heightened their awareness of Mizrahi identity. As Mira Eliezer experienced it: "They [the Ashkenazi women] made me understand that Ashkenazi feminism, namely Western feminism, is not like ours. They are Ashkenazi—well-established economically and living in prestigious neighborhoods. Our feminism remained implicit." Eliezer adds that each time she wanted to raise Mizrahi issues, she felt she had to apologize.[6]

Having challenged the ideological framework and values that underlay all the planned content of the 1994 conference, the discussion degenerated into a divisive struggle. A cacophony of Ashkenazi voices was heard, arguing that the fact that their origins are in the hegemonic sector of society does not automatically make them racist oppressors. They also argued that the issue of the ethnic divide in Israel is not at all relevant to feminism. In addition, they argued, the social gap between Ashkenazi and Mizrahi, though it might have existed in the past, no longer existed, so why open old wounds?

From the stage, a Mizrahi woman responded, "Is there a Mizrahi woman in the audience who can imagine how it would be to live in a society in which our dark skin, our curly hair, and our Arab names are respected and valued?"[7] Others went on to point out the hypocrisy of concepts like solidarity and universality as used by mainstream feminists, which amounted to systematic silencing whenever the ethnic problem was raised. As one participant put it,

> every attempt to tell us that there is no feminism is an attempt
> to hush us up. This is an attempt to dictate to us what is im-
> portant in our lives and what shape our struggles should take.
> This is your attempt to shape us according to the Ashkenazi
> feminist model. For, while our Mizrahi identity is attacked, the
> Ashkenazi identity is presented as the undoubted and obvious
> norm.[8]

When, in 1994, the issue of the ethnic divide was imposed on conference participants, the ethnic genie was out of the bottle—a genie that the Mizrahi women felt had until then been suppressed and silenced. It is no accident that the simple demand to discuss the issue was felt as a threat by many Ashkenazi women, since it brought into the open a demand for justice and redistribution of resources and power.

There were four components of the Mizrahi feminist challenge that the ruling elite found threatening. First, responding to the Mizrahi women's accusations meant considering one's own responsibility for the ethnic divide. Second, accepting responsibility entailed acknowledging and recognizing Ashkenazi hegemony. Third, accepting a more equitable redistribution of resources and influence necessarily meant that those who had would have less. Fourth, accepting responsibility required recognizing the tokenism of the Mizrahim and letting go of the belief there there was equal representation of Israeli women from all segments of society. These four components, whether consciously or unconsciously grasped, were altogether rejected by most of the Ashkenazi women present at the Tenth Annual Feminist Conference.

The fact that feminists have not found it easy to redistribute power more justly within the movement is not only because it is difficult to acknowledge the existing inequality, but also because that admission entails loss of power. Ashkenazi women are not only subordinated to the patriarchal order as passive objects, they are also active subjects who, to a certain extent, partake in, benefit from, and perpetuate that order. It is therefore not surprising that, when presented with the opportunity to accept responsibility and seek new directions in resolving the ethnic issue, the great majority of Ashkenazi women failed to do so.

The First Mizrahi Feminist Conference— The Beginning of Political Empowerment

Following the 1994 conference, several militant Mizrahi feminists ultimately felt that there was no way to return to the fold and that their only recourse was to leave the movement. In order to explore their experience of oppression as Mizrahi women, they decided to organize a Mizrahi feminist conference. This decision was a landmark in the development of Mizrahi feminism in Israel.

Though the declared intent of the nine organizers was to hold a conference in order to develop a Mizrahi feminist agenda, as the planning went on it became clear that the ethnic issue itself was what needed to be discussed. The program that resulted focused on the ethnic divide and the long history of Mizrahi oppression in Israel.

As the minutes of one of the meetings (19 July 1994) state, the group determined that, "We ought to learn our history, because it has been extinguished." The women brought their personal biographies into the process of conference planning and were determined, as the minutes indicate, to "focus on the experience of deprivation among themselves, free of the self-deception experienced in the presence of Askhenazi women."[9]

The topics chosen for discussion at the first Mizrahi feminist conference reflect two major concerns. First, there was a deeply felt need to close the gap between formal Zionist history as learned in school, and the women's personal biographies and what they had learned from their parents. The second common thread was another profoundly felt need—to expose and decry the hurtful experiences of Mizrahi women's parents and their own experience as children, which had yet to be recognized as painful by the rest of Israeli society.

Workshops planned for the Mizrahi Feminist Conference show that the two concerns described above were central: "The Children of Yemen—The Unbelievable Thought,"[10] "The Unreachable Past—The Mizrahi Experience as an Influence on Our Identity," "Where Has Mizrahi Medicine Gone?" "Mizrahi Women in the Media—The Marginality . . . of the *Freikhah*" [a derogatory name for a lower-class young woman; originally a female Moroccan name that means "joy"], "The Place of Mizrahi Culture in the Curriculum," "The *Aliyah* [Immigration] of the 50s from Mizrahi and Ashkenazi Points of View: The Hope and the Reality," "The Pursuit of Identity," "The History of Belly Dancing," "The Attitude of the Literary Establishment to Mizrahi Women Artists," "Mizrahi Women in the Protest Movements," "Single Mothers and the Welfare System."

The examination of Mizrahi history that was so prominent at the 1995 Mizrahi Feminist Conference was neither nostalgic nor a "return to roots." It was, rather, a painful process of the conference participants' exposing humiliating experiences of oppression in their own daily lives. The empowering and liberating quality of this process has often been described in feminist literature.[11] Thus, if such traditional feminist issues as employment, wages, or violence against women were not on the agenda, the more important feminist processes of self and social introspection and analysis did occur. These were the feminist issues that participants in the Mizrahi conference considered important, just as important as the issue of unemployment, for instance, and perhaps even more so when one's community has been the object of racism and cultural genocide.

As participants compared the textbooks from which they had learned Zionist history with the contents of their own socialization and experience, they participated in subverting "objective history" and deconstructing the hegemonic perceptions of the Zionist ethos. As a result, they became aware of the full complexity of their cultural and political lives. Inevitably, as the women revealed more and more instances of their personal exclusion from Israeli society, the process became one of protest. The discovery of a common experience of oppression was empowering. What occurred during the conference workshops can be described as feminist cognitive deconstruction and reconstruction of their experience as Mizrahi women, much as it has been discussed in the literature.[12]

The understanding of the matrix of oppression, says Patricia Collins, is an indispensable precondition for the process of liberation.[13] This is what the 1995 Mizrahi Feminist Conference achieved.

So What Is the Mizrahi Feminist Agenda?

The Mizrahi feminist agenda has evolved at the intersection of two strategic crossroads: one that focuses on the struggle against the subordination of Mizrahi women as a result of the ethnic divide and another that focuses on the struggle against their subordination as women. It includes two dimensions: discussion of the common but diverse (Iraqi, Yemenite, Moroccan, and so on) Mizrahi experience within the general population of Israel and discussion of the experience of Mizrahi women within the female population of Israel.

These dimensions are extremely significant to the liberation of Mizrahi women as Mizrahi women. Collins stresses the importance of this complexity in her elaboration of the experiences of black women. She notes, for example, the different contexts within which the same crime can be committed and hence be differently perceived: a black woman being raped by a white or a black man, or a white woman being raped by a white or a black man.[14] These are the kinds of analyses needed to illuminate and elaborate the causes of the marginalization of Mizrahi women. For example, Mizrahi and Ashkenazi women both face economic discrimination, but of a very different sort. Whereas Ashkenazi women (by and large, middle class) are held back by the sexist "glass ceiling," Mizrahi and Palestinian women (generally working in low-wage, unskilled jobs) are held back by racism, here in the form of insufficient education to qualify for skilled and professional jobs.

Thus the Mizrahi feminist agenda often defines a separate feminist arena: Mizrahi women must be enabled to escape from poverty and the conditions of life in city slums and outlying, economically depressed "development" towns that most Ashkenazi feminists never even see. The Mizrahi feminist agenda is not only different in content; it can also be different in the priorities it sets. As long as the majority of the children dependent on public services for welfare and education are the children of Mizrahi women, Mizrahi feminism will have to address issues of social policy more urgently than, for example, the issue of peace with the Palestinians, which has been a central concern of the largely Ashkenazi feminist movement. As long as most Mizrahi women are fighting for survival, these most basic issues will be the ones that define the boundaries of Mizrahi feminism.

The problems that must be resolved are those that contribute to the perpetuation of Mizrahi women's subordination to Ashkenazi women. Therein lies the first and daily hurdle Mizrahi women confront. A solution requires the cooperation of mainstream feminists, as well as the cooperation and effort of Mizrahi feminists, to find strategies to deal with the problems of childminders, housekeepers and other low-paid domestic service workers who are mostly Mizrahi women.

Strategies

Since the Tenth Feminist Conference two strategies have been adopted by Mizrahi feminists. One strategy has been to split off from mainstream feminist organizations and establish Mizrahi organizations, and the other strategy has been to avoid rejecting mainstream feminist activities altogether.

Each strategy has its advantages and its problems. The first, Mizrahi separatism, requires an elaboration of the specific issues of concern to Mizrahi women, as well as the development of aware feminist leadership at the grassroots level. It focuses on individual empowerment through consciousness-raising networks and the sociopolitical flow of information. It is that stage of feminist development in which the personal turns into the political, stimulating women to take more responsibility for their own lives. One advantage of this strategy is that Mizrahi activists are free of the competition and pressure they feel from the usually more educated, more successful Ashkenazi women who dominate mainstream feminist organizations. Without the sense of intimidation they had experienced in mixed organizations, they are free to share their experiences with one another and learn from them collectively.

For those who chose the second strategy and remained within mixed feminist organizations, thus far they find themselves still isolated as a group, though no longer as individuals, and they still do not have real political power within their organizations. These Mizrahi feminists must struggle for their piece of the pie, which, as Israeli feminist experience has shown, is never just handed to them. For this strategy to work, Mizrahi women must be involved in both formal and informal mainstream feminist organizations with an agenda that is similar to that of mainstream feminism: equality in the distribution of resources and representation in the decision-making process. Though there are disadvantages to this strategy, it is nevertheless indispensable to the empowerment of Mizrahi women.

Mizrahi Feminist Activists Facing Dilemmas

Some of the issues that Mizrahi feminists working in mixed settings have raised are:

Tokenism. Many progressive organizations, in the name of pluralism, often invite a Mizrahi woman to participate in meetings and other activities, representing Mizrahi women's interests. Implicit in the invitation is a commitment to Mizrahi feminism that the organizations often do not really intend to honor. Very soon, the Mizrahi woman understands that she has no power and finds herself in a grave dilemma: to continue playing the role without any real power, and thus colluding with a tokenist approach, or to resign and thus render Mizrahi women's issues invisible once again.

Affirmative action. To ensure that Palestinian, lesbian, Mizrahi, and Ashkenazi women have equal representation, some organizations within the Israeli feminist movement adopted the "four quarters" policy whereby every public feminist forum would have to include each of these four voices. Unfortunately, since there are very few Mizrahi feminist activists, this requirement sometimes creates ludicrous situations in which, for example, a Mizrahi feminist who never served in the armed forces is invited to talk on sexual harassment in the military. Again, the dilemma faced by Mizrahi feminists is whether it is worth rendering poor service to Mizrahi women's interests as opposed to rendering them invisible.

The professional Mizrahi feminist activist. Again, because there are so few Mizrahi feminist activists and because many organizations in the early 2000s invite Mizrahi women to participate in their activities, those who are active are known by all organizations and are frequently invited to participate in almost every activity. Thus a cadre of Mizrahi activists have become professional representatives of Mizrahi interests, hopping from one event to another and doing a necessarily superficial job.

The recruiter. Another issue Mizrahi feminist activists have encountered is being asked or expected to play the role of "recruiter." Very often mainstream feminist leaders appeal to their Mizrahi counterparts in the hope that, because of their contacts in the lower-class neighborhoods, they will help to recruit support from grassroots women for specific mainstream activities. A prominent recent example was the attempt of a women's peace organization to enlist neighborhood women to join their demonstrations. Those Mizrahi women who have joined peace organizations are frequently looked upon as the only ones capable of recruiting Mizrahi women, since they know the "native" language of the neighborhoods.

Kitchen cabinets. In many organizations, decisions are made informally, often in more social settings, and the Mizrahi activists often find out about them only after the cake has been divided. Thus, for example, an Israeli women's peace organization used Mizrahi women activists and slogans of social justice to raise funds for an ineffective project in a low-income neighborhood. Mizrahi women were never informed about the results of the campaign, not even when the money was earmarked for Mizrahi issues. Once the funds were raised, less money was allocated to the neighborhood project than had been budgeted for it.

The issues described above are not unique to the feminist movement. They are quite typical of Israeli social-change politics, which, throughout its history, has developed these mechanisms of tokenism, recruiting, co-optation, and decisions taken informally by ruling organizational elitists. Feminist organizations being constructed by women of the middle class replicate these norms and mechanisms, which together form a discriminatory system.

Signs of Change

The exposing of the ethnic divide in the feminist movement in 1994 and 1995 was the beginning of a conflictual and often personally painful period for Israeli feminists, but the fourteenth annual conference, held toward the end of 1999, may well mark the end of one stage and the beginning of another for Ashkenazi-Mizrahi feminist relations, at least in the grassroots women's movement.

It was evident in the planning leading up to the conference that the Mizrahi women were well organized as a group and had an identified leadership to represent them. For many years, the conference planners had adopted the "four quarters affirmative action policy. Though it had been effective in bringing new voices to the table, it was nevertheless true that the dominant voice at the annual conference was still Ashkenazi. In the planning for the fourteenth conference, the Mizrahi women demanded that the "quarters" actually be equal this time. Failing to find a common format that would meet that demand, the organizers decided to divide the two days of the conference into four quarters, with each group doing its own programming. Free to plan together and with no interference, the Mizrahi leaders developed a half-day of workshops on Mizrahi issues and identity and, instead of a panel, they staged a powerful performance. Mizrahi feminists provided the tone for the conference and embraced a large list of issues that concerned all sectors of women.

The Mizrahi women were also able to pressure the Ashkenazi "quarter" to relate to the meaning and consequences of being Ashkenazi. Some refused, but others took up the challenge of occupying only one quarter of the space.

The Mizrahi feminist victory, marked by the 1999 conference, is important, but it is not complete. Mizrahi feminism still remains a marginal concern to the Ashkenazi and largely Anglo-Saxon (from English-speaking countries) leadership of mainstream feminism in Israel. Mizrahi women have developed a strong voice in the Israeli feminist movement, but they are still not singing in the mainstream's opera.

Summary and Conclusion

Like all governmental and nongovernmental institutions in Israel, the feminist movement is infected by strains of racism, elitism, and Eurocentrism. Consequently, its agenda gives priority to issues of most concern to the dominant Ashkenazi majority of activists.

The beginnings of Mizrahi feminism are rooted in the tension between feminist rhetoric of equality and the reality of oppression within the movement. While feminists spoke of sisterhood and solidarity, Mizrahi participants felt implicit marginalization and exclusion. Mizrahi women's attempts to raise the issue and their rejection by the Ashkenazi majority in the movement served to distinguish them, to themselves, as a separate group. This in turn led to their coming to define the rest of the women as "Ashkenazi."

As a result of this failure by many Ashkenazi women to engage with these issues, some of the Mizrahi activists split off from the mainstream groups and organized their own conference, which attempted to relate to the multidimensional experience of oppression. But the most significant achievement of this gathering was the sense of liberation that accompanied the participants' reconstructions of their own experiences of ethnic discrimination. Since then, not only the Mizrahi separatists, but also the nonseparatist activists find it ideologically, personally, and strategically difficult to collaborate with mainstream feminist organizations. Yet their experience has strengthened them in significant ways. What remains to be done is to develop a clear formulation of Mizrahi feminist consciousness that makes sense to grassroots women and to continue the struggle for an equitable share of feminist resources.[15]

Notes

1. Alison Jaggar, *Feminist Politics and Human Nature* (Totowa, N.J.: Rowman and Littlefield, 1988); Iris Young, *Justice and the Politics of Difference* (Princeton, N.J.: Princeton University Press, 1990).

2. Young, *Justice and Politics*, p. 40.

3. *Hila News* (in Hebrew) (July 1994): 4; published in Tel Aviv by the Hila Organization.

4. Ibid.

5. Mira Eliezer, "We Have Come Quite a Distance," *Mitzad Sheni* #4 (in Hebrew) (July–August 1996) 25; published in Jerusalem by the Center for Alternative Information.

6. Ibid. There are additional testimonies on this topic in the reports from the Third and Seventh Annual Feminist Conferences in 1984 and 1988, respectively.

7. *Hila News*, (July 1994): 4.

8. Ibid.

9. Minutes from the preparation of conference meetings, July 19, 1994, the First Mizrahi Feminist Conference.

10. There are many in the Yemenite community who charge that during the 1950s the government, via social workers and nurses, took their babies from hospitals and put them up for adoption in Ashkenazi families, telling the parents that the babies had died. Two government commissions have been established to investigate the charges, and each concluded that such atrocities never occurred.

11. Catharine MacKinnon, *Toward a Feminist Theory of the State* (Cambridge, Mass.: Harvard University Press, 1989), pp. 84–105.

12. Ibid; see also Judith Butler, *Gender Trouble* (New York: Routledge, 1990).

13. Patricia Collins, *Black Feminist Thought* (New York: Routledge, 1990).

14. Ibid.

15. Feminist resources are those powers that women have as a result of their specific experiences as women, and these powers are employed for their liberation.

Bibliography

Aanzaldua, Gloria. *Making Face, Making Soul*. San Francisco, Calif.: Aunt Lute Foundation, 1990.

Ataliah. *Destroyed Yards* (in Hebrew). Jerusalem: Reshafim, 1989.

Bebbington, Clare. "Ladies Don't Climb Ladders." In *Frontiers of Leadership*, edited by Michael Syrette and Clare Hogg, pp. 496–500. Oxford, Eng.: Blackwell, 1992.

Ben-Gurion, David. *A Vision and A Way* (in Hebrew). Vols. D and E. (Tel-Aviv: Am-Oved, 1957–1962).

Bernstein, Deborah, "Oriental and Ashkenazi Jewish Women in the Labor Market." In *Calling the Equality Bluff*, edited by Barbara Swirsky and Marilyn Safir, pp. 186–92. New York: Pergamon, 1991.

Bikhler, Shimshon, and Shlomo Frenkel. *The Meukhassim* (in Hebrew). Tel-Aviv: Kadim, 1984.

Biniamini, Kalman, and Shlomo Ahronson. "Narcissism—Personal behavior and Political Culture" (in Hebrew). In *From Crisis To Chance: Proceedings of the Annual Confer-*

ence of Welfare Workers in Israel, pp. 161–74. Jerusalem: Association of Social Workers in Israel. 1982.

Butler, Judith. *Gender Trouble*. New York: Routledge, 1990.

Census of Population The Statistical Abstract of Israel 1972. Jerusalem: Central Bureau of Statistics, 1972.

Collins, Patricia Hill. *Black Feminist Thought*. New York: Routledge, 1990.

Dahan-Kalev, Henriette. "Oppression of Women by Other Women." *Israel Social Science Research* 12, no. 1 (1997): 31–45.

———. *Self-Organizing Systems: Wadi Salib and the Black Panthers—Implications on Israeli Society* (in Hebrew). Ph.D. diss., Department of Political Science, The Hebrew University of Jerusalem, 1992.

———. "Stereotype Discourse in Israel." Special edition: "The European Legacy—Toward New Paradigms," part 2. *Journal of the International Society for the Study of European Ideas*, 1, no. 2 (1996): 680–89.

Eliezer, Mira. "We Have come Quite a Distance" (in Hebrew). *Mitzad Sheni*, 4 (July–August 1996): 25. Published by the Center For Alternative Information in Jerusalem.

Etzioni-Halevi, Eva. *The Elite Connection and Democracy in Israel* (in Hebrew). Tel Aviv: Sifriat Poalim, 1993.

Feurstein, Karl, and Ruth Rischel. *The Children of the Melakh—On the Retardation of the Moroccan Children* (in Hebrew). Jerusalem: The Henrietta Szold Institute, 1956.

Fierman, Jaclyn. "Why Women Still Don't Hit the Top." In *Frontiers, of Leadership*, edited by Michel Syrette and Clare Hogg, pp. 501–10. Oxford, Eng.: Blackwell, 1992.

Firer, Ruth. "The Images of the Children of the Mizrachi in the Books of History" (in Hebrew). *Yiunim BeKhinukh* 45 (1986): 23–33.

Gelblum, Arie. "Ha'Aretz," (in Hebrew). As quoted in Tom Segev, *The Israelis*. Tel Aviv: Am-Oved, 1982.

Grant, Jan. "Women as Managers: What They Can Offer Organizations." In *Frontiers of Leadership*, pp. 307–12.

Hammond, Valerie. "Women Managers: Developing Their Full Potential." In *Frontiers of Leadership*, pp. 511–23.

Hila News (in Hebrew). Bulletins from June/July 1994 through 1996. Published by the Hila Organization in Tel Aviv.

Herzl, Theodor Benjamin Zeev. *Altneuland* (in Hebrew). Translated by Levensohn Lotta. New York: Bloch, 1941.

Hooks, Bell. *Feminist Theory From Margin to Center*. Boston, Mass.: South End Press, 1984.

Hophman, Yair. "Ethnic Identity of Youth in Israel" (in Hebrew). *M'gamot* 17 (1970): 5–14.

Iton, Akher (in Hebrew) 19–20. Published in *Kiryat Ata*, 1991.

Jaggar, Alison. *Feminist Politics and Human Nature*. Totowa, N.J.: Rowman and Littlefield, 1988.

Khakak, Lev. *Elyonim U'nekhutim* (Superiors and inferiors) (in Hebrew). Jerusalem: Kiryat Sefer, 1981.

Kimlika, Will. *Multicultural Citizenship*. Oxford, Eng.: Clarendon Press, 1995.

Kipnis, Levin. *Rumieh, the Little Nanny* (in Hebrew). Tel-Aviv: Lichtenfeld, 1983.

Kol Ha'Isha 11 (in Hebrew) (1983): 5. Newsletter.

Kol Ha'Isha 19 (in Hebrew) (1983): 1–3, 9. Newsletter.

Levitan, Dov. *Population Distribution* (in Hebrew). Jerusalem: The Ben-Tzi Institute, 1992.

Lipietz, Allen. "The Nation and the Regional: Their Autonomy vis-à-vis the Capitalist Crisis." In *Transcending the State Global Divide*, edited by P. Palan and G. Barry, pp. 23–43. London: Boulder, 1994.

MacKinnon, Catharine. *Toward a Feminist Theory of the State*. Cambridge, Mass.: Harvard University Press, 1989.

Mamman, Daniel. *The Connections between the Economic and the Political and Managerial Elites in Israel* (in Hebrew). Ph.D. diss., Department of Economics, The Hebrew University of Jerusalem, 1993.

Megamot, 3–4, (1951–52) (in Hebrew). Published in Tel Aviv by the Henrietta Szold Institute.

Minutes of the preparation of conference meetings, The First Mizrahi Feminist Conference. 19 July, 1994. (In Hebrew).

Mitzad Sheni, 1–6 (1996). (In Hebrew). Published in Jerusalem by the Center For Alternative Information.

Morris, Roz. "Management: Why Women Are Leading the Way." In *Frontiers of Leadership*, pp. 307–12.

Okin, Susan. *Women in Western Political Thought*. Princeton, N.J.: Princeton University Press, 1979.

O'Leary, Virginia. "Ambition and Leadership in Men and Women." In *Frontiers of Leadership*, pp. 313–17.

Protocols of the Third Annual Feminist Conference (in Hebrew), 1984.

Protocols of the Seventh Annual Feminist Conference (in Hebrew), 1988.

Raz, Hanitah, "Thoughts on the Closing of the Kol Ha'Isha Organization." *Kol Ha'Isha* 19 (1983). (In Hebrew). Newsletter.

Raz-Krakotzkin, Ammon. "Diaspora within Sovereignty" (in Hebrew). Part 2. *Theory and Criticism*, 5 (1994): 113–132.

Reports of the Adva Institute (in Hebrew). Tel Aviv: Adva Institute, 1994–1996.

Reports of Israel Central Bureau of Statistics, 1945–1956.

Said, Eduard. *Orientalism*. New York: Vintage Books, 1979.

Segev, Tom. *The Israelis* (in Hebrew). Jerusalem: Am-Oved, 1982.

Seri, Brachah. "An Outsider Guest." *Kol Ha'Isha* 19 (1983): 4. (In Hebrew). Newsletter.

Shiran, Vicki. "The Ninth Feminist Conference." *Noga* 26 (1983): 26. (In Hebrew).

Smooha, Sammy. *Israel Pluralism and the Conflict*. Berkeley: University of California Press, 1978.

Swartzwal, Yossi, and Yoav Rim. "Symmetry and Asymmetry in Perceptions" (in Hebrew). *Megamot* 24 (1978).

Young, Hugo. "Elected Unopposed." In *Frontiers of Leadership*, pp. 318–25.

Young, Iris. *Justice as Politics of Politics of Difference*. Princeton, N.J.: Princeton University Press, 1990.

Zameret, Zvi. *The Days of the Melting Pot: The Frumkin Committee Report*. Sde Boker, Israel: The Ben-Gurion Heritage Center, 1993.

The Women's Peace Movement in Israel[1]

Gila Svirsky

Women in Black, the largest and most visible of the women's peace movements in Israel, has existed since 1988. Although as of this writing (May 2002), it has shrunk to half a dozen vigils in as many locations in Israel, in its heyday (1988–1991) the movement attracted thousands of Israeli women to stand in vigils dressed in black and carrying signs advocating an end to the occupation by Israel of territory captured during the 1967 war. No other peace movement—women's or mixed-gender—has before or since so thoroughly captured the imagination and commitment of large numbers of Israeli women, who turned out week after week to declare their politics publicly and hence expose themselves to ongoing harassment and often physical attack.[2]

In this paper, I examine four main questions:

Why did women demonstrate as women during the period of the Intifada, more than during any other conflict in which Israel has been engaged?

Why do many women feel the need for "a peace movement of their own," when mixed-gender peace movements dominate the scene?

How is women's peace activism different from mixed-gender peace work? and

Is Women in Black a feminist movement?

I write as a participant in Women in Black and other women's peace movements, and as someone who has extensively researched and written

113

about the phenomenon. Most of this analysis is drawn from the period of the "first Intifada," December 1987 to Summer 1993.

A Brief History of Women in Black

The Women in Black movement was begun in January 1988 by a group of fifteen Jerusalem women who were members of the radical left, mixed-gender peace movement Dai LaKibbush (end the occupation). Although the first vigils were not originally designed to be gender distinct—the intention was to have women dressed in black and men dressed in white, for theatrical effect—the men failed to attire themselves in white, while the women's black costumes provoked attention from passers-by. The success of the gimmick to draw attention led the women to continue, and the "black" vigil soon became a specifically women's activity. The group of women dressed in stark black garb would stand silently in a bustling public square near the center of town. They would soon attract other women to join them who had heard of or seen the dramatic-looking spectacle. For one hour the women would hold hand-lettered signs, saying "Stop the Occupation." The vigil was also subject to a barrage of violent reactions from male passers-by.

Within weeks, the idea caught on in Tel Aviv and Haifa and, thereafter, at a total of thirty-nine crossroads throughout Israel. The Jerusalem vigil was always the largest of the Israeli vigils, though there were virtually only Jewish women there. In other vigils around Israel there was a sizable representation of Palestinian women citizens of Israel. Based on an informal census I conducted of the vigils, I estimate that during the heyday of the movement in Israel (1988–1991) there were some five thousand women who showed up at these vigils on any regular basis.[3]

A few months after Women in Black was founded in Jerusalem, solidarity vigils formed in other countries—first in Italy, then elsewhere. In some cities (including Amsterdam, London, Melbourne, and Sydney) the groups were mixed Jewish and Palestinian, and the women sought to develop a dialogue with each other as they jointly protested the Israeli occupation. A number of locations in the United States and Canada formed their own vigils, and eventually a North American coalition was created, called the "Jewish Women's Committee to End the Occupation."

In late 1990, the idea of these vigils took on a life of its own. Women dressed in black, calling themselves "Women in Black," formed vigils in many countries, the vigils now having nothing to do with the Israeli occupation. In Germany, Women in Black in Munich, Cologne, Berlin, Wiesbaden, and other cities originally protested the Gulf War and sale of chemicals by German firms to the Iraqi regime. After the war, German Women in Black broadened their mandate to protest neo-Nazism, xenophobia, racism against migrant workers, and other German social problems. Women in Black in southern India protested against religious fundamentalism focused against women. There were Women in Black in San Francisco to protest apathy about the homeless, Women in Black in Italy to protest war and organized crime, and Women in Black in Australia to protest domestic violence. One of the most vibrant movements was in Belgrade, where Women in Black protested their government's policies in the former Yugoslavia. Some of these groups have never even heard of Women in Black in Israel, where the movement began.

Feeling Invisible in Other Peace Frameworks

In the 1970s, when the contemporary feminist movement first began in Israel, most feminists had never addressed the question of the conflict between Israel and the Arabs.[4] This was not surprising, since even the liberal left in Israel had little to say about the conflict in those years. By the 1980s, however, when Israelis were polarizing into two opposing camps (proponents of "end the occupation" versus proponents of the "greater land of Israel"), the Israeli feminist movement made a deliberate decision to avoid the controversy. Although one plank basic to international feminist ideology has always been a pro-peace stance, many Israeli feminists (with several salient exceptions) felt that the fledgling Israeli feminist movement would never get off the ground if it assumed this controversial position. In those years (and even today to some extent), "peace talk" alienated many Israelis who might otherwise be interested in a more narrow agenda of equality for women. Thus, although the ideological inconsistency was obvious and painful, Israeli feminists sought ways to mute the geopolitical issues and to highlight women's rights, narrowly understood—leaving peace issues to peace organizations, even women's peace organizations, and excluding them from the general feminist agenda.[5]

Thus, women who wanted to engage the issue of the Arab-Israeli conflict in an NGO (nongovernmental organization) setting had to do so outside of the feminist movement. Most participated in the activities of Peace Now, the largest mixed-gender peace movement in Israel, and a small number found their way to the three women's peace organizations that existed before the first Intifada. These groups were either small (Gesher and WILPF) or mar-ginalized because they were comprised primarily of Arab women (TANDI).[6] Soon after the start of the Intifada, an additional seven women's peace or-ganizations appeared, and they managed to recruit many women who had never previously been politically active. In addition to Women in Black, these were Shani (Israeli Women Against the Occupation); the Women's Organi-zation for Women Political Prisoners; the Peace Cloth; Neled (Israeli Women for Coexistence); Reshet (Women's Network for the Advancement of Peace); and the Women and Peace Coalition.[7] (See the appendix of this essay for a description of each.) These women's peace organizations, known collectively as the Israeli women's peace movement, became the most vibrant and per-sistent part of the peace camp in Israel during the Intifada period, with conferences, rallies, lectures, parades, humanitarian activity, and a seemingly endless series of vigils. During these years, the incredible variety and fre-quency of activity often left women feeling that peace work had taken over all areas of their lives.

Why did this happen? Why did women in Israel feel the need for peace movements and organizations of their own when the Intifada began, rather than operating within traditional mixed-gender structures?

Prior to the Intifada, fewer women than men were active in Israeli peace work, and most of these participated in mixed-gender organizations, not independent women's groups.[8] From the outbreak of the Intifada, however, women seemed to form the majority of the rank and file in the mixed-gender peace organizations, as well as setting up their own peace movement. If you went to almost any peace demonstration in Israel, whether of thirty people on a street corner in Haifa or of a hundred thousand people in the municipal plaza of Tel Aviv, the predominance of women was noticeable. A number of researchers have made this observation, although I have found no data about it one way or the other.[9] Although women were often the foot soldiers of the peace movement, few headed these peace organizations or represented them publicly.

Peace Now was and is—by far—the largest and most visible peace or-ganization in Israel, and the absence of women on the speakers' platform was noticeable during the first dozen years of its existence. (Also missing were Jews of Mizrahi origin—from Muslim countries—and Israeli Arabs.) Peace Now was founded in 1978 to advocate for Israeli flexibility during the Camp David negotiations with Egypt, but it was not until the 1990s that women became a regular part of those who addressed their rallies. Women did have key roles inside the movement: Janet Aviad has headed Peace Now for years, and other women were leaders in setting policy and in decision making. But when it came to public spokes people, Peace Now either had no woman at all, a token woman, an unnamed woman moderator, or a woman whose job was to sing "The Song of Peace" at the end. There were no panels of female speakers, as there were of male speakers. Women were active but invisible.

There is one little-known detail in the story of the famous "officers' letter" that marks the birth of Peace Now. This was a public letter to the Israeli government signed by 350 army reservists, admonishing then Prime Minister Menachem Begin to embrace the opportunity to make "peace now." It was the first time in Israel's history that a bloc of army reserve officers had, albeit tactfully, linked the motivation of soldiers to fight with the government's willingness to pursue peace policies. Less known, however, is the fact that the name of Lieutenant Yael (Yuli) Tamir, one of the officers in the founding group and a key organizer, was deleted from the list prior to its publication. Why? It was because Lt. Tamir is a woman. The presence of a woman, they felt, would detract from the impact of an all-male lineup.[10] Years later, Yuli Tamir became Minister for Immigrant Absorption in Barak's administration.

Peace Now did begin to incorporate women (and Mizrahi Jews and Arabs) into the list of speakers around the third year of the Intifada.[11] Some of this democratization was a reflection of their decision to reach out to the non-Ashkenazi, nonprivileged sectors of the population, and some of it had to do with the persistent complaints presented by many, including Women in Black, to the leaders of Peace Now. But long before Peace Now got around to changing its patterns, women felt alienated.

This did not prevent all members of the peace camp, whether women or members of the more radical left-wing organizations, from attending Peace Now rallies. Everyone understood the need for large numbers. Because of its size and its closeness to the political and military establishment, Peace Now had the greatest direct impact on the changes in government policy of all the peace movements. Radical left-wingers might correctly claim that the radicals set the agenda that was later adopted by Peace Now. Indeed, because Peace Now was plugged into the establishment, they had the ear of decision makers more than the radicals did.

In short, when the Intifada broke out, women were not visible among the Peace Now leadership, let alone in political parties or the Knesset. Naomi Chazan, a peace researcher, Knesset member, and former deputy speaker of the Knesset, considers the invisibility of women to be one of the main factors in the rise of women's peace activism: "[W]omen have been blocked from leadership positions in other political organizations. . . . It is crucial for women to have the power to express themselves politically. That's why they've gravitated toward these new movements."[12]

And with regard to women in power, as Chazan noted in 1990:

> Women's representation in political life in Israel has been eroding for a number of years, and many of the formal channels are now blocked to women. . . . Any woman who wants to seriously express her opinion must do it through an extraparliamentary process. That is why you are seeing all of these groups.[13]

This invisibility of women in Israeli political life is one of the most frequently cited reasons for the need felt among women to organize on their own. The women who joined the vigil of Women in Black were certainly aware of this invisibility, and incensed about it. But this is only part of the story.

Emotional Impact of the Intifada

Another reason sometimes cited for the increased activism of women during the first (1987–1993) Intifada has to do with the nature of the Intifada itself. It was a popular uprising in which Palestinian children and women were full participants. Just one month into the conflict (on January 3, 1988), the first Palestinian woman was killed in the uprising, shot by Israeli soldiers as she tried to rescue a child from being struck by a soldier. This scene had a powerful impact on Israeli television viewers, especially other women. The footage of children being beaten, of women marching in front of the stone throwers, of poverty and oppression brought about by Israeli society, whether by omission or commission—all evoked strong feelings among Israeli women, some out of rising defensiveness and others out of compassion. These feelings were compounded by the distress that it was "our men"— brothers, sons, fathers—who were sent to put down the teenagers, the women, the mobs. Whether one regarded the Palestinian stone throwers as freedom fighters or not, they were surely not armed troops in those years, and sending Israeli armed troops against them raised complex feelings of confusion, if not shame.

Professor Galia Golan, coresearcher with Naomi Chazan and also a Peace Now and feminist activist, phrased it as follows: "Perhaps the Intifada spoke to women in a way that other wars had not. This was not only husbands and sons making war, not armies, but a rebellion of women and children. Perhaps this spoke to the hearts of women."[14]

There is an interesting debate about whether women have characteristic feelings about peace, bringing to situations of hostility such special sensitivities as motherliness, nurturing, and aversion to suffering.[15] Clearly the Intifada had an impact on women everywhere, feminist or not, evoking the human side of the conflict. One interesting observation about this was made by a (male) journalist, "While Peace Now and other left wing movements agonized over what the occupation was doing to Israeli society, women peace activists entered the territories in the early days of the Intifada to see what the occupation was doing to the local population, to express sympathy for their suffering, and to understand and dialogue with the Palestinians, based on personal contact."[16] Few male peace activists were engaged in this kind of peace work.

Women joined the Women in Black vigil for various motives. Some, especially those who came from the more radical left groups, had espoused the Palestinian cause for many years, and used the Intifada as an opportunity to raise the volume on the demand for Palestinian self-determination. The motivations of others who were relative newcomers to political activism (before they became further politicized by participating in the vigil) were more vaguely humanitarian (to end the violence) and self-centered (to protect our loved ones). Most activist women talked about "the corruption of the occupation," meaning what it had done to Israelis, but only some in the early period conceded the Palestinian right to a state. "End the violence" was a slogan useful for both camps, the more humanitarian and the more ideological.

Many analysts have grouped these together in listing the motivations for Israeli women's peace activism. Naomi Chazan has said, "This is not a struggle of tanks but a people's struggle. And the issues of self-determination and equality have special meaning for women."[17] Similarly, Ronit Lentin, who wrote an incisive analysis of the women's peace movement in Israel, observes that Israeli women could get "tuned in to the specifically feminist themes of that particular phase of the Israeli-Arab conflict: oppression, self-determination, human dignity, justice and security."[18] Debby Lerman of the Tel Aviv vigil strongly believes that "Women in Black was a specifically feminist response to political reality,"[19] though many women less familiar with or committed to feminism called it a "humanitarian response." But all these categories of women were represented at the Women in Black vigil and maintained an amiable coexistence.

For some, a specific feminist agenda mobilized them into action during the Israeli occupation. The vigils throughout Israel had a disproportionate representation of women from the rape crisis centers, the battered women's shelters, the women's health hot lines, and the antipornography groups. Those who were sensitive to the issue of violence against women applied that lesson to all forms of violence and oppression.

Excellent analyses have been written by several feminist academic researchers (Naomi Chazan, Erella Shadmi, Simona Sharoni, among others) pointing out the connection in Israel between the status of women, the ongoing conflict, and the growing militarization of society.[20] A number of observers have suggested that domestic violence dramatically increased in Israel with the attempts to quell the Palestinian uprising. Rachel Ostrowitz, coeditor of Israel's feminist *Noga* magazine, has noted, "Rape and violence against Israeli women are on the increase, and I have no doubt that it was the iron-fist policy that created the atmosphere and legitimacy for this."[21] The explanation was that violence becomes a way to solve problems: an Israeli soldier cannot club a demonstrator in the morning and not club his son or wife in the evening. I have not found research to substantiate these claims; however, it seems logical that violent behavior in one area carries through into all areas of life, including personal interactions and domestic relationships. On the other hand, one Israeli reserve-duty soldier guarding Palestinian detainees in a Gaza prison told me, "The Intifada is great for my marriage. I get out all my aggression on the prisoners, then come home to my family on the weekend completely relaxed."

Whatever the truth about the connection between different forms of aggression, discussions about this were not a significant part of Women in Black discourse and not a prime motive for the activism of most women. Nor were motherly or nurturing feelings what kept women involved in peace work, though they may have prepared the ground for the activism of some. On the other hand, most participants felt that they as women did have a message to convey about the geopolitical situation, and that Women in Black was a way that they preferred to convey that message.

The Structures and Formats of Women in Black

Women in Black was run very differently from mixed-gender peace organizations, and most women found this difference to their liking. These different structures and formats can be grouped into three categories:

First, the vigil form of demonstration: The image of women dressed in black and standing in silence bestowed a powerful symbolism of mourning, dignity, and conscience upon the event. A second huge advantage was that it was a simple and easily implemented tactic. A vigil could readily be organized far from the city centers, making it possible for women in the periphery to participate. Third, women appreciated the calm, nonaggressive nature of the vigil form of protest. One did not have to be pushy or shout or have slick, eye-catching slogans. And, finally, the women all gradually realized that their commitment to nonviolence was a source of strength. The more that nonviolence was practiced, the more they felt empowered by it and the stronger they appeared to outsiders.

Second, the nonhierarchical nature of the movement: Every woman was a peer, and not having a leader enhanced the individual commitment and increased the sense of collective responsibility. On a rainy day, more women would show up to the vigil than on a nice day, not wanting the women who came to feel alone. There was no official leadership, no official spokesperson, not even an official steering committee. The most developed institutional structure was a phone list, separate for each vigil. During intensely violent periods, some of the vigils met to deal with pressing issues (asking for a police presence, buying a first-aid kit, making sure at least one woman present was experienced in first aid, etc.), but any woman could attend these meetings. If the police chief wanted to speak with or meet "the leader," any women willing to volunteer would go, and that group would then share his words with everyone. If the media wanted to interview "the spokeswoman," the women talked among themselves about who the right person would be to represent them for that particular channel. And each woman, in speaking about the vigil, was expected to preface her remarks with the statement, "I represent only myself; there are many different points of view among Women in Black." In the Women in Black newsletter that I edited for two years, every issue carried the words: "This newsletter is an individual initiative and does not necessarily represent the views of Women in Black as a whole."

Third, consensus-seeking decision making for the vigil, whether informal or at meetings: Women in Black, like any movement, was often called upon to make decisions. These decisions sometimes concerned such major issues as whether the vigil should fly an Israeli flag, the advisability of adding new slogans, if men should be allowed to join. These were matters of heated concern and were potentially very divisive. However, a culture of discussion and consensus-seeking decision making evolved in almost all the Women in Black vigils, and this averted confrontation, invited full participation, and was a source of great pride. As noted by Naomi Chazan after observing one meeting, "I was very impressed by how well they listened to each other, the mutual support, and the absence of competitiveness. About sixty women participated, and just about every one asked a question or expressed her opinion."[22]

One tacit assumption underlying all the decisions was that the group would not adopt any position that would alienate a sizable number of women from the vigil. This assumption was the foundation of the supportive climate of decision making. Another basic principle was the format of the discussion itself. Many vigils developed a system called "making a round"—going around the room and allowing each woman to express her opinion unhindered. It would not be an overstatement to say that, by and large, women who spoke were not interrupted and there was a fundamental respect for each point of view.

It is unclear how this format of decision making was reached. How was it possible for Women in Black to have such amicable decision making, though all the women came from a culture of stormy battles over every trivial issue? Perhaps the women who came from feminist circles introduced some of the basic ground rules (e.g., not allowing someone to speak a second time until every woman who wishes to speak has already spoken once). Perhaps the women had built up enough trust for each other during the course of the vigil to enable a less ego-driven form of discussion. Whatever the source, the climate of discussion was open and thoughtful, and one would frequently hear women say that they had changed their opinion in light of the points that had been raised. The way the decisions were made fostered a strong sense of loyalty to the group.

Women in Black was a heterogeneous movement in terms of political background and involvement. Although the Tel Aviv and Haifa vigils were comprised of veteran feminists and peace activists, for most of the other women, the Women in Black vigil was a first political involvement. The structure and format of the movement made it possible for veterans and rookies, flaming radicals and comfort-zone liberals, to work together in harmony.

Was Women in Black a Feminist Movement?

Several of the founders of Women in Black were early and ardent feminists, but most were not. The Tel Aviv and Haifa vigils were avowedly feminist, but that was not true of the other vigils. Thus, statistically speaking, feminists were a minority in the early months and years of the Women in Black vigil.

This gradually shifted during the vigil years as feminist consciousness was raised. However, many women resented being designated "feminist," and that was sufficient reason for the women to eschew the label on most vigils. Nevertheless, although Women in Black never defined itself as a feminist movement, the themes of feminism eventually found their way in.

There is considerable evidence that a feminist awareness began to permeate the Women in Black movement. Many studies of the Israeli women's peace movement, including the sharp analysis of Simona Sharoni, testify to the conscious search for a feminist discourse among Women in Black.[23]

For example, at the first vigil in proximity to International Woman's Day (in March 1988), a group of women came to the Jerusalem vigil with balloons bearing feminist slogans. No one questioned their right to use the vigil to add a statement about women's issues. On International Woman's Day a year later, participation in the festive Jerusalem vigil surged to 160 women, and appropriate signs were added. This was already an initiative of the vigil as a whole.

Another example was the message sent by the National Conference of Women in Black to the Israeli and Arab participants in the Madrid peace conference held in October 1991. This message read in part: "We note with dismay that women are underrepresented in all the delegations; we believe that increased participation of women would significantly enhance the efforts toward dialogue and peace." This is certainly the statement of women who are aware of themselves as a force for "dialogue and peace," if not an out-and-out feminist message.

But I think the best evidence comes from the national Women in Black conferences that were held annually. With each passing conference, more and more sessions explored the connections between the occupation and feminism. Indeed, a feminist perspective was pervasive in the international Women in Black conference in December 1994, from the opening session ("The Israeli-Palestinian Peace Process: Feminist Views") through many of the workshops ("Peace, Pacifism and Gender," "Pacifism in Feminist Theory," "Revolutionizing Motherhood Toward a Culture of Peace," and "Feminist Views of the Peace Era and the New World Era," to mention just a few).

The growing feminism of participants in the Women in Black vigil was not coincidental, and it is not hard to explain. In my view, the following elements raised the feminist consciousness of participants in the Women in Black vigils:

First, the sexual and gender-oriented curses aimed at vigil participants helped alert women to the fact that they were being attacked not only for their political views, but for holding views at all. A strong woman or one with a political opinion was equated to a whore. The most polite chauvinist reaction was, "Get back into the kitchen." This can hardly fail to signal a woman that something is fundamentally askew between women and men in society. In the words of one journalist who witnessed it, "A woman has only to wear black and go to Paris Square to instantly become an ardent feminist."[24]

Second, the Women in Black vigil was virtually ignored by the media, while smaller and less interesting mixed-gender peace demonstrations were garnering media attention. And when the Israeli media did find their way to the vigil (inspired by seeing Women in Black appear in the foreign media), they often had questions that should have been embarrassing to pose: "Do you like the color black in your wardrobe?" asked one male reporter in an interview.[25] Being consistently ignored or patronized will eventually raise awareness.

Third, the formats, structures, and principles of the Women in Black movement (the vigil, nonviolence, lack of hierarchy, consensus decision making, etc.) were not only comfortable to the women, but were preferred to those of the mixed peace organizations. Many had never previously been active in all-women's organizations, and they found it a welcome change.

Fourth, inevitably, women were making the connection between war and the oppression of women. Some of the feminists among the women helped point this out, such as Nabila Espanioly and Dalia Sachs from the Haifa vigil: "War creates and legitimizes the norms of discrimination and oppression of women and other minorities in the personal, political and societal levels. For us women on all sides, this is not victory. We pay the price."[26]

Hanan Ashrawi credits the Intifada with helping women link gender and geopolitical issues:

> I think the most determining factor in the emergence of Israeli women's consciousness—of making the link between gender issues and national/political issues—came with the Intifada. The prominent role that Palestinian women played was, in a way, a challenge to Israeli women. They started trying to reach us on a feminist basis . . . to work together on common agendas—gender self-determination and national self-determination.[27]

Fifth, many of the women were appalled by the militarism of the Peace Now message. Some examples: the male leadership of Peace Now made a point of publicizing their army rank to prove that they were not shirkers of duty; leading Peace Now figures took public pride in their sons having combat roles (a few recoiled from service in the occupied territories especially during the second al-Aqsa Intifada, but most did not); and the speeches and ads of Peace Now reflected their acceptance of the underlying assumptions that wars do resolve conflicts, that strength coupled with peace is the best defense. Some of this attitude was passed off as packaging—the exigencies of having to market a plea for peace in a militant society—but much was rooted in Peace Now's fundamental agreement with military solutions, its belief in the Israeli army as an antidote to "the enemies of Israel."[28] But was it really necessary for the leading lights of a peace movement to publish a statement during the 1991 Gulf crisis in support of American military violence in Iraq? In the words of Tsali Reshef, spokesman for Peace Now, "We are not opposed to this war—strangely enough, a peace movement that is not opposed to war.... We never argued that Israel should not fight [or that] there's no such thing as a justified war—and this war, in our eyes, is a justified war."[29] Could Peace Now not imagine a response to Iraq's violence other than massive bombardment? Didn't anyone in Peace Now recall that in war, no one is the victor? Again, Nabila and Dalia capture well the alternative position of the woman's peace movement: "We are now even more strongly convinced that wars cannot solve conflicts; that they only create an illusion of power and victory, which creates more problems and conflicts. This illusion continues the cycle of death, destruction and male military dominance."[30]

Throughout the first Intifada, Peace Now failed to condemn the demolition of homes of the terrorists' families. In 1996, following a series of suicide bombers inside Israel, the main speaker at its rally in Jerusalem (the noted author David Grossman) called such demolitions "a necessary evil."[31]

The increasing awareness of the differences between Peace Now and Women in Black in their attitudes toward the conflicts was an important element in the growing feminist convictions of Women in Black participants.

The Second, Not-So-Hidden (Feminist) Message

The message of Women in Black was "end the occupation." The medium was women dressed in black standing at a weekly vigil. The latent message was the medium itself: these are independent, strong-willed women. Erella Shadmi, a Jerusalem Woman in Black, was one of the first to examine this in writing:

> [The Women in Black vigil] would appear to be a simple act of
> protest with a clear message. But under the surface, there is a
> layer in which the message is not the words but the act: the
> medium is the message. The unconventional combination of

being a woman, being in the public realm, and engaging in a struggle undermines the conventional perception of what is a woman and what is a political struggle, and redefines them.[32]

Erella, a lieutenant-colonel in the Israel Police, joined the vigil just days after taking early retirement from the force. A radical feminist theorist, Erella's analysis of the Women in Black movement helped make sense of the deep-seated opposition to that movement:

> Women in Black pulls the rug out from under the old symbols, founded on passive and dependent womanhood, whose honor is within the gates, and puts cracks in the wall between the public sphere, which belongs to the man, and the private, that of the woman. The concept of womanhood is juxtaposed with concepts believed to be competitive and contradictory—like politics and publicness—and this reawakens what human and Israeli history prefer to forget—the role of women in arenas of social and national struggle. In this way, Women in Black thwart conventional perceptions, break the traditional image of womanhood, and redefine the concept and its social context.[33]

Thus, Women in Black was defying consensus on two levels: political views and gender roles.

> SEEING BLACK: What is it about Women in Black that drives the average Kahanist scum out of his mind?[34] Not so much their politics as their stubborn perseverance, their vaunted arrogance, and the sense of sisterhood that leaves no room for men.[35]

As a result, the feminist consciousness of Women in Black was raised during the course of the vigil, both by reactions to the women and by their own analysis of the political situation. And as feminist consciousness expanded, so did the participants' pride in what they were doing and their courage about their convictions:

> It is sufficient to attend one vigil to understand the advantage of Women in Black over their attackers. It is easy to understand the terror evoked by dozens of women wearing black, intelligent and fearless, among those accustomed to seeing women as weak inferior creatures.[36]

Women in Black were not only perceived as strong and proud; in many ways, that is what they had become.

Appendix

Below is a brief description of each of the women's peace organizations mentioned above, separated into two groups—those founded before and those during the Intifada.

Three Women's Peace Organizations That Preceded the Intifada

1. *TANDI* (*Movement of Democratic Women in Israel*) was founded in 1948 as the local branch of the World Federation of Democratic Women. Although organized by women who were active in the more moderate of the two communist parties in Israel, TANDI is an independent movement. As an Arab-Jewish organization, TANDI works for "two states for two peoples, a just peace, women's rights, and children's rights." TANDI continues to be active, primarily among Arab women.

2. *Gesher* (bridge), founded in 1975 by a mother whose son was killed in war, was an organization of Jewish and Palestinian women who worked toward peace at the grassroots level through discussion groups, lectures, and cultural activities. Based in Haifa, Gesher eventually ceased functioning.

3. *Women's International League for Peace and Freedom (WILPF), Israel Section*. This international organization, founded in 1915 and two-time winner of the Nobel Peace Prize, has branches in forty countries, and an Israel branch founded in 1980. WILPF is committed to opposing all discrimination and works for a just peace between Israel and the Palestinian people (a negotiated two-state solution) as well as equality and coexistence between Arabs and Jews in Israel. WILPF's local activities include demonstrations, provision of food and clothing to disadvantaged Israelis and Palestinian refugees, and operation of kindergartens for disadvantaged children. Members of WILPF form the management and main constituency of the mixed-gender organization Gesher L'Shalom.

Seven Women's Peace Organizations Founded During the Intifada

1. *Shani (Israeli Women Against the Occupation)* was launched in Jerusalem in January 1988, in coordination with Women in Black. A second branch later developed in Tel Aviv. If Women in Black was the vigil component of the women's peace movement, Shani provided a critical forum for education and analysis of the issues from a woman's perspective. (I would have said "a feminist perspective," but several of Shani's main organizers were reluctant to use this word.)

Shani played a critical role in helping women become politicized about the the Arab-Israeli conflict. It provided a setting that encouraged questions and the exploration of issues without some of the ego issues that often inhibit women from participating in a mixed-gender context. Shani made a point both of inviting key Palestinian women from the territories to address Israeli women from their perspective and of holding meetings in the territories. It organized joint Palestinian-Israeli seminars for teachers, maintained contacts with Palestinian women under arrest and detention, and sponsored a seminar on the psychological effects of the Intifada on Israeli women. Shani also encouraged a boycott of products from the Jewish settlements in the West Bank.

2. *Women's Organization for Women Political Prisoners*, also founded in 1988 by Israeli Jewish women, sought to help Palestinian women who were imprisoned for Intifada activity. Members attended the trials of women charged with crimes, visited them in prison, and helped maintain contact between prisoners and their families. This organization addressed the special problems of women prisoners, from getting more nourishing food to pregnant prisoners to convincing prison authorities to allow infants to remain with their mothers; it also addressed complaints about sexual harrassment during interrogations. The organization was composed of two independent branches, one in Jerusalem and the other in Tel Aviv.

3. *Peace Cloth* (sometimes called Peace Quilt) was a project more than an organization, in which some 5,000 women from all over Israel sent in squares of cloth embroidered, painted, or otherwise designed with individual statements about peace. These patches were then sewn together into a tablecloth about 650 feet in length. The cloth was presented to the government by 500 women at a ceremony on the Knesset grounds, for use as a tablecloth on the future negotiating table. My sources report that the cloth was never used in Oslo, Cairo, Washington, Amman, or any other negotiating site.

4. *Neled (Israeli Women for Coexistence)* is a group of Jewish and Palestinian women which began in 1989 to meet for dialogue, social activities, and actions of solidarity with Palestinian women in the occupied territories. Most of the members were from the center (Tel Aviv) area of Israel. The organization is now dormant.

5. *Reshet (Israel Women's Peace Net)* grew out of the Israeli-Palestinian Women's Conference held in Brussels in 1989 and was initiated by prominent women, including members of Knesset. This organization made an effort to appeal to women in the political center or just left of center, bringing them into contact with leaders and members of Palestinian Women's Committees. Israeli women visited projects of the committees in the occupied territories, and held reciprocal "parlor visits" with Palestinian women. Reshet turned its mandate over to Bat Shalom as the peace process was getting underway.

6. *The Women and Peace Coalition* grew out of a 1988 conference in Jerusalem in which many new as well as veteran women's peace organizations participated, accentuating the need for a coordinating body of these groups. The Women and Peace Coalition became the common forum for communication among the many women's peace organizations, serving a critical role not only in coordinating and networking, but also in initiating joint actions and conferences. Almost all the major conferences (national and

international) held by the Israeli women's peace movement were initiated and sponsored by the Women and Peace Coalition. All the women's organizations described here (and the Haifa feminist center, Isha L'Isha, Woman to Woman) sent representatives to the coalition meetings, and unaffiliated women also attended. Members of the coalition were generally much more activist women and members of veteran and more radical peace organizations.

7. And, of course, *Women in Black*.

Notes

1. Adapted and expanded from chapter 4, "Why Women?" in *Standing for Peace: The History of Women in Black in Israel*, by Gila Svirsky, unpub. manuscript, 1996.

2. The Four Mothers Movement for Peace in Lebanon was not exclusively a women's movement, and never at any point mobilized thousands of women to its events, as did Women in Black.

3. Gila Svirsky, "Standing for Peace: The Story of Women in Black in Israel," unpub. manuscript, 1996.

4. There were some important exceptions, but the thrust of the women's liberation movement in Israel was then—and generally still remains—to avoid the issue of peace. For a fascinating overview of the early years of the women's movement, see the account of activist Gilberte Finkel, *A History of the Women's Liberation Movement in Israel*, unpub. manuscript, June 1981; or Gilberte Finkel, "Von der Kibbuz: Bewegung zum Schweige-marsch" in *Argument-Sonderband* 176 (1990): 56–80.

5. As recently as January 2000, at a Jerusalem conference sponsored by the Israel Women's Network (Israel's main feminist advocacy organization), the subject of the Arab-Israeli conflict was neither raised nor discussed, even though this conflict has broadly acknowledged ramifications for the equality of women in this country.

6. Mothers Against Silence was a small women's group founded in the 1970s to end the Lebanon War, but they soon incorporated men and changed their name to Parents Against Silence.

7. Some of these have since passed out of existence and new groups have formed—among them, Bat Shalom of the Jerusalem Link, Mothers and Women for Peace, and New Profile.

8. For data on this, see Gadi Wolsfeld, *The Politics of Provocation: Participation and Protest in Israel* (Albany: State University of New York, 1988).

9. See Naomi Chazan, "Israeli Women and Peace Activism," in *Calling the Equality Bluff: Women in Israel*, ed. Barbara Swirski and Marilyn P. Safir (New York: Pergamon Press, 1991), p. 153.

10. Based on the author's interview with Yuli Tamir, June 21, 1996.

11. This strategic decision was taken in December 1988—see Reuven Kaminer, *The*

Politics of Protest, (Sussex, England: Sussex Academic Press, 1996), p. 110–14—but it took time to implement. Ronni Kaufman, who took on most of the organizing duties at Peace Now for three Intifada years (1989–1992), helped Peace Now diversify its public representation and shared some of his observations in an interview with the author on June 20, 1996.

12. Randi Jo Land, "A Separate Peace?" *Jerusalem Post*, 29 June 1989.

13. Tom Hundley, "The Vigils Are Black and White, Not the Issue," *Chicago Tribune*, 17 July 1990.

14. Michal Sela, "Five Years of Roses and Rotten Eggs" (in Hebrew), *Davar* (January 1993).

15. See, for example, Betty Reardon, *Sexism and the War System*, (New York: Teacher's College Press, 1985); Adrienne Harris and Ynestra King, eds., *Rocking the Ship of State: Toward a Feminist Peace Politics*, (Boulder, Colo.: Westview Press, 1989); and Sara Ruddick, *Maternal Thinking: Toward a Politics of Peace*, (New York: Ballantine Books, 1989).

16. Yoram Harpaz, "They Don't Shoot, They Don't Cry," *Kol Ha'Ir*, 10 March, 1989.

17. Land, "A Separate Peace?"

18. Ronit Lentin, "Woman—The Peace Activist Who Isn't There: Israeli and Palestinian Women Working for Peace" (1995): 26. From the quarterly newsletter of the Irish Peace Institute Research Center, University of Limerick.

19. Interview with the author on May 2, 1996.

20. See Naomi Chazan, "Gender Equality? Not in a War Zone!" *Israeli Democracy* 3, no. 2 (1989); Erella Shadmi, "Occupation, Violence, and Women in Israeli Society," *Women in Black National Newsletter*, no. 5 (spring 1993); Simona Sharoni, "Homefront as Battlefield: Gender, Military Occupation and Violence Against Women," in *Women and the Israeli Occupation: The Politics of Change*, ed. Tamar Mayer (London: Routledge, 1994), pp. 121–137; and again Simona Sharoni, "Every Woman Is Occupied Territory: The Politics of Militarism and Sexism and the Israeli-Palestinian Conflict," *Journal of Gender Studies* 1, no. 3 (1992): 447–62, (special issue: *Gender and Nationalism*).

21. Rachel Ostrowitz, "Dangerous Women: The Israeli Women's Peace Movement," in *Jewish Women's Call for Peace: A Handbook for Jewish Women on the Israeli/Palestinian Conflict*, ed. Rita Falbel, Irena Klepfisz, and Donna Nevel (Ithaca, N.Y.: Firebrand Books, 1990).

22. Harpaz, "They Don't Shoot, They Don't Cry."

23. See Simona Sharoni, "Search for a New Feminist Discourse," *Challenge*, 4, no. 5 (September–October 1993).

24. Neri Livne, "Letter from the Front: The New Israeli Left: It Looks Like a Comeback for Jerusalem" (in Hebrew), *Koteret Rashit*, 20 April 1988.

25. Arnon Lapid, "Just a Question" (in Hebrew), *Davar*, 31 October, 1991.

26. Nabila Espanioly and Dalia Sachs, "Peace Process: Israeli and Palestinian Women," *Bridges* 2, no. 2 (fall 1991): 112–119.

27. "The Feminist Behind the Spokeswoman: A Candid Talk with Hanan Ashrawi," *Ms.*, (March/April 1992), 14–17. The interview was conducted by Rabab Hadi, cofounder of the Union of Palestinian Women's Associations in North America.

28. In *The Politics of Protest*, his excellent survey of Israeli protest movements during the Intifada, Reuven Kaminer provides an astute and balanced evaluation of the strengths and flaws of Peace Now.

29. Vernon Loeb, "A Cause at a Loss," *Philadelphia Inquirer*, 11, February 1991, Daily Magazine section.

30. Espanioly and Sachs, "Peace Process."

31. This was at the Peace Now rally on March 9, 1996, in downtown Jerusalem, following a succession of bombs in Jerusalem, Tel Aviv, and Ashkelon that took the lives of almost seventy people.

32. Erella Shadmi, "Politics through the Back Door," (in Hebrew), *Ha-aretz*, 24, February 1992.

33. Ibid.

34. Kahanism is the generic term for movements that followed the extreme right-wing views of Rabbi Meir Kahane.

35. Ibid., p. 24.

36. Ibid.

Violence Against Women

Irit Umanit

An Overview

Violence against women is, in Israel as in all other places, about power and control. In a patriarchal society, as Israel is, those who make the rules and rule are men with power over the ones whom they perceive as powerless (mainly women). Are there unique characteristics, then, to the issue of violence against women in Israel? If so, what are they?

The answer to this is related to the unique history of this relatively young society, built on ideology and on the fundamental shift of a Jewish people from a minority to the ruling majority. The pioneers (many of them socialists) who built Israel as a Zionist state were highly invested in their belief that they were creating a new and different society—a just and gender-equal society, free from oppression for a new Jewish people. Alas, thousands of years of male domination, well rooted in the Jewish tradition, proved stronger than sociopolitical ideology; and other than the myth of equality, which the men in power were invested in maintaining, the actual sharing of power was nearly nonexistent. The foreparents of Israel were mainly forefathers.

One can understand this reality when one looks at the kibbutz movement,

I wish to express my gratitude to Mrs. Tall Korman from the Association of Rape Crisis Centers in Israel, for her help. Statistics were gathered from the National Association of Rape Crisis Centers, the National Toll-Free Hotline for Battered Women, the Women's Network of Israel, and the Ministry of Labor and Welfare.

where the share of wealth was indeed equal. Did it bring about a gender-equal society? It did not, for status in the kibbutz came not from wealth but rather from the division of roles, and virtually all roles of high status were occupied by men. The myth of equality remained until recent years. Since the kibbutz movement is currently undergoing privatization and traditional male roles are priced significantly higher than those of women, this myth has become even more apparent.

Thus, when in the early seventies the issue of violence against women was first brought to the public's attention by women who opened the first shelters for battered women, the response of the authorities was to proclaim that no such problem existed in Israel. For the first fifteen years or so of the shelters movement in Israel, the establishment refused to give the shelters any support. Policies changed dramatically about ten years ago, and I will address these changes later in this article.

Another situation unique to Israel, as the Jewish and Zionist state, is its ongoing state of war, enduring from its very first day of existence to the present time. This reality had to, and did, put men in this society in an advanced status as soldiers and protectors at the expense of women, who were expected to cater to and worship the macho image of the frontline soldiers—their brothers, sons, and husbands. This unique order has forced both men and women to pay a high price over the years. The men, on the one hand, are being ordered to risk their lives and to build the tough male identity of a soldier. The women, on the other hand, are expected to step aside and allow the former soldier to advance in society much faster than they because he risked his life for the state. Also, the built-in hierarchy of the military machine does not lend itself to education about gender equality or a total ban on the use of violence.

A last point to be raised on a unique feminist agenda in Israel is the core issue of a Jewish state. As Israel's government has always been a ruling majority based on religion, there was a decision at Israel's outset not to separate religion from state. This political decision has influenced all matters relating to women, including the formal attitude concerning violence against women in marriage, in a deeply suppressive way. "Men's superiority" is a fundamental tenet in Judaism, as in other religions. Also, since Israel has been declared a Jewish state, all non-Jewish citizens of Israel are automatically put in a less-than-equal status. A Jewish woman citizen is better off than is an Arab man. In this respect Jewish women are part of the ruling majority, and their suffering and lack of rights, including the right to safety, are relative.

The Emergence of Shelters for Women Victims of Violence

In 1976, a group of feminists from Haifa, led by Marcia Freedman (later a member of the Israeli Parliament), opened the first shelter for battered women in Israel. These women were met with ridicule and the worst kind of stereotyping. It has always been, as was true in this case, easier to disparage women by calling them whores, lesbians, or ugly man-haters, than to deal with their demands for justice and for equal power. A second shelter opened a few months later in the town of Herzeliah, near Tel Aviv, founded by a group led by Ruth Resnick. The shelter was created with a clear feminist ideology, volunteer time, donations, and a strong sense of radical and pioneer enthusiasm. Over the next fifteen years, six shelters were opened in Israel.

Real change in services took place only when a shift occurred in the public's awareness of the magnitude of the phenomenon of violence against women in Israel. This change took place due to the willingness on the part of the Labor Party, in power in the early 1990s, to play a much larger role in financing services relating to violence against women. In addition, the Ministry of Labor and Welfare, under the guidance of its minister, Ora Namir, became actively involved.

There are now thirteen shelters for battered women in Israel. Of these, one is for Arab women only, one for Orthodox Jewish women, and one a short-term emergency shelter with a multicultural staff. Two more were expected to open in the year 2000, however, due to the financial burden placed on the state by the security situation associated with the present Intifada, these shelters were not begun nor is it likely that any new shelters will open in the next few years. The shelters are run by nonprofit organizations in contract with and under the supervision of the Ministry of Labor and Welfare. During negotiations between the Forum of Shelter Directors and the ministry, a compromise was reached on womanpower per shelter size, upkeep cost, etc. The government finances 75 percent of each contract and the organizations raise the other 25 percent of the cost. Any additional money they are able to bring in goes to expansion of services for the women and to benefits for their employees that are not covered in the contract. In reality, the government finances about 60 percent of the actual cost of the shelters.

This change from totally independent ideological NGOs (nongovernmental organizations) creating and running the shelters to the institutionalization of selling services to the government does not come without a price. Of the thirteen shelters now in operation, only six claim to hold a feminist ideology and the others outwardly declare themselves social service oriented, and some even antifeminist. This change in the source of funding is an important issue, and the impact of this change is worthy of in-depth research. What are the differences made in the lives of the women residing in one shelter or another, if any? Could it be that where empowerment and gender equality are an integral part of the shelter's philosophy, the women would be more likely not to simply replace one violent partner with another upon leaving the shelter?

On the positive side, with the institutionalization came a dramatic increase in services for women victims of violence. Examples of these services are legal aid, rent subsidies, halfway apartments, treatment centers for the violators, family courts, and specialization in the treatment of women victims of violence in the Faculty of Social Work and in the police force. None of this would have happened without the radical and pioneer work of the feminist movement for the last twenty-five years, to whom credit is due but not given.

The estimation is that every seventh woman in Israel is a battered woman and every third has suffered some kind of violence related to her gender. The issue is "out of the closet." Nobody here would now dare to say that there is no violence against women in Israel, as was the belief some twenty years ago. The media covers the incidents up front, and it is politically correct to be against violence against women. The legislature is constantly dealing with the issue, mainly through the Committee on Gender Equality. Legislation in Israel is very progressive, relating not only to physical violence but also to sexual harassment at the workplace, the severity of the punishment, etc. Despite the fact that some of the new shelters are not feminist, feminism is "in." It has been internalized as an ideology and a way of life, particularly for some of the "elite" women in society—such as parliament members, artists, and media celebrities—who join hands with grassroots women to eradicate all forms of violence against women.

Approximately twenty-five women are killed by their male partners each year in Israel. Although the shelters are mainly filled with women who are victims of both violence and poverty (those who can afford other solutions and hiding places do not usually take advantage of shelter services), violence occurs in every socioeconomic sector. Two years ago, a highly publicized complaint was filed against a parliament member for violence toward his wife; also of notoriety was the complaint filed against a university professor by his wife. A young woman kibbutz member was killed last year by a stalker. A gang rape of a high-school girl by her peers in a very affluent neighborhood of Ramat Hasharon was fully covered by the media, and an investigation of a minister is now underway following a complaint of sexual harassment by a worker in his office. Finally, and most unfortunately, the myth of children's safety was shattered with the revelation, in six separate incidents in 1999, of men murdering their children, five of the incidents occurring as revenge on women who had left the men.

Israel is a multicultural society and the predicaments of each woman vary, depending on their culture of origin. The degree to which each individual internalizes and accepts that culture is also different. What we see in the shelters is that the commitment of the woman's family of origin to support her and her road to freedom from violence is imperative to her success. When a woman is a second or third generation of battered women and her mother, grandmother, and sisters stayed with their batterers, she will be less likely to move away from her abuser. Some of the women arriving at the shelters suffer almost unbearable pressure from their own family of origin to return home. The belief in these cultures is that violence against women by their husbands is a plight a woman may expect and even must accept. In some cases the woman's flight to a shelter is perceived as "a shameful act" by her family. Sometimes it is seen as so shameful that it is "worthy" of revenge by death. In less extreme cases a woman's "abandonment" of the batterer can influence the future of her sisters in a matchmaking for a good marriage.

All of this cultural baggage is put on the shoulders of the battered woman by her own family members. This pressure is on top of the already heavy load of her attempt to escape violence. I constantly find myself in awe at the courage of these women, and the determination that many of them demonstrate in their journey.

Rape Crisis Centers in Israel

The first rape crisis center in Israel opened in 1978 in Tel Aviv; today, there are ten rape crisis centers scattered throughout Israel. With a history very similar to that of the shelters, these centers began as a feminist movement initiative, led by Esther Eilam and others. The heart of the rape crisis centers is the operation of an anonymous hotline for victims of sexual abuse of any kind. Since their inception, the services they provide have grown to include support groups, advocacy throughout police and court procedures when applicable, and an educational program, which they provide to schools and other agencies.

The taboo on the subject of rape was much stronger than that on domestic violence. For many years the burden of proving "no provocation" was on the victim, and sentencing of the rapist was very lenient. A group of women celebrities, mainly from the arts, media, and Parliament, has formed an organization, "Ezrat Nashim," to support the centers and advocate for the issue. After about two years of negotiation, with strong support from the Parliament Committee on Women's Status, a significant increase in government financial aid to the rape crisis centers was agreed on and implemented. The national association of the rape crisis centers decided that in order to assure this financial aid they would let go of the principal argument about the ministry under which they would function, thus ending up under the Ministry of Labor and Welfare. This, in my opinion, was a grave ideological mistake because it connects victims of sexual assault and rape with neediness and welfare instead of law and justice.

In the case mentioned earlier of the gang rape in Ramat Hasharon, an important phenomenon became clear. There was a large gap between the support that the teenage victim received from the rape crisis center in Tel Aviv, the media, and Ezrat Nashim, versus the "outcast" status she received in school from her peers, both boys and girls, who chose to support the popular teenage rapists. This was quite a shocking revelation for feminists, who believed that we were much farther advanced in educating the younger generation to understand that the blame of rape is always and only with the rapist, and has nothing to do with the victim's behavior.

Statistics

About eight hundred women and twelve hundred children arrive at shelters each year, and an uncounted number of women are turned away due to lack of space. The need for shelter is particularly high during the summer months. Residents stay at the shelters for anywhere between a few days and one year.

In 1999, the rape crisis centers throughout Israel received 16,680 calls. Of them, 7,073 were directly about sexual assaults and rapes. The completed statistics for the year 1998 show that 5,236 calls were made concerning sexual assault, and may be broken down based on type of assault, as follows: 28.3 percent concerned rape, 4.6 percent attempted rape, 3.3 percent gang rape, 2.6 percent continuous forced sex, 6.2 percent incest by a father, 3.3 percent incest by a brother, 8.9 percent incest by other family members, 28.5 percent general sexual assault. The rest of the calls were about different types of sexual harassment, with 5.3 percent unqualified inquiries. In 1999, there was an astounding 35 percent increase in the number of calls to the rape crisis centers.

Thirteen percent of the calls were regarding attacks by strangers, 23.5 percent did not reveal the identity of the attacker, 27.7 percent concerned attacks by family members, and 35.8 percent concerned attacks by acquaintances. Forty-two percent reported assaults against minors (younger than eighteen), 24.2 percent against women aged nineteen to forty, with 32 percent not reporting the age. Eighty-eight percent of assaults were against women, the rest mostly against minor boys. Jewish women made 94.8 percent of the calls. This was most likely due to concern about the depth of secrecy kept, lack of use of existing services by Arab women, and lack of services in languages other than Hebrew. The victim made 55.2 percent of the initial calls, the victim's family made 18.8 percent, a close friend made 12 percent, the police made only 2.2 percent, and other government agencies made 7.5 percent. Of the calls to rape crisis centers that were not related to sexual assault, and are not counted in the above statistics, 25.6 percent were from battered women, and 6.7 percent from women undergoing divorce.

There is a clear sense in Israel that there is indeed an increase in violence in society. However, it is important to point out that the 35 percent increase in cases reported to the rape crisis centers is very probably due in part to increased reporting, a result of the issues of rape and sexual assault being more widely addressed by the media and the legislature. Prime-time television has broadcast ongoing ads with a toll-free number to call for reporting sexual assaults. The most renowned women journalists and other celebrities appeared in these ads, encouraging women to call and to seek aid and counseling. The media widely covered the case (mentioned earlier) of the gang rape and that of the minister who temporarily resigned and was under investigation, as well as the support given to the victims. Parliament passed a new law on sexual harassment in the workplace, despite some vociferous opposition. All of these events influenced the huge increase in the number of calls to the rape crisis centers. It is difficult to tell at this time exactly how much of this was a real increase in violence and how much was due to increased awareness and reporting.

Hotlines for Battered Women

The hotlines for battered women also have been used primarily by Jewish women, with only 10 percent of all calls being from Arab women. Recently, there has been an increase in the number of immigrants from the former

Soviet Union calling the hotlines. About 11,480 women called the three main hotlines for battered women in 1999. Since there is no way to discern how many of these calls were from the same person to different hotlines, this number is an approximation. For all three of these hotlines there has been a decrease in the average age of the women calling. Hotlines started in the late 1980s. The national hotline began as a regional one in 1990 and became national in 1996. Thirty percent of the calls are now from women ages twenty-one to twenty-five, and a total of more than 70 percent under the age of forty. This is an encouraging change, proving success in awareness-raising efforts.

In the last three years, the police have opened approximately twenty-one thousand new cases each year, following specific complaints of domestic violence. Women made 75 percent to 78 percent of the complaints, and men made the remaining complaints (against their woman partner). However, most of the complaints by men were made during divorce procedures or following the woman's complaint. The police, without any court procedure, closed approximately 25 percent of the complaints. This, too, was an improvement due to a change in the police policy regarding domestic violence. In the past, the police attitude and policy regarding domestic violence was that it is an individual's issue. Instructions for personnel dealing with such issues was simply to calm things down. One officer often took the man outside for a talk, while another spoke with the woman about her "violence-provoking behavior." Now that domestic violence has been identified as a crime, police personnel are instructed to arrest the violator, press charges, and, when necessary, help the woman find a shelter for herself and her children. Most police stations in Israel now have a division for domestic violence with personnel specifically trained about the issue.

Family Treatment Centers

There are eighteen family treatment centers for the prevention of domestic violence in Israel, again under the Ministry of Labor and Welfare. As expected, many more women than men turn to them for help. Most men receiving treatment do so under court order, in lieu of prison time. The centers offer individual, couple, and family counseling as well as support groups. These centers are more family focused than women oriented. They provide an opportunity for family members to attempt seriously to rebuild their home lives free from violence, and at the same time help women to get out of relationships and the men to accept this, if and when the women so choose.

A first "shelter" for men batterers opened in 1997, where men reside for three months of intensive treatment. Most of them go there instead of serving a prison sentence. While the shelter can only take in eight men at a time, it is an interesting attempt at moving the batterer, instead of the victim, from home. The long-term results are yet to be evaluated.

Final Thoughts

We have come a long way in the fifty-four years of the statehood of Israel in dealing with violence against women. The most important advance is a shift in the awareness of violence against women as a social and as a gender issue, rather than as a personal one. Much more must still be done to expand that awareness and to end this abuse.

It is yet to be seen what impact an end to war will have on this issue. Also of equal importance will be the impact that a separation of state and religion may have on women's issues generally and on violence against women in particular. How will the change in attitude and services, which has taken place at the legislative level as well as in the media, affect society at large? How and will "governmentalizing" the services influence ideology, and thus affect the treatment of the problem? And what, then, are the new challenges and agenda of the radical feminist movement in Israel in this new millennium?

Tami Katz-Freiman

In memory of the artist
Meira Shemesh

Preface: To be (political) or not to be?

Since this essay is being written during the Festival of Sukkoth (Tabernacles), against the backdrop of the recent political turmoil in our battle-fatigued region (this time, the El Aksa Intifada), the following question cannot be avoided: What is the significance and impact of artistic practice in a permanently volatile country? During times of peace, visual art is last on the list of Israel's cultural agenda. Resources, budgets, institutional and market infrastructure are not self-evident in a place where the political conflict overshadows any attempt to operate according to codes of "normality." In times of conflict, these circumstances are radicalized ad absurdum, for there is nothing farther or more detached from the Israeli-Palestinian conflict than the preoccupation with sexual identity and the body. Within this context, writing about artistic practice is likewise perceived as petty. Notwithstanding, perhaps the very engagement with the "normal" is, in itself, a political statement highlighted by the cry "live and let live."

Those who are not familiar with the visual art scene in Israel naturally have all sorts of presumptions and expectations. What kind of culture does Israel produce? What are the themes Israeli artists are expected to confront? Many foreign curators and professionals from the art field whom I met in

Israel preferred and appreciated artists whose work was explicitly political, while disdainfully dismissing anything that was not explicitly political.[1] This implies that in a country where the legendary "political pot" is always boiling, and at times even overflowing, there is no justification for the individual's preoccupation with normal, individualistic "trivialities," such as sexual identity, gender, sexuality, or the body. I hope that the following text will not only illustrate the options of representation of women by women in Israel, but also link the works to the sociopolitical reality in which they were created.

As I will attempt to illustrate, the binary opposition implied by the above, concerning a pair of dichotomous options, namely "political" and "apolitical," is not entirely accurate. The choice made by women artists currently operating in Israel—to express either a quintessentially political voice, one that is often perceived as superficial and propagandist, or a personal, individual, ostensibly apolitical one, which in any event declares itself as political—is a dynamic, flexible, circumstance-related and multifaceted choice.

The filter through which I will discuss these issues is that of an exhibition I cocurated in 1994 (together with anthropologist and sociologist Dr. Tamar El Or) for the Ein Harod Museum of Art in Israel.[2] Entitled *Meta-Sex 94: Identity, Body and Sexuality*, the exhibition presented fifteen artists—thirteen women and two men—who featured their paintings, photographs, videos, installations, and objects. It reflected a local as well as an international tendency that culminated in the 1990s: a preoccupation with issues of sexuality and identity that challenged conventional definitions and political expectations.

The following paragraphs will combine a discussion of works from the show as well as later works exhibited in other frameworks. It will attempt to anchor artistic practice in Israel on the borderline between the personal and the political.

Background and facts—here and there

The following introduction to my essay for the *Meta-Sex* catalogue relates a signal episode:

> The car began to cough and choke, it bounced and stopped. We came out, four women—three of the artists participating in the exhibition and myself, the curator. We were on our way back from the Ein Harod Museum of Art, midway, just past Wadi Ara.[3] Darkness was growing. We lifted the engine cover and once again were compelled to admit that the "constructiv-

ist relief" uncovered in front of our eyes was like a riddle to us. Were it not for the men, who stopped their car and within seconds located the source of the problem, we could not have gone on. We could not ignore the grotesque coincidence that put the feminist theory and all those academic texts we read to the test of reality. We thought of history, that kept us away from the car engine, of the progress we made towards it, despite everything, and of the long way still ahead of us. Can this story serve to uphold an anti-feminist argument? Is this an essential scene or is it merely a coincidental episode?[4]

Some of the crucial burning issues related to cultural gaps and tensions, on both the local and the universal levels, emerged already in that depiction. Naturally, *Meta-Sex* was feminist in its orientation. Against the backdrop of the political situation and the flourishing myths of masculinity, heroism, and machoistic patriotism, exhibitions of this kind are still rare in Israel.[5] Even though the present essay does not purport to review the history of the feminist voice in Israeli art, one ought to mention one precursor of *Meta-Sex*, an exhibition considered a trailblazer in art research and curatorship.

In the summer of 1990, the Tel Aviv Museum of Art held the first feminist exhibition, *Feminine Presence* (curator Ellen Ginton), which set out to explore the beginnings of the "feminist era" in Israeli art. In retrospect, it seems that the exhibition paradoxically pointed out the problematic issues inherent in the feminine voice within the local artistic context. What the curator exhibited was, in fact, a chronology of denial, often accompanied by an apologetic tone, both on her part and on the part of the women artists. Curator Ellen Ginton skillfully analyzed the history of the denial discourse and showed how it corresponded to the earliest phase of feminism—the phase of imitating men and talking in male-minded terms. Dganit Berest, a prominent Israeli artist, wrote in the exhibition catalogue, "First, I knew that feminine identity or sexual identity had not occupied me at all in my works. . . . [A]n interpretation which would try to distill a common component, a 'feminine' one, from the works of the various artists represented in this exhibition would seem to me forced, even offensive."[6] Tamar Getter, another leading Israeli artist, articulated the axiom, "Just as there is no male and female mathematics, so there is no masculine and feminine art."[7] It seems to me that both would have agreed with Virginia Woolf, who wrote in 1929, "It is fatal for a woman to lay [in her work] the least stress on any grievance; to plead even with justice any cause; in any way to speak consciously as a woman."[8] The curator's conclusion was that there is no point in looking for a formal, behavioral, or mental common denominator in women's art, since "these artists have nothing in common, apart from the fact that they are women, and Israeli women artists."[9]

This assertion implies that art is a universal, autonomous field, operating beyond sexuality and unrelated to gender. Nevertheless, *Feminine Presence* marked a turning point. It was a significant exhibition, if only for exposing the extensive power held by women in Israeli art from the seventies to the present day. One may argue that *Feminine Presence* made *Meta-Sex* possible, by introducing a legitimate channel of discussion, placing these concerns on the agenda, and inspiring a discussion.

The four years that passed between *Feminine Presence* and *Meta-Sex* reflect a deep generation gap, attesting to a real change in perception and expression of sexuality and gender within the artistic context. Unlike *Feminine Presence*, *Meta-Sex* did attempt to point out a common denominator, perhaps not a formal one, but certainly a mental one, that reflects the transformations in current feminist thought. A certain normality could be detected, a maturation. Israeli art, which previously refrained from exhibiting its sexual facets, began to rid itself of embarrassment. The art of the seventies in Israel was characterized by repression and denial of sexuality (being conceptual, intellectual art). The eighties stressed sexuality. This is one of the reasons that the gap between the participants in *Meta-Sex* and the women artists of *Feminine Presence* is much greater than the four years separating them, since it conceals at least twenty years. Most of the women artists that exhibited in 1990 (with the exception of the younger ones) were a product of the seventies, years in which they grew and matured as artists. In their art and, moreover, in their statements as expressed in the catalogue (except the artist Michal Ne'eman, who explicitly stressed gender/semiotic issues) they internalized the denial of the significance of gender to the work of art. The young artists of *Meta-Sex*, in contrast, internalized the flourishing of sexuality characterizing the late eighties. For them, feminism had ceased to be an object for battle. It was now possible to talk about art in feminine or masculine terms, just as it was possible to deal openly with the sexual aspects present in the work.

Beyond the generation gap and the differences in attitude, there was a fundamental difference in artistic language. Of the seventeen women artists who participated in *Feminine Presence*, only three exhibited sculpture; painting was clearly the dominant medium. In *Meta-Sex*, most artists applied technologies related to mass media: photography, video, installation, and object. Only a few exhibited paintings, and even then they evaded the traditional definition, the "painting" being part of an installation or disguised as photography. This tendency can be explained in terms of trend or zeitgeist. But it may also reflect the exhaustion of painting as a leading privileged masculine discipline. For the craft of picture making—a translation of the world into its material being—was throughout art history the heritage of men; these pictures functioned as "portholes to the safe," where "the visually desired" was deposited. Among the various treasures lying in this safe were representations of women.[10]

Consequently, from the beginning of the seventies (both in Europe and the U.S.), women artists focused on alternative modes of expression that could replace painting, such as photography, installation, earth works, and performances. These strategies aimed at undermining the representational systems, reducing the translation gap, and bringing forth "the real thing."[11] The feminist discourse offered art history a reflection and interpretation from the perspective of the margins (the "others"). It sought to divert the mainstream toward new directions, to offer yet another analytic tool for looking at the world. Rational, hierarchic, linear thinking—which characterized the modern era—collapsed, along with absolute utopian and ideological belief systems. The feminine voice offered a different rationale, containing a variety of multifaceted, experiential alternatives. Feminist reading has integrated successfully into the general discourse of postmodernism. Its contribution to the discussion of contemporary art is immeasurable.

The Meta-Sex (dirty) body

Naturally, the preoccupation with identity issues introduced the body as a central object in *Meta-Sex*, both as a biological organism disintegrating into parts, and as demanding, physical matter that can be experimented upon and transformed—the last front of ideological battles, in the sense of how to employ and how to represent it in a way that would make a difference.

Meta-Sex revolved around several thematic axes: the body, the abject, the domestic function, and the autobiographical-personal link. The inventory of images consisted of body parts, sexual implements, personal articles, domestic objects, hygiene-related items, purification, eating and secretion, kitchenware, motherhood, women soldiers, brides, feeding instruments, biological mutations, and consumption products. The works in *Meta-Sex* challenged the accepted relationships of woman-mother, woman-nature, woman-home, woman-dirt, and woman-man, concurrently undermining feminine conventions.

Miriam Cabessa: subverting Nature/Culture dichotomy

Miriam Cabessa chose to exhibit in *Meta-Sex* one of the most moving attractions, borrowed from the neighboring museum of natural history—a showcase displaying errors of nature: a two-headed calf, a lamb with six legs, an egg within an egg, chicks with three and four legs, and other mutations— products of nature's cruelest imagination (*There Is Nothing to Do*, 1994; fig. 1.) The clinical, scientific language of the original labels was used as part of the work. By dislocating and transferring an item from a nature museum to an art museum the artist rendered a cynical, amusing, and cruel shift that undermined the validity of taxonomic categories as well as all other socially constructed categories. The representation of nature's failure could be interpreted as corresponding to the conservative concept of the woman as the "other"—as inferior, lustful, and nonspiritual.

FIGURE 1. Miriam Cabessa, *There Is Nothing to Do*, 1994. Glass cabinet with taxidermied animals.

Simone de Beauvoir, a representative of the early phase of feminist discourse, described women as "prisoners of their womb." She argued that in order to obtain liberty and equality women must first liberate themselves of bodily processes, especially those connected with childbirth, which she perceived as the root of their subjection to biology, of being a passive instrument of life. "Trapped by nature, the pregnant woman is plant and animal. . . . a collection of sticky materials, an incubator, an egg . . ."[12] The miserable creatures in the glass cabinet of Miriam Cabessa's work seemed like this "collection of sticky materials." They, too, produce embarrassment because of their anomaly.

One of the basic assumptions posed by the feminist discourse is that woman's social presence is different from that of man. The traditional research of art history is paved with texts that strip the body of its sexuality and remove its social and psychological context. In this process, the nakedness of the body, the erotic charge carried in its nudity, its sexual identity, and its modes of presentation within a context of social discourse, were submerged and erased.

Anat Zahor: the abject Mother Nature

The most subversive representation of the female body in *Meta-Sex* was Anat Zahor's *Urination* video (fig. 2). It was set in a very dark room, close to the museum's Judaica collection; the floor was covered with red soil and in the center there was a monitor displaying a video film that documented a woman urinating. The soundtrack was a combination of gushing water and nuns

Figure 2.
Anat Zahor, *Urination*, 1994. Video still from a room installation: monitor, soil, electric bulb, and soundtrack.

singing. The woman, shown in the natural and comfortable position of kneeling in nature, is seen from behind, so that only the lower part of her body and the shower of urine being absorbed in the earth are exposed. The screening of the video in a loop engendered a sense of endless urination—an act of voiding, a sense of release. In exposing this intimate act, in peeping into the most discrete, taboo parts of the female representation, the artist undermined centuries of canonical "proper" female representation.

Urination and other works in *Meta-Sex* related to a key term in feminist theory—the *abject*—coined by scholar and psychoanalyst Julia Kristeva. Abject is "that which disturbs identity, system and order. That which does not respect borders, positions, and rules. The in-between, the ambiguous, the composite."[13] Underlying this notion is the body as a symbolic system of interior and exterior, administered through a regime of prohibitions that constitute the symbolic order: what is clean and what is dirty, what is proper and what is despicable, what is approved and what is rejected, what remains within the system and what is discharged and cast out. In this context, dirt is perceived as a violation of the body's integrity, threatening to dissolve the soothing division between the body's interior and the external casing of the skin.

According to Kristeva, this process of rejection, exclusion, elimination, or removal of waste occurs, first and foremost, on the basic level of body tissues: blood, urine, saliva, vomit, breast milk, trimmed hair, perspiration, and semen—all these are organic materials excreted from the body. However, from the private level of bodily tissues, Kristeva expanded the principle of abjection, applying it to more generic levels of social order: the dirty, the defective, the abnormal have always represented the borderline, the peripheral, the bestial, that which occupies the margins of the dominant culture and in any case belongs to the female domain. The efforts invested in preserving the categories as well as those invested in exclusion are called "culture." The term "abject art," derived from this context, refers to art that deals with a body that has ceased to be an object of passion and has become abject—a despised object, exposed in its basest, most contemptible aspects. Urination in the Western world is a matter of secrecy, an act locked behind restroom doors. Anat Zahor brought urination out into the open. This may be her version of the representation of Mother Nature.

Ariane Littman-Cohen: from biography to politics

Another work that dealt with the notion of the abject and the concepts of dirt and contamination, although from a different point of view, was Ariane

Littman-Cohen's sterilizer (*Interior*, 1994). A sterilizer is usually designed for cleansing and sterilizing, neutralizing the virus that threatens to contaminate the body. An assortment of personal items was inserted into the sterilizer: a photograph of the artist as an infant, curled in her mother's arms; cosmetic products for preventing premature wrinkles; a Manet reproduction; a photograph of a street in Prague; some sweets, condoms, and dried flowers. These articles resembled laboratory samples from outer space, exposed to ultraviolet lighting, to a sterilizing and purifying mechanism, that neutralized them of the "real," of childhood memories and remnants of life that clung to them.

Interior reminded me of the bubble metaphor formulated by French philosopher Jean Baudrillard when he compared our lives to the life of a sick boy who grew up in a sterile, medical environment, a vacuum barring any possibility of germ penetration that protected his vulnerable body.[14] His mother caressed him with rubber-gloved hands through a sterile sleeve built into a glass tent. He grew up in an exterritorial atmosphere, under the constant supervision of science, threatened by his mother's kiss. According to Baudrillard, we are all bubble children; we are all afraid of touch. Our brains and bodies have already become analogous to this sanitized sphere, a transparent envelope within which we seek refuge in vain. "The extermination of mankind begins," he said, "with the extermination of germs." For "man, with his humors, his passions, his laugh, and his genitalia, is nothing more than a filthy little germ disturbing the universe of transparency."[15]

The biographical (local) element in *Interior* was even more powerful in another work by Littman-Cohen, *Mother and Daughter, 1963*, a thousand-piece jigsaw puzzle modeled after an old photograph of herself as a baby embraced in her mother's arms (fig. 3). The romantic-ideal scene of mother-daughter relationships against the backdrop of the snowy Alps stood in contrast to the deconstructive potential of the picture split into a thousand pieces. Littman-Cohen was born in Switzerland and immigrated to Israel on her own, after her brother committed suicide when she was eighteen. The deconstruction and reconstruction of familial harmony were congruent with her personal story. Analyzing this process of deconstruction, the artist wrote, "The smile of my mother especially was striking to me, it embodied a spontaneous and free happiness, something that belongs only to youth and great expectations. . . . [The puzzle] represented my revolt against the inexorability of time and against life that had not, as it slipped past, materialized the expectations embodied in my mother's smile. . . . When the [puzzle] machine instantly closed, exercising a pressure of a few hundred tons upon the image,

Figure 3. Ariane Littman-Cohen, *Mother and Daughter, 1963,* 1994. A thousand-piece jigsaw puzzle.

fragmenting the image into one thousand pieces, I felt the physical crushing of time. The fetishization of time and memory was blown up into one thousand pieces and I felt a sudden terror inside."[16]

A more direct feminist tone was embedded in another work by Littman-Cohen (*Untitled,* 1994) in which she dealt bluntly with sexist representations of the female body as objects used for sales promotion in advertising (fig. 4). A pair of straddled legs belonging to a display window mannequin emerged from the wall and in between the legs, at eye level, a peephole invited the viewer to peep in. Looking in, one could see an inscription embroidered on a floral lacework, a famous quote from Alexander Pope: "Women have no character at all."

Concurrent with Littman-Cohen's scrutiny into her own biography, she conceived a body of work referring more specifically to her Israeli identity. In *Holy Land for Sale* (executed for the exhibition *Desert Cliché: Israel Now—Local Images*)[17] she exported one hundred and fifty bags of sacred soil to America, marketing holy earth in easy-to-carry, handy-sized packages (fig. 5). The work was executed in collaboration with the Israeli company Arim (meaning cities or towns), a government-owned national development corporation whose logo was printed on each bag. Arim represented Israel's technological development in recent years. The "blooming of the desert" is no

FIGURE 4. Ariane Littman-Cohen, *Untitled*, 1994. Wall installation with female mannequin legs, slide viewer, fabric, and wood.

FIGURE 5. Ariane Littman-Cohen, *Holy Land for Sale*, 1996. Fabric, soil, wood, linen string.

FIGURE 6. Ariane Littman-Cohen, *Virgin of Israel & Her Daughters*, 1994. Beehives, electrical wiring, bulbs.

longer a metaphor for planting forests, but rather an expression of advanced technological urbanization. Packaged like holy water or religious souvenirs, *Holy Land For Sale* referred to Israel's growth and to the Holy Land as a potential real estate venture. *Holy Land for Sale* can also be viewed as a metaphor for transferring areas of land from hand to hand.

In *Virgin of Israel & Her Daughters*, Littman-Cohen reacted to the Israeli masculine myth of heroism. A dozen beehives, lit in red from within, were scattered around with their top panels wide open (fig. 6). This installation was originally created for *Tel Hai '94*, an exhibition taking place every few years in Tel Hai, the fortress of the Israeli myth of heroism, in the Upper Galilee. In 1994, the curator, Gideon Ofrat, chose to exhibit the works in military tents. As a monarchy headed by a "queen mother," the beehive embodies an advanced level of cooperation and nurturing, where the male members play a secondary role. In *Virgin of Israel & Her Daughters*, Littman-Cohen chose the beehive as a metaphor, shedding new light on women's place within the Israeli legend of heroism. At the same time she drew attention to the private mother who sends her sons to war, and the public mother (motherland) who claims her victims. The empty, functionless beehives, reminiscent of sarcophagi, evoked a memorial site. A close observation of the open beehives revealed mysterious signs carved on each of the inner walls: scratches and engravings in the wood. These were the tracks of the wax moth, a beehive parasite that leaves its gnawing marks on the honeycombs, evidence of the slow process of death in the beehive. Paradoxically this piece tied together two biblical myths, the myth of plenty, "the land of milk and honey," and the biblical extinction myth of "a land that devours its inhabitants."

Hilla Lulu Lin: between body politics and Middle Eastern politics

Another artist whose works incorporate both the personal and the political is Hilla Lulu Lin. In *Meta-Sex* she presented a video installation, *No More Tears*, in a room with yellow walls and a ceiling fan. A wrapped, coated heavy stone was suspended from a hook in the most irritating location in the room, threatening the viewer. The video documented the endless journey of an egg yolk, which crawled slowly up the artist's arms, climbed to her shoulder, entered her mouth, reemerged fully, reverted to rolling on the palm of her hand, and so on and so forth (fig. 7). It was a never-ending loop of an autoerotic act, "anorectic acrobatics"—reception and emission, between pleasure and strangulation, which demanded a kind of acrobatic skill so the yolk would not burst in her mouth.

Through the act of nearly swallowing the yolk, Lin tried to unravel the common affinities among woman-food-body, and to take control over anything likely to penetrate. The choice of an egg yolk, an archetypal feminine-organic element, brings to mind erotic cinematic scenes, exhibiting a similar use of organic materials. The linkage between body and food also corresponds with Janine Antoni's chocolate and soap castings and Jana Sterbak's meat-dress works.

A different kind of association between food and existence was manifest in *Cold Blood (A Poem in Three Parts)*, a chilling work produced by Lin in 1996, in the wake of Prime Minister Yitzhak Rabin's assassination and prior

FIGURE 7. Hilla Lulu Lin, *No More Tears*, 1994. Video stills from a room installation.

FIGURE 8.
Hilla Lulu Lin, *Cold Blood (A Poem in Three Parts)*, 1996. Computer-generated images on paper (2 details).

to the ascent of the right-wing Likud party.[18] It consisted of three parts, all
of them photographs: the Tel Aviv seashore, based on a postcard image of
Tel Aviv; a manipulated image of the Dome of the Rock in Jerusalem; and
the artist's eyes (figs. 8a, 8b). The hedonistic character of Tel-Aviv's seashore
was juxtaposed with the sacredness of the Dome of the Rock, the most sacred
Muslim site in Jerusalem. Both iconic landscapes were depicted under raw,
bloody skies. In between these two scary images the artist planted a postcard-
size photograph: her own two eyes, blinding in their emptiness.

Anat Betzer-Shapira: back to normality—
stereotypes of domestic territories

In the *Sisters* series Anat Betzer-Shapira used stereotypes of children's paintings, as they appear in psychology books—pictures that depict the family
institution, the motherly and fatherly functions from a child's point of view
(fig. 9). She processed these childish representational stereotypes of "mommy
in the kitchen," enlarging them to form "bad" and "dirty" childlike paintings,

FIGURE 9. Anat Betzer-
Shapira, *Sisters,* 1992–1993. Oil
on canvas.

FIGURE 10. Anat Betzer Shapira, *Sister Within a Brain Storming*, 1994. A view from a room installation with doormats and woven-wool tapestries.

and added inscriptions: "sister washing dishes," "sister digging in the dirt," "sister cooking," or "sister is doing it for herself." One got the impression of solidarity with these feminine functions, as if the artist sought to sanctify the despised works of all the anonymous "sisters" sharing the same fate, wherever they may be.

Betzer-Shapira's second piece was a room installation in which she covered the museum floor with doormats and hung tapestries on the walls (*Sister within a Brain Storming*, 1994; fig. 10). The latter, produced in a weaving factory, meticulously reconstructed original paintings executed by the artist depicting fresh, pure brides. The bulky, rough doormats holding the dirt and mud at the threshold belonged in the domestic territory, albeit from the other side of the door. The symbolic meaning was clear: the romantic aura of the bride, the object of universal yearning—the wedding night ideal—had become a farce. "Beyond the doormats is where dream and movie brides were always carried. Inside the house they often found filth and dirt, which they turned into a flourishing garden. In this garden the beautiful brides faded, assumed the face and flavor of their cleaning detergents."[19]

Ganit Mayslits-Kassif: the feminine voice of architecture

Another expression of "staining" and "negotiating with dirt" was offered by architect Ganit Mayslits-Kassif, whose work expressed her "feminine voice" through architecture. In *Building Components* she used the museum's standard building components in a manner which subverted its architectural hygiene (fig. 11a, 11b). The walls, ceiling, and columns were manipulated by use of such inferior, "feminine" materials as milk, rice, candies, feathers, latex, nipples, and rubber. These unorthodox materials stained the whiteness of the walls, introducing an unconventional texture, rendering flexible the rough lines of the "white cube." The "window" blocked the view with candies, the glass ceiling was covered with feathers, and one of the walls acquired phallus-like extensions covered with synthetic fur on either side.

Mayslits-Kassif perceives her architectural and academic work as a laboratory where she explores the interrelations between architecture and the body, order and randomness, cleanliness and dirt. Architecture is considered the queen of all disciplines, associated mainly with the masculine tradition. The encounter between gender and architecture allowed her to apply critical thinking. Architectural values such as rationality, order, efficiency, linearity, functionality, and clarity are all considered part of a male, modernist architecture. Ganit Mayslits-Kassif tried to violate the tranquillity of the ordered, clean architectural space. She wanted to reconsider the materiality of our everyday, constructed environment through sensual motivation. She chose to rebuild the functional clean space and transform it into an erotic, unmediated, inviting, and seductive environment.

Galit Eilat and Max Friedmann sharing a fantastic bedroom

Intervention in the details of the architectural envelope was extended to the architectural territory in Galit Eilat and Max Friedmann's joint work. The two situated their work (*Those in the Yard*) in a storage shed in the forest behind the museum. Eilat and Friedmann transformed the old wooden shack into a bedroom: two single beds, a table, shelves, an armchair, and an open closet. They decorated the mahogany beams of the walls with a wallpaperlike pattern and covered the floor with a tiger-patterned, wall-to-wall synthetic fur carpet. Inside the room they planted such subversive elements as a reproduction of a medieval painting of tortured women, and an open closet exposing garments printed with bodily impressions—a man's underwear with the image of the upper body of a woman and a full slip printed with an image of a masculine body.

By situating the bedroom, an explicitly domestic territory, outside the

Figure 11a and 11b. Ganit Mayslits-Kassif, *Building Components*, 1994. Details from an installation.

museum (the museum itself is located within the socialist territory of a kib-butz), the artists created a feeling of a fictional lodge, like period rooms in history museums that preserve the collective memory of the past through exhibiting elements of the individual's daily life (the king's bedroom, the servants' room, etc.). In this case they wanted to create an atmosphere of middle-class, rococo-style taste, referring to the most decadent European culture. Rococo art objects were intended to entertain the rich, bored, tired, and passive members of society, who turned to art for pleasure and leisure. The rococo represented the final phase in a culture of taste in which "beau-tiful" and "artistic" were still synonymous. Transforming the kibbutz shack into a rococo-style bedroom was an ironic social comment on socialist values in contemporary consumerist culture.

Meira Shemesh: the false splendor of the trivial[20]

The same kind of fake splendor, albeit more personal, was evoked by Meira Shemesh's restored childhood living room, which consisted of three com-ponents: *The Hanger* (1994)—a richly decorated chandelier in which she replaced the lightbulbs with colorful stuffed balloons (fig. 12); *My Mother's*

FIGURE 12. Meira Shemesh, *The Hanger*, 1994. Chandelier, iron wire, colored balloons (detail).

FIGURE 13. Meira
Shemesh, *My Mother's Dress,*
1994. Fabric, crystal, plastic
beads, and wooden hanger.

Dress (1994)—a silvery evening dress belonging to her mother (fig. 13); and
Thingies—banal objects placed on a shelf. All three elements belonged to the
"female realm."

The empty garment concealed the body's memory, with its smell, its
touch, and its secret passions, like an absent-present. The elegant fifties dress,
as well as the chandelier, could be read as nostalgic items. However, it seems
that Shemesh was rather interested in sabotaging the memory: she deepened
the already deep décolleté, added the necklace, stuffed the breasts with balls,
and thus violated the authenticity of the nostalgic personal remnant, rendering it grotesque.

Such shifts were also typical of the series *Thingies*, which crowded the two
wooden shelves set on the third wall. The remains of the formica sideboard
previously occupying her parents' living room, the realm of kitsch, were populated by a rare collection of utterly useless objects: souvenirs, cheap orna-
ments, parts of toys—all retreated and reprocessed through an obsessive handi-
craft of occupational therapy. A careful and pedantic work, as though one
were attempting to preserve the nostalgic qualities, to heal and stitch together

the memory fragments. These unimportant objects, which radiated a cheap and scorned beauty, sought to undermine the concept of "home" as the ideal construction of a good woman, and to challenge definitions of good taste.

Shemesh offered here a new concept for the still life genre—the genre of the minor themes. Unlike the genres of the major themes, which are placed in the public sphere of history, the sphere where subjects constitute themselves by action, the genre of the minor themes is pushed to the margins, to the domestic sphere of kitchen. Norman Bryson, who studied the still life genre, argued that it is the silent, hidden side, the voiceless side of material life.[21] According to Bryson, domestic artifacts convey a sense of familiarity, as they situate the spectator in a close and identified space; therefore, in their presentation lies a dimension of comfort. Bryson also pointed out that still-life paintings correspond to the sensations of the hand rather than the eye. In this context, it may be argued that Meira Shemesh's manipulated mundane artifacts deny the dominating power of the (masculine) gaze, and are far more receptive to the touch than to the gaze.

Tamara Masel's choice of silence

Tamara Masel's photographs, too, denied the dominating power of the masculine gaze (*Untitled*, 1994). She showed anonymous portraits, photographed from behind, from an angle that revealed the neck and hair and concealed the face (fig. 14). One could not tell whether it was an older woman or a

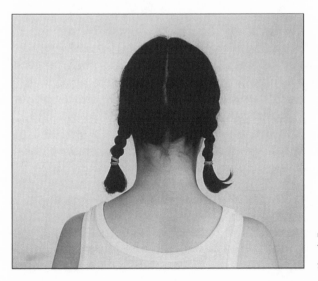

FIGURE 14.
Tamara Masel, *Untitled*, 1994. C-print.

young girl. Both turned their backs on the viewer, avoiding exposure, refusing to return a gaze. Sexuality was restrained, embarrassing. The braiding implied something innocent, taking one back to adolescence; yet it was, in fact, another kind of bodily regime, a routine operation performed by mothers on their daughters in order to render a clean, disciplined appearance. Turning the back also implied not being associated with anything considered "feminine," with materiality, beauty, or any other emblem of temptation.

Michal Shamir and the erotic (conceptual) dialogue with the viewer

Temptation and dialogue were the core of Michal Shamir's conceptual work (*Sign-Post*, 1994; fig. 15). Shamir inserted signs into such visible locations as the restroom and the building's entrance, and assimilated them so that they were integrated "naturally" into the architectural components: tin signposts were attached to the entrance walls and to the building's central columns, while other signposts were planted in hidden niches in the museum. The camouflaging, simulative strategy—assimilating the "artistic" signpost among

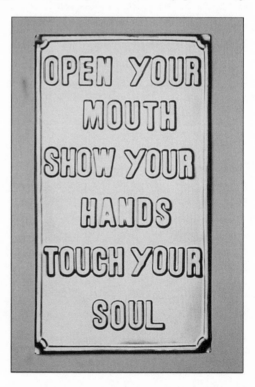

FIGURE 15. Michal Shamir, *Sign-Post*, 1994. Detail from a site-specific installation, mixed media.

"regular" signposts—operated in contradiction to the very visible, functional essence of signposts. The inscriptions on the signposts were mainly instructions for bodily activity ("open your mouth," "close your eyes," "lean forward") or intimate, erotic commands ("lick your knees," "touch yourself," "press your thighs," "inhale," "exhale," "open your mouth," "suck your toes," "smell your sweat"). Under the cover of the intimate tone these imperative sentences tell us what to do. They convey authority, power, and discipline, and their syntax corresponds to the familiar structure of "Insert a disk into drive A, and press enter" or "apply shampoo to your hair and massage gently." The power of the instructions was derived mainly from the surprisingly intimate content and, of course, from our inability to respond.

Merilou Levin promising not to fake orgasms

The idea of linking bodily discipline to recipes for freedom and happiness was also manifest in Merilou Levin's works—a realist painting of a bra fastener on a cutting board (fig. 16), and a small blackboard. On the blackboard

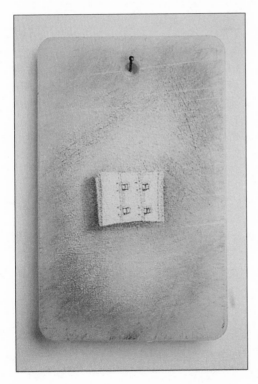

FIGURE 16. Merilou Levin, *Oil on chopping board*, 1993.

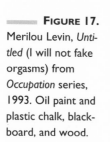

FIGURE 17.
Merilou Levin, *Untitled* (I will not fake orgasms) from *Occupation* series, 1993. Oil paint and plastic chalk, blackboard, and wood.

(the realm of expression for millions of teachers) the artist wrote repeatedly, in docile handwriting—as if she were a punished pupil—the promise: "I will not fake orgasms" (fig. 17).

This subversive text alluded to all those "right" and "wrong" sexual modes of behavior, according to Dr. Ruth. No longer a woman as a supplier of sexual services, no longer satisfying by pretending to be satisfied, no more denial of a woman's own authentic self as a woman. The obsessive repetition strives to restore a childhood memory of an "educational" punishment, an assignment that involved self-taming, obedience, submission, and repetition. The same ambiguity reflected in the painting of the bra hooks on a cutting board, a painting that can be read as metaphor for what is left of the struggle for women's liberation. Foucault talked about good handwriting as one of the common technologies within the mechanism of subject production: "a specific practice and training, that focus on the hand in order to teach it to produce punctual movements, thus discipline the entire body to create a new, better and more docile self."[22] Likewise, it can be claimed that, through good handwriting or the pedantic, delightful realist painting, the artist seems to train herself to submit to her liberated self, declaring its explicit unwillingness to fake orgasms.

Nir Hod: undermining the myth of heroism

Discipline and falseness were also manifest in the series *Woman-Soldiers* by Nir Hod, the only male artist in *Meta-Sex*.[23] In a glittering, golden-framed

FIGURE 18. Nir Hod, *Woman-Soldiers*, 1994. Central part of a triptych, photo transfer, oil on canvas, glitter.

triptych Hod depicted three women soldiers, each directing her gaze toward eternity, conveying pride, glamour, and patriotism—a visual convention in official photographs of male and female soldiers in Israeli historical propaganda.[24] The woman soldier at the center of the triptych was the artist himself, employing his own body dressed in drag to characterize the stereotype of the woman soldier, rendering her both kitschy and exotic (fig. 18).

For Hod, the woman soldier is an archetype of femininity, a symbol of the total woman. By using his own image, holding a cellular phone and wearing a seductive unbuttoned uniform shirt, Hod wanted us to reexamine this ultimate Israeli cliché: a woman soldier in obligatory military service, an essential Israeli invention—a unique, matchless model of equality between the sexes, a model which has been officially marketed to the world as a pure Israeli brand. Hod questions the myth of women's equality, particularly in light of the traditional role division so common in a society that lives from war to war. This ironic description of the women soldiers added a new dimension to the constant criticism in Israeli society regarding discrimination of women in the army, where they serve a shorter period of time and their promotion in many of the branches is blocked due to their sex.

FIGURE 19. Tiranit Barzilay, *Untitled*, 1993. C-print from the *Bomb Shelters* series.

In *Soldier and Woman Soldier* (1996) the soldier is enacted by popular Israeli rock singer Aviv Geffen, who was quite a controversial figure in the nineties, an object of adoration to a great many Israeli youths. His androgynous appearance and the fact that he did not serve in the army, along with his pacifist songs, marked him as a symbol of a "lost" generation.[25]

These investigations in gender politics represent the social, sexual, and cultural transformations currently taking place in Israel. They reflect a basic discomfort with the state of women in Israeli society, where equality between the sexes has always been a myth. Discrimination against women is manifest in nearly all aspects of the country's social life.[26] The attitude of Israelis toward the integration of women into society has always been ambivalent, and the root of this ambivalence lies in the role of the Orthodox parties and the Jewish religion in Israeli political life.

Tiranit Barzilay: from postmodernism to post-Zionism

I started this essay by analyzing works that address universal gender issues, and I would like to conclude with Tiranit Barzilay, a photographer whose works are saturated with sociological and political local content. In Barzilay's *Bomb Shelters* series (*Untitled*, 1993), consisting of staged youth in ceremonial blue and white clothing, engaged in repetitive Sisyphean functionless actions, one can identify Western postmodern issues transformed into local concerns (fig. 19). The official Western voice talks about the disintegration of meaning and self, while the local voice talks about post-Zionism and the disintegration of national identity. The ritualistic activities carried out in bomb shelters

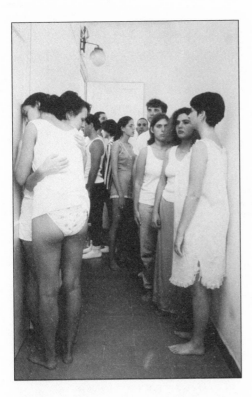

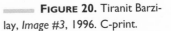 **FIGURE 20.** Tiranit Barzilay, *Image #3*, 1996. C-print.

echo the official national memorial ceremonies: Holocaust Day, Memorial Day, Independence Day.

Tiranit Barzilay's photographs echo the shattering of the two heroic Israeli myths: the myth of solidarity and the myth of the "safe shelter for the Jewish people." The latter was the core of Zionist ideology, but this safe haven was questioned with every new war. It was seriously challenged during the Gulf War when missiles landed on Tel Aviv. In another series of photographs (*Image #3*, 1996, and *Image #6*, 1996) Barzilay depicted young people in underwear occupied in mundane group rituals taking place in empty rooms in Tel Aviv (figs. 20, 21). These photographs reflect generational conditions of anxiety, loss of identity, solitude, passivity, impotence, weakness, and detachment. The hugs seem more like mechanical gestures, devoid of feeling. The passivity, the acts' lack of apparent function, the body's intimate exposure—created an apocalyptic atmosphere. Within the Israeli context, these photographs may bring to mind associations of the Holocaust—people squeezed into corridors or lined up for the shower.

In the photograph of the dance scene (*Image #6*), one may observe the

FIGURE 21. Tiranit Barzilay, *Image #6*, 1996. C-print.

radical change Israeli society had undergone from the years of heroic Zionism to contemporary post-Zionism. The circle dance recalled the hora—the celebratory Israeli circle folk dance, choreographed during the early, optimistic phase of Zionism, a popular dance at Jewish weddings until this very day. For Barzilay, a young secular leftist Israeli, these figures are frozen in time. The solidarity is established through being in the same boat, as it were. There is no eye contact among the girls and the women who dance, even though they hold hands. The famous Israeli togetherness and solidarity collapsed, deconstructed into an empty pattern of a staged ritual.

In conclusion, one may learn a great deal about gender interrelations, social issues, and politics via art. This holds true universally, and particularly in Israel, where one may draw parallels between the private body of the individual and the public body of Zionism. The "right" body, according to Zionist ideology, was a working body, a fighting body, a healthy one, a "macho" one, the so-called "new Jew"—the Israeli. In this sense, the young generation of women artists whose work reflects the feminist discourse of the body's deconstruction offers a different post-Zionist voice within the discourse of deconstructing the mythical heroic "public body."

Notes

1. The most radical in this perception was Katherine David, curator of *Documenta X* *(1997)*, who, as a guest of honor for the opening of *Meta-Sex*, chose to ignore most of the participating feminist-oriented women artists, asserting that they were "not political enough."

2. A unique museum located on a kibbutz in the Jezreel Valley.

3. A stretch of Arab villages on the way to Hadera, which is currently considered somewhat dangerous due to the recent violent demonstrations of Israeli Palestinians.

4. Tami Katz-Freiman and Tamar El Or, *Meta-Sex 94: Identity, Body and Sexuality* (Tel Aviv: Ein Harod Museum of Art and Bat Yam Museum, June 1994, p. 152; exhibition catalogue.

5. Around the time of *Meta-Sex* and immediately thereafter a change occurred in the legitimacy given to the feminine voice, and more female artists began to exhibit under various feminist umbrellas. In this context one should mention the show *The Full Part of the Sign* (curator Ilana Tenenbaum), held at the Borochov Gallery in November 1993. This exhibition offered a critical opinion regarding the modes of production and representation of the female self. The issue "Female Time" of the historical quarterly *Zmanim* (winter 1993) and "The Dirty Issue" of the Israeli art magazine *Studio* # 51 (March 1994) joined this trend. A few years later *Oh, Mama: Representation of the Mother in Israeli Contemporary Art* was shown (curators Yehudit Matzkel and Hadara Scheflan-Katzav), the Museum of Israeli Art, Ramat Gan (March 1997), an exhibition that dealt specifically with the myth of the Israeli mother. In this context one should also note the welcome activity of Antea Gallery, a Women's Artspace, operating since 1994, which focuses on critical issues related to women, art, society, and culture. In February 2000, Antea in collaboration with Kol Ha'Isha, an association committed to promoting a feminist model of social change, produced the exhibition *Sister: Mizrahi Women Artists in Israel* (curators Shula Keshet and Rita Mendes-Flohr), which dealt with personal identity and sociopolitical aspects revolving around the theme of the Mizrahi (Sephardic) woman. The objective of the show, according to the catalogue, was "to constitute the beginning of a different cultural proposition, one that can be translated into an alternative order of priorities and a new vision of society." See Shula Keshet and Rita Mendes-Flohr, *Sister: Mizrahi Women Artists in Israel* (The Artists' House, Jerusalem, February 2000, p. 45; exhibition catalogue.

6. Dganit Berest, *Feminine Presence: Israeli Women Artists in the Seventies and Eighties* trans. Richard Flant (Tel Aviv Museum of Art, summer 1990), pp. 167–68; exhibition catalogue.

7. Tamar Getter, *Feminine Presence*, p. 184, as quoted from an article by Sara Breitberg-Semel, "Women's Art in Israel," *Ariel* (1979).

8. Virginia Woolf, *A Room of One's Own* (1928; rep. London: Penguin, 1945), pp. 102–3.

9. Ellen Ginton, *Feminine Presence*, p. 179.

10. For a comprehensive analysis of the "porthole to the safe" syndrome, see Lea Dovev, "The Eye and the Body: Malaise in the Feminist Aesthetics," *Zmanim* 46–47 (in Hebrew) (winter 1993): 93. Dovev referred to the fifth chapter in John Berger's book, dealing with the oil painting medium. See John Berger, et al., *Ways of Seeing* (London: BBC/Penguin, 1974):, pp. 83–112.

11. In the early nineties numerous exhibitions concerned with body and sexuality were held throughout the world. The most significant among them were the three versions of *Bad Girls* held in London (Institute of Contemporary Arts), New York (the New Museum of Contemporary Art), and Los Angeles (University Art Gallery). One should also mention the two exhibitions held at the Whitney Museum of American Art, *Dirt and Domesticity: Constructions of the Feminine* (summer 1992) and *Abject Art: Repulsion and Desire in American Art* (summer 1993), as reflecting these tendencies.

12. Simone de Beauvoir, *The Second Sex* (1949; rep. New York: Random House/Vintage Books, 1974), p. 553.

13. Julia Kristeva, *Powers of Horror: An Essay on Abjection*, trans. Leon S. Roudiez (New York: Columbia University Press, 1982), p. 3.

14. Jean Baudrillard, "Rituals of Transparency," in *The Ecstasy of Communication*, (Semiotext(e): New York, 1988), pp. 29–44.

15. Ibid., p. 38.

16. From an unpublished text by Ariane Littman-Cohen; refer to her website, www.alc.art.co.il.

17. *Desert Cliché: Israel Now—Local Images* was a group exhibition curated by Tami Katz-Freiman and Amy Cappellazzo, which traveled in Israel and the U.S. between 1996 and 1998: Bass Museum of Art, Miami Beach, (April 1997); Grey Art Gallery and Study Center of New York University, New York (November 1997); Nexus Contemporary Art Center, Atlanta (May 1998); Yerba Buena Center for the Art, San Francisco (September 1998).

18. Hilla Lulu Lin executed *Cold Blood (A Poem in Three Parts)* in 1996 for the exhibition *Desert Cliché*; at that time it was perceived as an alarming prophecy.

19. Tamar El Or, *Meta-Sex* p. 78.

20. Meira Shemesh died in 1996 while waiting for a heart transplant in Belgium.

21. Norman Bryson, *Looking at the Overlooked: Four Essays on Still Life Painting* (Cambridge, Mass.: Harvard University Press, 1990).

22. Michel Foucault, *Discipline and Punish*, trans. Alan Sheridan (Middlesex, N.Y.: Vintage Books, 1979), pp. 135–69.

23. Except Max Friedmann, who operated in a team with Galit Eilat.

24. By the 1990s, the images of "the soldier" and "the woman soldier" had already become visual clichés in Israeli culture. The stereotype of the Israeli macho became yet another marketing tool, both commercial and ideological. For further reading on the transformations of the myth of heroism and military strength, see Tami Katz-Freiman, *Desert Cliché: Israel Now—Local Images*, pp. 49–57; exhibition catalogue. Published by the Israeli Forum of Art Museums, 1996.

25. During the mass rally for support of the peace process in which Israel's Prime Minister Yitzhak Rabin was assassinated, Aviv Geffen was the last artist to perform on stage, singing his song *Forever Brother*; shortly after Geffen received a warm hug from Rabin, the latter was shot.

26. Matrimonial laws and labor laws do not really protect women. Very few women are among the decision makers or hold prominent positions in the Israeli economy. Women in politics amount to no more than 9 percent. Among Western democracies, Israel is seventeenth on the list of women in politics, after Spain and Portugal.

Epilogue

Melanie S. Rich

As is often the case, one's preconceived notion of a place is inalterably changed by visiting it, by seeing it with open eyes, and by getting to know the people. Fantasies seldom mirror reality when it comes to the integration of everyday life. So has it been with my experience of traveling to Israel and working with women there. I was struck by the number of pressing issues that remain on the forefront of Israeli feminism. In a recent telephone conversation with Terry Greenblatt, the director of Bat Shalom, an Israeli feminist organization, I was reminded that any feminist issues we discuss at this time must be considered within the context of the "insane reality" of a country in an ongoing and escalating violent conflict. This particular phone conversation followed the horrifying event of the first female suicide bomber the previous day in Jerusalem.

In an interesting example of parallel process, after we touched on the reality that constantly exists for Israelis, and although I had troubling images in the back of my mind throughout the exchange, we proceeded with our agenda for the conversation and continued with the business at hand. The major challenge Ms. Greenblatt identified for feminists in Israel today is to integrate and internalize the lessons learned from identity politics. Feminist leaders do not believe that, beyond consciousness-raising, there has been tremendous progress in true inclusiveness or recognition of the strengthened position of all women by having all voices heard at the negotiating table. Because understanding identity politics is not an end in itself, but rather a method by which a safe place can be provided for marginalized factions, much further evolution is required to gain shared leadership and decision-making power for all representatives of feminist positions.

A second major agenda item for Israeli feminists is the challenge of this particular political climate. In this period of increasing aggression by both sides, it becomes especially apparent how difficult it can be to reach a middle ground, as demonstrated by as narrow an issue as whether women from a Palestinian group will even sit with women from a settlement, and vice versa. Meetings between Israeli and Palestinian women were temporarily halted as the political climate and logistics became too dangerous; however, there is a desire and willingness on both sides to resume activities, even though there is serious doubt about whether they have had any impact on the powers that be to influence policies on peace.

It is difficult to integrate the current reality of violence and death with the fantasy of security and ambience associated with the concept of a home-land. As a diaspora Jewish woman, I retain certain images with which I grew up that are indelible impressions of Israel. One of those impressions is the miracle of a people who transformed the desert into green, lush lands. Another is the "Never again!" posture of a people who, for the first time since perhaps the Macabees, stand strong, invincible, and unafraid. After thousands of years of persecution, the post-Holocaust reality of Israel gave to Jews around the world an enhanced self-image that ceased to depend solely upon self-esteem from learnedness and education, values of family, and ethics, but had now come from a self-esteem based on strength, virility, and power.

I recall feeling confused after attending my first lecture by an Israeli feminist on the development of feminism in Israel. She spoke harshly about the concept of occupation and, in the context of feminist language, the immorality of any people subjugating another. For the first time I was asked to stretch my imagination in thinking about the image of the young macho Israeli soldier who was not cast in the usual cloak of a handsome hero, but rather in that of an impressionable young person learning to use violence and force. We were invited to ponder the possibility of that young man being able to compartmentalize his "work life" and "work persona" and prevent his work personality from spilling over into his interactions with the people around him in his nonmilitary life. Images of men armed with weapons interrogating civilians at checkpoints, speaking in authoritative or disrespectful tones to the elderly or to women, clouded my earlier conception of military personnel being strictly necessary protectors. For the first time ever, I had to question the images of my childhood, to question the immense pride I felt in the victory of the Six Day War. I had always believed in Israel's right of ownership of the territories won in war, viewing them as the spoils of defeating rather than of being defeated. I believed then, as I do now, that much of the militarism of Israel is out of necessity in the fight to exist; however, the more I learn, the more ambivalent I become about this issue. I still think the experience of being surrounded by enemies is one that few Americans can conceptualize, much less live with for an entire lifetime. And yet, how do we resolve this attitude within the context of the feminist position that no people have the right to subjugate another people? Implicit in any understanding of the dynamic of occupation is the idea of an environment that equivalently contaminates both sides of the relationship.

Violence against women sadly appears to be a universal phenomenon, and is another major agenda item for Israeli feminists currently. Due to some consciousness-raising around this issue, it is now more recognized as a social issue, however, feminist leaders are adamant that it must be viewed as a political issue as well. This question notwithstanding, the concept of violence against women in Israel is one that barely can be comprehended when juxtaposed against a culture that greatly promotes family values, and a country that stands as a safe haven for the downtrodden. However, such violence is occurring in Israel, not in small numbers, and most certainly not just as a problem associated with a particular group, socioeconomic situation, or ethnic faction. It is only after a number of highly publicized tragedies in which women were victimized in "unexpected" social circumstances that this issue emerged as one of Israel's major social problems. The disgrace of this issue is what makes me most uncomfortable on multiple levels and most confronts my earlier, idealized version of Israeli society and the values professed in this country.

There are many passionate activists involved in the issue of violence against women. Irit Umanit is one who has devoted her professional life to trying to make a difference for all women who are victims of violence in Israel. It is through her tireless efforts, and that of many other women like her, that the shelter system in Israel exists today. For some, the cruelest irony in this issue is the paradox posed by the need for special shelters for Orthodox women who are the victims of domestic violence. It is incredible that a people observing kosher food laws, ostensibly to avoid the cruelty of mixing a slain offspring with its mother, could also be a community of religious people with abusers in their midst. One cannot help but wonder about the collusion with the abuser through silence by the witnesses. If, however, one thinks about the issue from a feminist perspective, analyzing the role and status of women in the Orthodox culture, suddenly the existence of this problem is perhaps not so surprising. If it is impure to shake the hand of a woman who is not a man's own wife, then is not every woman viewed as little else than a sex object? Feminists believe that such objectifying of any human leads to the disrespect and devaluing that is a necessary component in domestic violence or any other violence toward another human being. As long as the silence is maintained, a fermenting environment for violence against women is propagated. While thinking about this issue is unpleasant and talking about it considered by some as poor manners, there cannot be a continuation of the denial and lack of activism by the society as a whole, if it is ever to be eradicated. As is true in the United States, violence against women in Israel today is a symptom of something much bigger that is fundamentally wrong within the culture. Until those fundamental principles and values are examined, and especially the allocation of responsibility for the violence (which obviously does not lie with the victim), change cannot and will not take place.

It has been equally baffling, as an actively practicing diaspora Reform Jew, to understand the rift that religion has caused in Israel. It is disconcerting to experience the discord between secular Jews, Reform/Conservative Jews, and Orthodox Jews. This prejudice and conflict is foreign to those of us who grew up in small American Jewish communities, where out of necessity Jews have to get along. On an emotional level, it is rather easy to understand why after years and years of trying to fight and work within the system, Dr. Alice Shalvi, a feminist, professor, author, and devout Jew, has finally left the Orthodox practice of Judaism to become a Conservative Jew.

It is refreshing that so many opportunities now exist for women to study and practice Judaism, and yet the insult to women by ulta-Orthodox men continues in their daily practice of contempt, disrespect, and exploitation of women, beginning with their morning prayer, in which God is thanked for making them neither slaves nor women. It is difficult to remain respectful and generous, with an attitude of appreciation of diversity, toward any group that does not reciprocate such respect. It was a disheartening experience to travel to the Wailing Wall for the first time with my children and be separated due to the gender requirements of one side or the other, rather than to experience this incredible place as a family. I remember with sadness observing an Orthodox bar mitzvah at the Wall, where the mother and female family members of the young man being celebrated stood on chairs and watched from afar. I resolved at that moment that when my son chose to repeat his bar mitzvah in Israel it would not be at that holy place, where neither his own mother nor his sister could stand by his side. And while many creative outlets for women wishing to worship and express their religious voice have evolved in Israel in the past decade, the discord between the religious factions cannot be denied.

One of the successes of the feminist movement is moving the issue of economic empowerment from a level of elitist political discussion to the much more pragmatic issue of whether or not a woman can put food on her table. The question of how a woman grows and empowers herself in the face of everyday life is a priority issue, and such discussions, as well as information sharing with women, have now begun. For example, now, while in a shelter, a woman might have the opportunity to receive employment counseling or training (such as a computer class) rather than having to wait until she has left the shelter. Women have also been empowered through the initiative of specific employment rights groups going into workplaces to educate women workers about their rights. Information is being used as a tool for empowerment.

The women's peace movement in Israel stands as a model for the developing style of feminism in Israel today. It is no accident that pluralism, inclusion, and a democratic foundation are at the heart of the movement. While the ride is sometimes a bumpy one—and the feminist movement has had its growing pains—in general there now appears to be an extremely open and welcoming posture toward all women interested in the mission. This accessibility is extended even to outsiders such as myself, a non-Israeli. Both my work with Partnership 2000, a joint venture between the United Jewish Communities of North America and the Jewish Agency for Israel, as well as the work on this book project have repeatedly demonstrated this openness.

Most conversations I have had with women in Israel rather immediately focus on the issue of peace in the Middle East. I was struck by the fact that the Partnership 2000 Women's Forum in the Kinneret has a twofold focus. There is certainly a wish to improve conditions for women of their own region by enhancing the opportunities for volunteerism, and by promoting women's empowerment through leadership training and peer counseling (at a women's growth center called Tse'ela in Tiberias). However, these endeavors have shared from the beginning a focus of promoting peace through dialogues with Arab women neighbors. The project is called "Women Across the Borders" and is a critically important endeavor because women on both sides of the Israeli-Arab conflict are heartsick over the loss of their husbands, sons, and brothers in wars. While the American women (from Tulsa, St.

Paul, Minneapolis, and Milwaukee) cannot directly relate to being in a state of war, any woman can identify with the depth of the bereavement and despair that such losses cause.

While I have felt bafflement and at times ambivalence during my personal transformation from seeing Israel as an idealized utopia to experiencing the reality of Israel today, I have also felt a genuine connection to the Jewish homeland. This connection is at times surprising and at other moments so familiar that I am filled with a sense of collective belonging. Despite the problems that women and feminists encounter, and even our despair at feeling unheard in the larger arena of Israeli-Palestinian politics, it is important that we maintain a tenacious spirit in working together and addressing those problems. This must remain our ongoing and committed mission.

Page numbers in italics refer to illustrations.

Acker, Joan, 77
Adler, Rachel, 25
Aloni, Shulamit, 6
Arab-Israeli conflict, 1–2, 115–16, 118–19, 124–25, 127–29nn.4, 5, 6, 176–77
Arab women: in Islam, 64, 65–66, 75n.43; Palestinian women, xviii, 13, 62–63, 73n.19, 127–28, 173; peace organizations and, 127–28; rape crisis center use by, 138
Art: abjection in, 147–49; authority, images of, 162–63; body images in, 147–49, 153, 157, 170n.11; dirt, images of, 157; domestic images in, 149–50, 155–61; equality represented in, 166, 171n.26; feminist identity in, xvii; food images in, 153–55; national identity and, 150, 166–67, 170n.17; nostalgia in, 159–61; sexuality in, 144, 145–47, 161–64, 170n.11; soldier images in, 152, 164–66, 170n.24
Art exhibitions: artistic media in, 145–46, 170n.12; *Desert Cliché: Israel Now—Local Images,* 148–52, 153–55, 170nn.17, 18; *Feminine Presence,* 143–45; *The Full Part of the Sign,* 169n.5; *Meta-Sex,* xvii, 142–

43, 145–47, 153–54, 164–65, 169n.5; *Oh, Mama: Representation of the Mother in Israeli Contemporary Art,* 169n.5; *Sister: Mizrahi Women Artists in Israel,* 169n.5
Ashkenazi women, xviii, 12–13, 100–101, 104, 107–8
Ashrawi, Hanan, 124
Aviad, Janet, 116–17

Barak, Ehud, 60, 117
Barukh She'asani Ishah? (book), 45, 50n.26
Barzilay, Tiranit, 166–68
Baudrillard, Jean, 149
Beauvoir, Simone de, 147
Begin, Menachem, 117
Berest, Dganit, 143
Betzer-Shapira, Anat, 155–56
Bina, Malka, 38
Black Panthers, 3–4
Bomb Shelters series (Tiranit Barzilay), *166,* 166–67
Brin, Deborah, 30
Broner, Esther M., 48n.14
Bryson, Norman, 161
Building Components (Ganit Mayslits-Kassif), 157, *158*

Cabessa, Miriam, 146, 147

Cappellazzo, Amy, 170n.17

CEDAW convention (United Nations Convention on the Elimination of All Forms of Discrimination against Women), 59, 72nn.4, 7, 74nn.29, 30, 75n.45

Chazan, Naomi, 117–18, 119, 120, 121

Christianity, 67, 73n.40

Cohen, Shaye, 46n.2

Cold Blood (A Poem in Three Parts) (Hilla Lulu Lin), 153–55, *154*

Collins, Patricia, 104

Conferences, women's, 44, 99–101, 103, 107–8, 109n.10, 123

Conservative Judaism: Americans in, 20; army service and, 39; batei midrash of, 31; haggadah, feminist, 26; Torah reading in, 21, 22; *Va'ani Tefillati* (Masorti prayer book), 24, 25, 48n.17, 49nn.22, 23; women rabbis in, 40, 41. *See also* Liturgy and ritual

Dahan-Kalev, Henriette, 12, 13

Divorce, xv, 19–20, 46, 52n.64, 65–66

Dovev, Lea, 170n.10

Dror, Gilah, 41

Druze Religious Courts Law (1962), 18

Education: academic courses on women, 9, 35; batei midrash, 31–32; conferences, 29–30, 44; for Haredi women, 32–33; hevruta method of, 35; *hesder* programs, 39; kibbutz women and, 78, 79; Nechama Leibowitz and, 34; in peace organizations and, 127; Tali schools (Ma-

sorti), 31; Talmud study for women, 33–34; tracks in, 18–19; women's text study, 32–39

Eilat, Galit, 157–58

Eliezer, Mira, 100, 101

Ellenson, David, 49n.23

El Or, Tamar, 32, 33, 142

Elper, Ora Wiskind, 46

Employment: choice in, 80; class and, 104; economic empowerment, 176; equality legislation/equality in, 62; gender divisions in, 79–81, 86; glass ceilings in, 104; housework, xvi, 7; on kibbutz, 78–80, 82–85, 89–91; of Mizrahi women, 99; part-time, 2; professional barriers, 13; wages and, 2, 59, 80–81

"The Empowerment of Women," 29–30

Equal Rights for Women Act (1951), xv

Eshel, Shuli, 7

Espanioly, Nabila, 124, 125

Falk, Marcia, 48n.15

Family: in art, 149–50; children and, 2, 5, 25, 26, 65–66, 79–80, 84–85, 89; domestic violence and, 136, 139–40; gender roles in, 69; on kibbutz, 84–85, 89–90; labor divisions in, xvi, 7, 11; reproductive technology and, 5, 61; right of formation, 63–64, 73nn.26, 28; structure of, 63–64; women's employment, 2. *See also* Marriage

Feigelson, Mimi, 32

Feminine Presence (art exhibit), 143–44

Feminism, Israeli: American influence on, 3, 5, 9–10, 11–12, 20; on the

Arab-Israeli Conflict, 115–19, 129nn.4, 5, 6; Ashkenazi bias in, 12–14; economic empowerment and, 176; invisibility of oppression, 97–98; Israel Women's Network, 129n.5; kibbutz women and, 86–88; lesbian, 8–9; liberal, 10–11; militancy of, xvi–xvii, 3–4; in national kibbutz movements, 86–88; professionalization of, 9–10; radical, 4, 11–12; religion-state connection and, 133–34; religious role models and, 42–43; second wave (1980s), 9–10; women in political life, 5–8, 60–61, 137. See also Art; denominational headings (e.g. Conservative Judaism); Israeli government; Mizrahi women; Peace organizations; Zionism

Ferris, Helene, 30

Finkel, Gilberte, 129n.4

Foucault, Michel, 164

Freedman, Marcia, 6, 134

Fried, Nurit, 36

Friedmann, Max, 157–58

Frymer-Kensky, Tikva, 24, 49n.20

The Full Part of the Sign (exhibition), 169n.5

Furstenberg, Rochelle, 19–20

Geffen, Aviv, 166

Getter, Tamar, 143

Getz, Shlomo, 80

Ginton, Ellen, 143

Golan, Galia, 10, 118

Goldberg, Monique Susskind, 41, 46

Goldsmith, Karni, 26

Golinkin, David, 46, 49n.22, 52n.64

Graetz, Naomi, 45, 48n.17

Greenblatt, Terry, 172

Greenfield, Tzvia, 43

Gribetz, Beverly, 38

Grossman, Susan, 49n.20

Halpern, Micah D., 45

Handelman, Susan, 46

The Hanger (Meira Shemesh), 159

Haredi communities, 32–33

Hartman-Halbertal, Tova, 50n.30

Haut, Rivkah, 30

Health care, 61

Henkin, Chana, 36, 37

Heschel, Susannah, 46n.2

Hod, Nir, 164–65

Hoffman, Anat, 42

Holy Land for Sale (Ariane Littman-Cohen), 150–51, 151

Hotlines, 138–39

Human Dignity and Freedom Law (1992), 59

Human rights: Arab women and, 62–63; CEDAW convention, 59, 72nn.4, 7, 74nn.29, 30, 75n.45; Christian law and, 67; employment equity, 61; health care, 61; Islamic law and, 66–67; Jewish law (halakah) and, 65–66, 71; legislation, 58–59; patriarchalism and, 69–70; personal status and, 63–65, 68; religious freedom and, 70–71, 73nn.27, 28; women in elective office and, 5–8, 60–61, 72n.5, 117–18, 137, 171n.26

Hyman, Paula, 48n.15

Ilan, Tova, 43

Image #3 (Tiranit Barzilay), 167, 167

Image #6 (Tiranit Barzilay), 167–68, 168

Interior (Ariane Littman-Cohen), 148–49
Intifada, 118–19, 124, 125, 127–28
Islam, 64, 65–66, 75n.43
Israeli government: equal rights legislation, 58–60, 72n.5; Jewish religious law and, 64–66, 73n.28, 133–34; rape crisis centers, support for, 137; religious councils and, 19; women in, 5–8, 60–61, 72n.5, 117–18, 137, 171n.26. *See also* Zionism
Israel Women's Network, 29–31, 129n.5

Jewish law (halakah). *See* Family; Legal system; Liturgy and ritual; Marriage
Jewish Legal Writings by Women (Halpern and Safrai), 45
JOFA (Jewish Orthodox Feminist Alliance), 23–24, 28–29, 47

Kagan, Rachel, 6
Katz, Yael Levine, 45
Katz-Freiman, Tami, 170n.17
Kaufman, Debra, 33
Kayan (Palestinian feminist organization), 13
Kehat, Chana, 44
Kelman, Na'amah, 20, 41
Keshet, Shula, 169n.5
Kibbutz: child care on, 79–80, 84–85, 89; education on, 77–78, 79, 80; feminism and, 86–88; gender inequality on, xvi, 86–90, 133; management positions on, 82–83, 90; wages on, 80–81, 133; work assignments on, 78–80, 84–85, 89–91
Klagsbrun, Francine, 30
Klein, Amy, 41
Kook, Leah, 41

Kristeva, Julia, 148
Krug, Marion, 30

Landes, Danny, 31
Lebowitz, Maya, 50n.26
Lederhendler, Amy, 21, 48n.11
Legal system: advocacy for women in, 36–37; and *agunot*, 19–20, 46, 52n.64, 69; divorce, xv, 65–66; Jewish law (halakah) in, 65–66, 71, 133–34; personal status in, 64–68, 73n.40, 75n.43; religious courts, 18, 19; sex discrimination in, 64, 73nn.27, 28; Yad ha-Ishah (legal aid), 36; yoatzot halakah (women halakic consultants), 37–38
Legislation: for equal pay, 10; Equal Rights for Women Act (1951), xv; military service options and, 10–11; national identity and, 57–58; Prevention of Violence in the Family Act (1992), 58; Property Relations Between Spouses Act (1990), 58–59; sexual harrassment, 10
Leibovich, Maya, 41
Leibowitz, Nechama, 34
Lentin, Ronit, 119
Lerman, Debby, 119
Levin, Leah Simmons, 7–8
Levin, Merilou, 163–64
Levine, Sarra, 38
Levmore, Rachel, 36
Life on the Fringes: A Feminist Journey toward Traditional Rabbinic Ordination (Ner-David), 45
Lin, Hilla Lulu, 153–54
Littman-Cohen, Ariane, 148–52
Liturgy and ritual: in bat mitzvah, 27, 50nn.27, 28; gendered language in, 23–24, 48nn.15, 17, 49n.18; haggadah, feminist, 26; *imahot* (matri-

archs) added in, 25; kaddish, 23, 26, 27–28, 48n.14; *K'vod hatzibbur* and, 22; literacy and, 30–31; in marriage ceremony, 27; megillah reading (Scroll of Esther), 29; prayer books (siddurim), 24, 25, 26, 48nn.15, 17, 49nn.18, 22, 23; prayer leaders, women as, 21; for Rosh Hodesh, 29; *tallitot* (prayer shawls) and, 21, 49n.23; *tefillin* (phylacteries), 21, 25–26, 49n.22; *Tehinnat ha-Nashim le-Vinyan ha-Mikdash* (Katz), 45–46; Torah reading, 21, 22, 27, 47n.5; traditional Jewish sources on, 20–22, 23, 47n.7; women-only prayer groups, 22, 48n.12; women's life events and, 25, 27, 45n.7, 49n.20, 50nn.27, 28; Zeved habat, 25, 26

Magnus, Shulamit, 30
Marriage: and *agunot*, 19–20, 46, 52n.64, 69; children and, 65–66; civil options for, xv, 65–66, 71–72; divorce, xv, 65–66; in Islam, 66–67; legislation, 58–59; property and, 58–59; religious identity and, 64–68; sexuality in, 37, 61, 68; women's rituals and, 27
Masel, Tamara, 161–62
Masorti. *See* Conservative Judaism
Matzkel, Yehudit, 169n.5
Mayslits-Kassif, Ganit, 157
Mazor, Yoram, 50n.26
Meir, Golda, 4, 60
Mendes-Flohr, Rita, 169n.5
Meta-Sex 94: Identity, Body and Sexuality (art exhibition), xvii, 142–43, 145–47, 153–54, 164–65, 169n.5
Military service: equality in, 10–11; heroism, xvii, 60, 152–53; images in

art, 152, 164–66, *165;* machismo in, 1–2, 133, 170n.24, 173; *nachal* units in, 39; national security and, 57–58; Peace Now and, 120, 124–25; *sherut leumi* (national service), 39; violence and, xvii, 120, 133, 173; women in, 164–66, 170n.24; and the Yom Kippur War, 1–2
Millen, Rochelle L., 48n.14
Mizrahi women: Ashkenazi women and, xvii–xviii, 12–13, 100–101, 104, 107–8; conference attendance of, 99–101, 103, 107–8, 109n.10; discrimination and, xviii, 12–13, 97, 100, 103–4, 106–7; feminist activism of, 15, 99–100, 105, 106, 107; as religious role models, 40; Rosh Hodesh rituals, 29; *Sister: Mizrachi Women Artists in Israel* (exhibition), 169n.5; social policy and, 13, 104–5; Zionism and, 103–4, 109n.10
Mother and Daughter, 1963 (Ariane Littman-Cohen), 149–50, *150*
My Mother's Dress (Meira Shemesh), 159–60, *160*

Namir, Ora, 134
Nashim (journal), 44–45
National Religious Party, xv
Ne'eman, Michal, 144
Ner-David, Haviva, 45
NILAKHEM (Women for a New Society), 4
No More Tears (Hilla Lulu Lin), *153*

Ofrat, Gideon, 152
Oh, Mama: Representation of the Mother in Israeli Contemporary Art (exhibition), 169n.5
Oil on chopping board (Merilou Levin), *163,* 163–64

Oriental Jews. *See* Mizrahi women
Orthodox Judaism: ba'alot teshuva in, 33; bat mitzvah in, 27, 48n.14; domestic violence and, 174–75; hegemony of, 73n.28; JOFA (Jewish Orthodox Feminist Alliance), 23–24, 28–29, 47n.5; leadership roles for women, 19; marriage and, xv, 65–66, 70–72; personal status in, 68; rabbinic authority in, xv; reading of Scroll of Esther (the megillah) in, 29; religious councils, 19; religious courts, 18, 19; text study, women's, 32–34; Torah reading, women's, 22; women as rabbis in, 45; women role models in, 40, 41; women's conferences, 44; women's tefillah groups, 22, 27. *See also* Education; Liturgy and ritual; Schools
Or va-Derekh le-bat Yisrael (Orthodox women's prayer book), 24
Ostrowitz, Rachel, 120

Palestinian women: discrimination against, xviii, 62–63, 73n.19; feminism and, 13, 173; peace organizations and, 127–28
Patriarchalism in religion, 17–18, 46n.2, 65, 69–70
Peace Now, 115–17, 119, 120, 124–25, 131nn.28, 31
Peace organizations: Arab-Israeli conflict, 1–2, 115–16, 118–19, 124–25, 127–29nn.4, 5, 6, 176–77; Bat Shalom, 129n.7, 172; Gesher, 127; Intifada and, 118–19, 124, 125, 127–28; leadership training and, 176; Neled (Israeli Women for Cooexistence), 128; Palestinian women and, 127–28; Parents Against Silence,

129n.6; Peace Cloth, 128; Peace Now, 115–17, 119, 120, 124–25, 131nn.28, 31; Reshet (Israel Women's Peace Net), 128; SHANI (Israeli Women Against the Occupation), 127–28; TANDI (Movement of Democratic Women in Israel), 127; The Women and Peace Coalition, 128; Women in Black, xvi, xvii, 4, 114–15, 118–28; Women's International League for Peace and Freedom (WILPF), 127; Women's Organization for Women Political Prisoners, 128
Peli, Pnina, 44
Plaskow, Judith, 46n.2
Political office, women in, 6–7, 60–61, 137
Prayer books (siddurim): gendered language in, 24, 48nn.15, 17, 49n.18; matriarchs *(imahot)* added in, 25; *Or va-Derekh le-bat Yisrael* (Orthodox women's prayer book), 24; *Va'ani Tefillati* (Masorti prayer book), 24, 25, 48n.17, 49nn.22, 23; women-centered prayers in, 25, 26
Prevention of Violence in the Family Act (1992), 58
Property Relations Between Spouses Act (1990), 58–59
Puterkovski, Malka, 38

Rabbinical Courts Jurisdiction (Marriage and Divorce) Law (1953), 18
Rabin assassination, 153–55, 166, 171n.25
Raday, Frances, 59, 72 nn.3, 4, 74n.40
Ragen, Naomi, 42–43
Ramon, Einat, 41
Rape crisis centers, 136–38

Ravitsky, Ruth, 45
Reform Judaism: Americans in, 20; *Barukh She'asani Ishah?*, 45, 50n.26; Beit Shemuel *(beit midrash)*, 31; religious councils, 19; synagogues in Israel, 31; women rabbis in, 40, 41. *See also* Liturgy and ritual
Rein, Natalie, 2, 5
Reshef, Tsali, 125
Resnick, Ruth, 134
Riskin, Shlomo, 34, 36
Robins, Rochelle, 38
Rosen, Michael, 31
Ross, Tamar, 23–24
Roublev, Hagar, 4

Sachs, Dalia, 124, 125
Safrai, Chana, 35, 44, 45
Scheflan-Katzav, Hadara, 169n.5
Schoenfeld, Stuart, 50n.28
Schools: Bat Kol (feminist yeshiva), 38; beit ya'akov, 32, 50n.39; Beit Shmuel (Reform *beit midrash*), 31; Evelina De Rothschild High School, 51n.49; Judith Lieberman Institute, 34–35; Kerem (teacher training institute), 35; MaTaN, 38; Ma'yan, 48n.14; Midreshet Lindenbaum, 35–36, 39; Nishmat, 36–37, 51n.47; Pardes, 31; Pelech, 38; Tali schools (Masorti), 31; Yakar *(beit midrash)*, 31–32
Selvidge, Marla, 46n.2
Sered, Susan, 29, 30, 40, 41
Shadmi, Erella, 120, 125–26
Shakdiel, Leah, 26, 29, 42
Shalabi, Shahira, 13, 14
Shalvi, Alice, 10, 38, 42, 175
Shamir, Michal, 162–63
Sharansky, Meir, 32

Sharoni, Simona, 120, 123
Shelters for battered women, 8, 134, 137
Shemesh, Meira, 159–61
Shenhav, Sharon, 46
Sherut leumi (national service), 39
Shiryon, Kinneret, 41
Sign-Post (Michal Shamir), *162,* 162–63
Silence Is Deadly: Judaism Confronts Wifebeating (Graetz), 45
Sister: Mizrahi Women Artists in Israel (exhibition), 169n.5
Sisters (Anat Betzer-Shapira), *155,* 155–56
Sister Within a Brain Storming (Anat Betzer-Shapira), *156*
Smith, Dorothy, 77
Soldier and Woman Soldier (Nir Hod), 166
Survivor services: government funding of, 137; hotlines, 136, 138–39; rape crisis centers, 136–38; shelters for battered women, 8, 134, 137; statistics of, 137–38; Yad ha-Ishah (legal aid), 36
Synagogues: Beit Daniel (Reform), 31; Kehilat Yedidya, 28, 50n.30; seating arrangements in, 21–22; Shira Hadasha, 50n.30; women's leadership roles in, 21

Tabory, Ephraim, 22–23, 48n.13
Tamir, Yael (Yuli), 117
Tehinnat ha-Nashim le-Vinyan ha-Mikdash (Katz), 45–46
Tenenbaum, Ilana, 169n.5
There Is Nothing to Do (Miriam Cabessa), *146,* 146–47
Thingies (Meira Shemesh), 160–61

Those in the Yard (Galit Eilat, Max Friedmann), 157–59, *158*

Torah of the Mothers: Contemporary Jewish Women Read Classical Jewish Texts, 46

Tzemel, Leah, 4

Umanit, Irit, 174

UN Committee on the Elimination of Discrimination against Women, 62–63

Untitled (Ariane Littman-Cohen), 150, *151*

Untitled (Merilou Levin), 163–64, *164*

Untitled (Tamara Masel), *161,* 161–62

Urination (Anat Zahor), *147,* 147–48

Va'ani Tefillati (Masorti prayer book), 24, 25, 48n.17, 49nn.22, 23

Vila, Diana, 46

Violence against women: cultural issues in, 136–37; Ezrat Nashim, 137; family treatment centers, 139–40; military service and, xvii, 120, 133, 173; Orthodox Judaism and, 174–75; Palestinian women, 63; as political issue, 174; public awareness of, 135, 136, 138, 139, 174; *Silence Is Deadly: Judaism Confronts Wifebeating* (Graetz), 45; statistics on, 137–38; survivor services, 8, 36, 134, 136–39

Virgin of Israel & Her Daughters (Ariane Littman-Cohen), *152,* 152–53

Weiss, Susan, 36

Weissman, Deborah, 28–29, 35, 50n.39

Western Wall (Kotel), 11, 21, 29, 30, 47n.5, 175–76

Wolfsfeld, Gadi, 129n.8

Wolowelsky, Joel, 49n.24

Women in Black, xvi, xvii, 4; decision-making in, 121–22; feminism and, 122–24, 126; history of, 114–15; Intifada and, 118–19, 124, 125, 127–28; leadership in, 120–21; in the media, 124; Peace Now militarism and, 124–25; vigils of, 120–24, 125–26; on war and women's oppression, 124

Women of the Wall, 21, 29, 30, 47n.5

Women Reading from Genesis (Ravitsky), 45

Women's Equal Rights Law (1951), 58

Women-Soldiers (Nir Hod), 164–65, *165*

Women's Organization for Women Political Prisoners, 128

Women's Party (NES), 5, 6–8

Women's Tefillah Network, 22

Yoatzot halakah (women halakic consultants), 37–38

Young, Iris, 97–98

Zahor, Anat, 147–48

Zimmerman, Deena, 37, 51n.48

Zionism: in art, xvii, 167–68; Mizrahi women and, 103–4; myths of, xvii, 166–68, 170n.24, 171n.26, 173–74; women's role in, 5, 11

Zohara (Rabbanit), 41

Zornberg, Aviva Gottlieb, 38